Chicken Sunday
and Other Great Tales
Best-Loved Writers and Their Work

by Gay Lynn Joseph
and
Jan Koger

Fearon Teacher Aids

We lovingly dedicate this book to
our husbands and children,
who sacrificed to make this book
possible.

Dennis Joseph
Bo, Donnie, Ras, and Audrey

Dennis Koger
Mandy, Michael, and Melody

In memory of
Rev. Robert L. Wimpee, Sr.
1928–1995

Senior Editor: Susan Eddy

Editor: Lisa Trumbauer

Design: Catherine Calamia and Michele Episcopo

Illustrations: Doris Simone

Fearon Teacher Aids
An Imprint of Modern Curriculum
A Division of Simon & Schuster
299 Jefferson Road
Parsippany, NJ 07054-0480

ISBN 1-56417-906-0

1 2 3 4 5 6 7 8 9 MAL 01 00 99 98 97

Contents

Introduction

Welcome to author studies! This approach will not only excite students about books, but will give you a refreshing avenue to teach reading, writing, and the love of literature. As elementary classroom teachers ourselves, we have made this book teacher-friendly and have included everything you need to successfully present and manage author studies in your classroom. Take a quick trip to your local library, and you will be on your way!

This book is designed to teach one author each month of the school year. Each author section highlights four books, one for each week of the month. A week's worth of enriching activities geared for teaching reading, writing, and the love of literature, as well as cross-curricular projects, are specifically laid out with clear, easy-to-follow instructions. Also included are photos and interesting biographical information about each author.

As classroom teachers and mothers of children with special needs, we are aware that the abilities and interests of students vary greatly. With this in mind, we have modified activities so that your least advanced first grader to your most advanced third grader will enjoy each activity and achieve success.

A Few Suggestions

Following are suggestions we found helpful and effective when implementing these author studies. They are suggestions only. Apply those that are appropriate for your class.

Sequence of Author Studies

The author studies in this book are in no particular order. Pick and choose as you see fit. After you have chosen your author, visit your school or local library to obtain book selections and any other books the author has written.

Classroom Display

Choose a specific place in your classroom, such as a bulletin board or a blank wall, to display biographical information and the photograph of your featured author. Use the area throughout your author study to display students' writing activities and art projects.

Reading Corner

Set up a comfortable area in your classroom for students to enjoy the books as you read to them. We recommend you read the weekly selection each day to get students back into the book. You might invite some students to read the book aloud to the class.

Book Reports

To help students understand and grasp the themes and messages of these stories, the first activity for each selection is a book report. These reports include shape books, mobiles, and story cubes, to name a few. Most of the book reports suggest that students write the sequence of story events, which we have included. Some students, depending on age or ability, may need to draw the events. Lines can be deleted from reproducible writing pages by placing white paper over the lines before photocopying.

Writing Journals

One of the purposes of this book is for students to not only learn and appreciate individual author's writing styles, but also to incorporate them as they develop writing styles of their own. Several activities focus on a Writing Journal. Provide students with notebooks in which to record literary techniques you explore. Encourage students to refer to their Writing Journals as they write. It is exciting to see similes, onomatopoeia, and other interesting language arts appear in students' writings!

Memorable Story Quotes

We have included a quote from each literature selection that is poignant and reflects the main idea of the story. Suggest that students memorize them. By the end of the year, students will be able to recite story quotes from over 30 titles!

Author Portfolios

To remember the authors and books they read, invite students to start an author portfolio. In folders, have students keep a sample item, such as a writing project, from each book you study. Students will enjoy remembering the books and authors they discovered as they read through the collected items in their author portfolios.

We hope you and your students enjoy the literature selections and activities of this author studies book. Our goal is to open students' minds to all sorts of literature and to foster a love for reading and writing. We hope this book achieves that goal and that you and your students find these author studies rewarding and enriching experiences.

Patricia Polacco

Get ready to fall in love with the books of Patricia Polacco! Her graceful use of the English language, combined with her charming illustrations, will delight and entertain your students. Through her stories, Polacco subtly introduces readers to her rich heritage and traditions.

Interesting Facts About the Author

Birth: Patricia Polacco was born on July 11, 1944, in Lansing, Michigan.

Childhood: Born in Michigan, Patricia moved to Oakland, California, after her parents divorced, at which time she and her brother, Richard, lived with their mother. She and Richard spent summers in Michigan with their father and grandparents. The setting of many of her stories reflects both places. Patricia was also influenced by her grandparents, who were excellent storytellers.

Today: Patricia lives in Michigan, with her husband, Enzo. They have two grown children.

Background: Patricia comes from Russian and Irish heritages. Her mother's people were from Russia, and her father's people were from Ireland.

Education: School was not easy for Patricia, who had a difficult time with reading and math. Realizing at an early age that she learned things differently than other people did, she was able to compensate for these differences. She graduated from college and earned a Ph.D. in art history.

Beginnings as an author:

Patricia started writing and illustrating children's books when she was 41 years old. Her love of writing, as well as of her family, flows through her books.

Common threads to look for throughout her books:

- Consistent and detailed illustrations of family members, for example, Richard.
- Photographs of friends and family mixed in with her illustrations. Some books have family photos inside the book covers.
- Similes as a literary device.
- Adjectives that provide explicit mental pictures.
- Story elements, such as setting, characters, conflict, and plot, that are clearly defined.

Pastimes: Patricia enjoys relaxing in her rocking chair as she listens to music and daydreams, thinking up new ideas for her books. She also runs for exercise and enjoys spending time with family and friends.

Books by Patricia Polacco

- *Chicken Sunday*
- *Just Plain Fancy*
- *My Rotten Redheaded Older Brother*
- *Babushka Baba Yaga*
- *Tikvah Means Hope*
- *The Keeping Quilt*
- *The Bee Tree*
- *Uncle Vova's Tree*
- *Meteor*
- *Picnic at Mudsock Meadow*
- *Applemando's Dreams*
- *Firetalking*
- *I Can Hear the Sun*

- *Mrs. Katz and Tush*
- *Pink and Say*
- *Some Birthday!*
- *Thunder Cake*
- *My Ol' Man*
- *Rechenka's Eggs*
- *Boat Ride With Lillian Two Blossom*
- *Aunt Chip and the Great Triple Creek Dam Affair*
- *Babushka's Mother Goose*
- *In Enzo's Garden*
- *The Trees of the Dancing Goats*

Chicken Sunday

Start your Patricia Polacco journey with Chicken Sunday. In this story, Patricia Polacco explores what happens when three children receive and give unconditional love as they try to please their neighbor, Miss Eula.

Points of Interest Not Mentioned in the Story

- After you read the book, point out to children the six-digit number that has been tattooed on Mr. Kodinski's left arm. Explain that these digits once identified Mr. Kodinski as a prisoner in a Jewish concentration camp established by the Germans during World War II. This fact is not directly stated in the book. However, this background explains Mr. Kodinski's attitude and Miss Eula's comments about him. Additionally, it offers great opportunities to discuss the Holocaust and prejudice in general.

- The pysansky eggs are of special interest to Patricia Polacco. Her Ukrainian grandmother taught her how to make the beautifully decorated eggs as a child. These eggs inspired her to write another book, *Rechenka's Eggs*.

- Stewart and Winston Washington, part of the trio in *Chicken Sunday*, were actually Patricia's neighbors when they were children. Stewart is still her neighbor today. They enjoy sitting and talking on the porch, and she considers him one of her best friends.

Memorable Story Quote

"How we loved to hear Miss Eula sing. She had a voice like slow thunder and sweet rain."

Activities for *Chicken Sunday*

ACTIVITY 1: Similes

ACTIVITY 2: Easter Hat Shape Book Report

ACTIVITY 3: Pysansky Eggs

ACTIVITY 4: Fancy Newspaper Hats

ACTIVITY 5: Design a Hat

ACTIVITY 6: Writing Extension 1—Blame

ACTIVITY 7: Writing Extension 2—Special Friends

ACTIVITY 1

Similes

Patricia Polacco skillfully uses similes throughout her literature. Encourage children to begin a list of similes to "borrow" for their own writings.

Procedure

1. Create a coat-hanger chart for your classroom. Cut a length of butcher paper, and fold and glue the corners over the hanger, as shown on page 261.

2. Write the word *simile* on the chalkboard. Explain that a simile is a figure of speech that compares things using the words *like* or *as*. For example: "He was as brave as a lion." "She screeched like a cat."

3. Reread *Chicken Sunday*, and have students listen for similes. ("She had a voice like slow thunder and sweet rain." "You'll be as flat as a hen's tongue.") List them on the coat-hanger chart while students list the similes in their Writing Journals. Encourage children to add to the lists when they read other books.

ACTIVITY 2

Easter Hat Shape Book Report

Invite students to write book reports in a shape book modeled after Miss Eula's hat.

Assembling the Books

1. Reproduce one hat pattern for each student.

2. Have children trace the pattern onto nine sheets of construction paper and cut out.

3. Explain that one hat serves as the cover for their shape books. Instruct children to glue writing paper onto the other pages and staple them together on the left-hand side.

The Writing Process

Encourage children to think about the story with such guiding questions as:

- *Who* was in the story?
- *Where* did the story take place?
- *What* were the main problems? (For example, the children's desire to buy Miss Eula a hat.) *How* were they resolved?

With the class, list or draw on the chalkboard, overhead, or chart paper the events of the story. Keep the events short, simple, and to the point. Some suggestions follow.

1. Miss Eula admires a hat in Mr. Kodinski's hat shop.

2. The children plot to get the hat for Miss Eula.

3. The children are blamed for eggs that were thrown near Mr. Kodinski's shop.

4. The children have a confrontation with Miss Eula.

5. Mr. Kodinski allows the children to sell pysansky eggs in his shop.

6. Mr. Kodinski gives the children the Easter hat for Miss Eula.

7. On Easter Sunday, Miss Eula proudly sings in church, wearing her new Easter hat.

Encourage children to tell about the story events in order, one for each page of their shape books. On the last page, have children write or draw the message they received from this book.

Miss Eula Hat Pattern

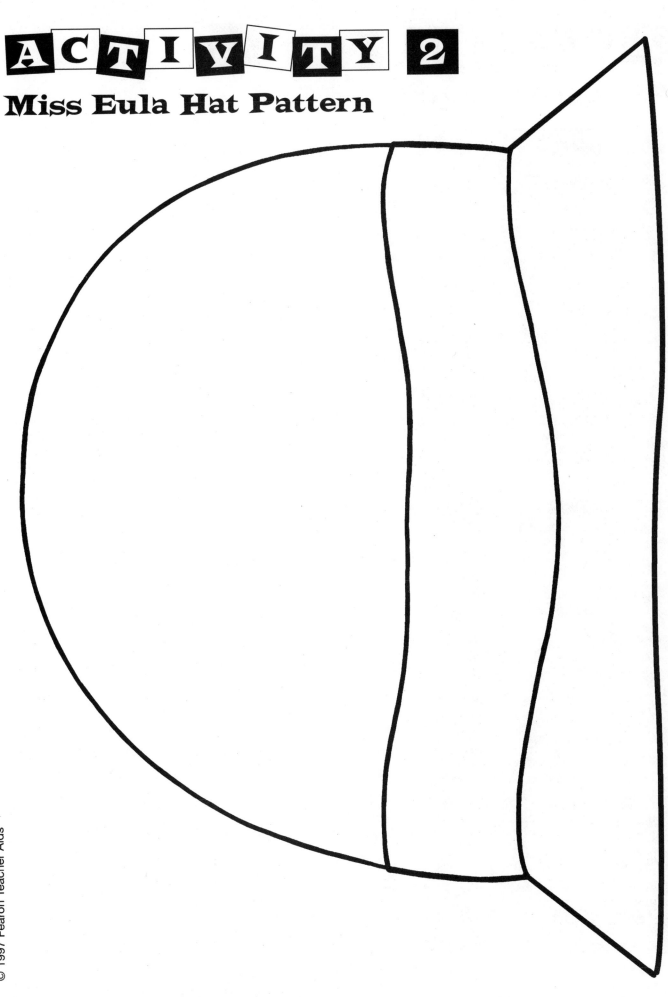

ACTIVITY 3

Pysansky Eggs

Pysansky eggs come from the Ukraine. At Easter time they are given to family and friends as a symbol of love. The eggs get their name from the Ukrainian word *pysaty* which means "to write." The Ukrainian people treasure the eggs for good luck. They once believed the eggs could heal the sick, protect their homes, and bring a good harvest.

The tradition of making pysansky eggs has been passed down from mother to daughter for generations. After blowing the egg out of the shells, the artist uses a *kistka*—a tiny funnel on a handle—to drip a melted beeswax design onto the egg. The egg is then dipped into a pastel-colored dye. More wax is added, and the egg is dipped into another color. This process is repeated, with the final color being either black or red. After warming, the wax melts and is wiped off the egg. Revealed is a colorful pattern with white lines. A final coat of lacquer is used to preserve it. One common decoration on the egg is a wide band with designs.

This activity invites students to make their own pysansky eggs. A simpler variation is included to make the process easier for younger students.

Supplies

- hard-boiled eggs, one for each student
- newspaper
- white wax crayons
- egg cartons
- four bowls for dye
- yellow, blue, red, and black egg dye
- candle
- soft cloth

Procedure

1. Prepare enough hard-boiled eggs so each student in your class has one. Also prepare the egg dyes according to the directions on the package, putting one color in each bowl. Let the dyes completely cool.

2. Give each student a hard-boiled egg and a white wax crayon.

3. Show how to use the crayon to draw designs on the egg.

4. Instruct students to dip the egg in yellow dye, then place it in the egg carton to dry.

5. Have students apply another design on the egg with the crayon. Dip the egg into red dye, and return it to the carton to dry.

6. Repeat the procedure with the remaining dyes, or until students are satisfied with their designs.

7. After the eggs are completely dry, the wax needs to be removed. You might enlist help from an adult aide for this part. Children should not work with the lit candle! Carefully hold the egg next to, not on top of, the candle flame. When the wax has softened, invite the child whose egg you hold to wipe the wax off the egg with a clean, soft cloth. Their beautiful designs will be revealed.

8. Very young students may draw designs on their eggs with permanent markers or acrylic paint as an alternative.

ACTIVITY 4

Fancy Newspaper Hats

Encourage students to make fancy hats of their own. Afterward, let children use their hats to create a window display for Mr. Kodinsky's hat shop.

Procedure

1. Provide each student with four unfolded newspaper pages.
2. Demonstrate how to place each sheet on top of the other so that all the corners are sticking out.
3. Tell students to roll all the sides toward the middle, creating a large brim.
4. Show children how to push the middle section of newspaper up, creating the crown portion of the hat.
5. Have children lightly tape the rolled edges to the crown.
6. Now invite students to decorate their hats with glitter, sequins, ribbon, and other art scraps.
7. Hold a hat parade through your school or within your classroom. You might provide appropriate music for students to march to. After the parade, let students display their hats in a showcase to represent "Mr. Kodinsky's Hat Shop."

ACTIVITY 5

Design a Hat

Challenge students to be creative as they design a new Easter hat for Miss Eula.

Procedure

1. Have children draw pictures of Miss Eula on a large sheet of paper.
2. Instruct students to arrange hat cutouts over their drawings to come up with a pleasing design for a new hat. Tell them to tape or glue their new hats to their Miss Eula drawings.
3. After completing the hat, give students writing paper. Have them title the page, "Miss Eula's Hat Is . . ." Challenge students to list words to describe their hat designs.
4. Tell students to tape the describing words to the bottom of their Miss Eula pictures and hats. Display students' work around the room.
5. Were some describing words used more than others? Start a bar chart for children to compare the different adjectives they used.

ACTIVITY 6

Writing Extension 1— Blame

How would students feel if they were blamed for something they did not do, like the characters in the story? Invite students to reflect upon such an experience by writing a journal entry for a character in the book.

The Writing Process

1. Discuss with the class the experience of the children in *Chicken Sunday* when they were wrongly blamed for throwing the eggs. How would students feel if they were in this position? Encourage students to share their ideas.

2. Invite students to imagine they are one of the children in the story. What would that child write if she or he kept a journal?

3. Challenge students to write about it. Invite volunteers to share their journal entries with the class.

ACTIVITY 7

Writing Extension 2— Special Friends

People in your community can be important or special to your students. Challenge students to write a short story based on such a person.

The Writing Process

Share with students that the character of Miss Eula is based on someone who was special in Patricia Polacco's life. Discuss with students people they know who are special or important in their own lives or communities.

Invite students to write short stories about these special people. Guide their writing with the following questions:

- *How* is this person important or special?

- *What* is your most memorable experience with this person?

- *How* has this person influenced you?

- *How* might you show him or her that he or she is special or important to you?

Just Plain Fancy

In Just Plain Fancy, *Patricia Polacco mixes Amish values with childlike curiosities and natural desires. After finding an egg that is not a plain ol' chicken egg, Naomi and Ruth, two young Amish sisters, strive to hide the unusual bird that hatches from it. Because the bird is not ordinary and plain, they are afraid of being blamed for having something "fancy." After a series of exciting and intriguing events, the girls come to realize that some things are not made fancy by man but are a part of God's handiwork.*

Points of Interest Not Mentioned in the Story

- The book never states how this unusual egg got to Naomi and Ruth's farm. However, on the title page, a van is shown going down a country road with its back door wide open. An egg is flying out of the open door toward the soft grass on the side of the road. This is a valuable point for students to notice, showing them how important illustrations can be.

- A number of Amish communities are located in Michigan. Since Patricia Polacco spent much of her life there, she probably observed the ways of the Amish. Suggest to students that this gave her the background she needed to write the story. Encourage them to think about things in their own communties about which they could write.

- In this story the Amish community has a frolic. A frolic is when families and friends from local and neighboring communities join together to help another family build a barn. Such a barn raising is vividly depicted in the film *Witness* (Warner Brothers, 1985), which features the Amish community. The film is certainly not one that is appropriate to show from beginning to end in any classroom! However, this short portion lends enrichment, giving students a clear picture of a barn raising. This portion can be found approximately halfway through the film and is about five minutes long.

Memorable Story Quote

"Plainly it was a miracle . . . and sometimes miracles are just plain fancy!"

Activities for *Just Plain Fancy*

ACTIVITY 1: Peacock Book Report

ACTIVITY 2: How Many Ways Can You Say "Said"?

ACTIVITY 3: Children's Play

ACTIVITY 4: Amish Lifestyle Venn Diagram

ACTIVITY 5: Writing Extension 1—Fancy

ACTIVITY 6: Writing Extension 2—Feelings

ACTIVITY 1
Peacock Book Report

Your students will never forget this wonderful story as they discover the simpler ways of life and the wonders of nature depicted in *Just Plain Fancy*. Invite students to make a peacock and its feathers in which to record the sequence of events of the story.

Supplies
- patterns on page 271
- colored construction paper
- pencil
- scissors
- writing paper

Assembling the Peacock

1. Instruct students to trace the peacock's body onto colored construction paper and cut it out.

2. Tell students to trace the peacock feathers seven times on light-colored construction paper and cut them out, too.

3. On a separate sheet of paper, have students write seven main story events. (See below.) Ask students to write each event on one of the seven feathers.

4. Show students how to arrange the feathers around the peacock's body, gluing them in place.

The Writing Process

Brainstorm with students the following questions.
- *Who* was in the story?
- *Where* did the story take place?
- *Why* is there a story at all?
- *What* were the problems? (For example, the girls' desire to have something fancy.)
- *How* were the problems resolved?

With the class, list the sequence of story events on the chalkboard. Below are seven suggested events, numbered in order.

1. Naomi and Ruth find the unusual egg.

2. The egg hatches a fancy chick.

3. The girls are afraid that Fancy will keep Naomi from receiving her white cap.

4. Fancy reveals he is a peacock to Naomi and Ruth.

5. During the community frolic, Fancy escapes.

6. Martha, the oldest of the gathering, explains that the peacock is a gift from God, not one created by man.

7. Naomi receives her white cap.

ACTIVITY 2

How Many Ways Can You Say "Said"?

Share with students that to make writing more colorful, authors often use a variety of words to relay the same thing. Patricia Polacco cleverly uses different words to show how something has been said. This activity encourages students to begin a list of words they can use in place of *said*.

Procedure

1. Make a coat-hanger chart for your classroom. (See Appendix, page 261.) Write the label, "Many Ways to Say Said" across the top.

2. Go through the book with the class, looking for the different ways that Patricia Polacco relays speech as she quotes her characters.

3. List these words on your chart. Invite students to record them in their Writing Journals. Your list might include *asked, complained, scolded, sang, whimpered, cried, called, chirped,* and *squealed.*

4. Add to this list as you read each Patricia Polacco book and others in your studies. Encourage students to use the words in their own writings.

Extra! Check out Patricia Polacco's book, *My Rotten Redheaded Older Brothe*r for other unique ways to say "said."

ACTIVITY 3

Children's Play

Further enjoy the story by inviting children to put on a play.

The following pages include the play script as well as suggestions for costumes and props. Encourage everyone to participate, either by taking a role or by working behind the scenes to create scenery.

Just Plain Fancy

A Children's Play

Characters

- Kaleb (papa)
- Naomi
- Ruth
- Aunt Sari
- Martha
- Cousin Hannah
- Peacock
- Four chickens
- Members of the Amish community

Costumes

- Characters should wear plain, Amish-type clothings. Blue bonnets are necessary for Naomi and Ruth. A white bonnet is needed for Naomi at the end.
- The peacock costume could consist of brightly-colored clothing.
- Chicken costumes could be solid white clothing.

Props

- stuffed chicken to be Henny
- egg made of soft material, such as a sponge
- 4 chairs
- hen house constructed from a large appliance box or other cardboard
- baskets for egg-gathering
- other eggs (these can be balls of wadded white paper)

Scene 1

(The hen house is sitting on one side of the stage. Paper eggs are scattered about. The sound of a truck or car is heard offstage. (Pre-record the sound of a car.) Suddenly an egg flies onto the stage from the direction of the car sound.)

Scene 2

(Four chairs are placed on the stage—two in front, and two in back. Papa, Ruth, and Naomi are in the chairs, which serves as a buggy. Papa pretends to be holding a horse's reins.)

Naomi: Papa, why don't we have a car like the English?

Papa: It is not our way, child. We are in no hurry.

(The buggy stops, Papa gets out and pretends to unharness the horse. Papa exits the stage. Naomi and Ruth get out of the buggy and skip toward the hen house.)

Naomi: Everything around here is so plain. Our clothes are plain, our houses are plain, even our chickens are plain. It would pleasure me—just once—to have something fancy.

Ruth: Shaw, Naomi. You aughtn't to be saying such things. Let's look for eggs.

Naomi: *(bending down beside the large egg)* This egg looks different from any I have ever seen. It is still warm. Let's put it in Henny's nest. This one needs to be hatched.

(Naomi puts the egg in her basket. The girls begin to walk toward the hen house.)

Ruth: You are so good with chickens. I just know you are going to get your white cap this year. Mama says you are ready.

Naomi: Oh, I hope so. I really hope so.

Ruth: Ain't we pleasured. You wanted something fancy and now you've got it.
(Naomi puts egg under Henny, who is sitting on hay just outside the hen house.)

Scene 3

Narrator: As the days pass, Naomi and Ruth check Henny's nest. Every day they looked at the eggs, watching for signs of cracks in the shells. Then, one day the eggs hatch.

(Naomi and Ruth enter the stage walking toward the henhouse. They bend down, realizing that the eggs have hatched.)

Ruth: Look at the little chick from the fancy egg, Naomi.

Naomi: That egg was fancy inside and out, wasn't it? Fancy. That's just what we will name this chick.

Ruth: *(dancing and skipping around)* FANCY. FANCY. FANCY.

Scene 4

Narrator: Weeks pass. Henny's chicks grow quickly and are soon scratching around in the dirt. They have all lost their yellow downy feathers and have grown bright white ones. All of them except Fancy. Fancy looks very different from the others. There is no doubt about it. This chick isn't plain!

(Five children waddle onto the stage. Four are dressed all in white. They are the chickens. One is dressed in a solid bright color. He or she is the peacock. Naomi and Ruth enter the stage with baskets full of feed.)

Naomi: Fancy, you're still fancy. You're the only thing around here that's not plain.

Ruth: I love you, Fancy.

Scene 5

Narrator: One afternoon in the wash house, the girls hear Aunt Sari talking about a person in the neighboring Amish community.

Sari: She dressed too fancy. She had to be shunned.

Naomi: Is it wrong to be fancy?

Hannah: Indeed, yes! We are just plain folk. It is in our laws, the Ordnung, that we must be plain.

Ruth: What does shun mean?

Sari: Someone who is shunned is shamed in front of the elders. After that the friends and neighbors are told not to speak to that person. They are no longer one of us.

(Naomi and Ruth look at each other with worry and exit the stage.)

Scene 6

Narrator: The girls are worried about Fancy. Not only could Fancy be shunned, but they could be shunned for having Fancy. As soon as they are finished with their chores, the girls run to the hen house.

(The girls are standing by the hen house surrounded by chickens.)

Ruth: What are we going to do? Fancy is too fancy to be Amish.

(At that moment, Fancy ruffles his "feathers" and shows his peacock costume. The girls look astonished.)

Naomi: Stay here just a minute, Ruth. I'll be right back.

(Naomi exits the stage and returns with a big quilt. She places it around Fancy.)

Naomi: We'll have to hide him until we know what to do. The elders will be here for the frolic tomorrow.

Ruth: He'll be shunned. Maybe we will be, too.

Scene 7

(During the narration, the frolic is going on. Men are working, women are talking, and children are playing. Everyone is silent as they act out the scene while the narrator is speaking. As soon as the narration stops, the frolic continues, but the actors adlib words. Ruth and Naomi look worried.)

Narrator: The next morning, the neighboring Amish folk arrive for the frolic. The men and boys help add a stable to the Vlekes' barn. They work hard in the sun while the women work and talk. Naomi and Ruth help serve food, pour lemonade, and thread needles for the women who are quilting. This day should be happy for them, but the girls are worried about Fancy. When she has served the last ladle of lemonade, Naomi starts toward the hen house.

(Fancy runs toward the gathering, flapping his wings.)

Naomi: OH, NO! This is all my fault. I wanted something fancy. I should have known better than to make that kind of wish.

Ruth: Poor Fancy. Now he'll be shunned.

(Fancy runs all through the gathering—over, under, around, and through people—while Naomi chases him. He lands right in front of Martha, the oldest member of the gathering, and spreads his wings. Everyone looks at the bird, stunned.)

Naomi: Please don't shun him. I did this. I made him fancy.

Martha: Dry your tears, child. This isn't your doing. This be God's handiwork. Only He could think up colors like that.

Ruth: You mean you aren't going to shun him?

Martha: One can only be shunned for going against the ways of our people. This is no plain chicken. This be one of God's most beautiful creations. He's fancy, child, and that's the way of it.

(Everyone cheers.)

Martha: *(holding out a new white cap to Naomi)* I believe you have this coming child. Your family believes you have earned this well, and I agree. Not only have you given good and faithful care to your flock of chickens, but you have raised one of the finest peacocks I ever did see.

(Naomi hugs Fancy, proudly.)

Narrator: No one ever knew why Fancy was hatched by Henny. Plainly it was a miracle. Sometimes miracles are just plain fancy!

ACTIVITY 4

Amish Lifestyle Venn Diagram

Encourage children to compare and contrast information using a Venn diagram. This activity will allow students to compare their way of life with the Amish in the story. Share the following information with your class.

History

In the 1690s Jacob Ammann (whom the Amish were named after) led the Amish away from the Swiss Mennonites because of disagreements over church discipline. The Amish wanted more control and simplicity in their lives and felt that the Mennonites were pulling away from original religious beliefs. The Amish even went to the point of shunning those who did not follow their rules. These rules are called the Ordnung. The Amish came to America around 1727.

Locale

The Amish live in farming communities in 23 states and in Ontario, Canada. The largest groups live in Ohio, Pennsylvania, Indiana, Iowa, and Illinois.

Lifestyle

Simplicity is the key to Amish life. They are taught total separation from the world. Their code of living requires farming in the simplest of ways—horse-drawn plows and manual labor. They do not use cars. Transportation is by horse-drawn buggies. Electricity and telephones are not allowed. There are also forbidden activities such as going to war, swearing, and holding public office. The women wear plain clothing, usually long dresses and bonnets. The men are bearded with wide-brimmed hats. Worship is very important to the Amish, and they are extremely family and community oriented. They often help each other with everyday chores as well as major projects. (For more information, check out *The Amish* by Doris Faber, Doubleday, 1991.)

Procedure

1. Brainstorm with students the ways of the Amish. (for example, plain clothing, no electricity, grow their own food, worship, sharing, and so on) List their ideas on the chalkboard.
2. Then brainstorm with children the lifestyles they have. (for example, choice of clothing, electricity, food is purchased, worship, sharing, and so on) Make another list to record these ideas.
3. Now let students complete the Venn diagram. (See the Appendix for a Venn diagram template.) Have children list the Amish ways on one side, and their own ways on the other. In the middle where the circles intersect, encourage students to list the things they have in common.

ACTIVITY 5

Writing Extension 1: Fancy

The word *fancy* means different things to different people. Invite students to share what they think fancy means.

The Writing Process

1. Discuss with the class their ideas about what the word *fancy* means. What do students consider fancy? List their ideas on the chalkboard. For example, fancy can be used to describe objects, occasions, places, people, ideas, and so on.

2. Now challenge students to write a paragraph about something they think is fancy. Suggest that they illustrate their paragraphs, too.

3. Encourage volunteers to share their work with the class.

ACTIVITY 6

Writing Extension 2: Feelings

Invite students to explore the feelings of the characters in the story by writing new situations in which others might have similar emotions.

The Writing Process

1. Conclude with students that Naomi and Ruth felt embarrassed and ashamed at points in the story. Why did they feel this way?

2. Brainstorm with students other instances in which someone might feel the way Ruth and Naomi did. List them on the chalkboard.

3. Invite students to choose one of the instances and to write a first-person account of it, explaining how he or she feels and why. Let students come up with other instances, too.

4. Encourage students to use the following questions as a guide.

- *Why* does the character feel ashamed or embarrassed? Was it the situation, a person, or something she or he did?
- *How* does the character act or react to these feelings?
- *How* is the situation resolved?
- Did the character learn a lesson from the situation? *What* was it?
- *What* might the character tell a friend in the same situation?

The Keeping Quilt

The Keeping Quilt uses a simple piece of fabric to take the reader on a journey through generations. The journey begins with Patricia Polacco's great grandmother arriving in America from Russia with a babushka, or shawl, gently draped over her head. After taking the reader through four generations, the book ends with pieces of the original babushka enveloping a new life, Patricia Polacco's daughter. The Keeping Quilt will not only warm students' hearts, but also enrich their love and curiosity of family heritage.

Points of Interest Not Mentioned in the Story

- This quilt is a real article of treasured history in Patricia Polacco's family. Patricia is the present keeper of the quilt. She still uses it as a tablecloth on special occasions, as a chuppa in weddings, and as a blanket to welcome new babies into the world.

- Throughout the book the babushka and the fabrics that make up the quilt are the only parts in the illustration that are in color. This technique draws the reader's attention to the main focus of the story.

Memorable Story Quote

"We will make a quilt to help us always remember home. It will be like having the family in backhome Russia dance around us at night."

Activities for *The Keeping Quilt*

ACTIVITY 1: Class Quilt Book Report

ACTIVITY 2: Family Traditions Cookbook

ACTIVITY 3: Class Keeping Quilt

ACTIVITY 4: Family History Museum

ACTIVITY 5: Artist Technique

ACTIVITY 6: Creative Dramatics

ACTIVITY 7: My Time Line

ACTIVITY 1

Class Quilt Book Report

Quilts usually have a story of their own, just as *The Keeping Quilt* does. Explain to the class that they will be making a class quilt that retells the story of *The Keeping Quilt*. Begin the activity with the writing process, culminating with the class quilt.

Assembling the Quilt

1. Spread out a length of mural paper, preferably in a bright color, such as red, green, or blue.
2. Invite students or groups to arrange the completed quilt squares on the paper to represent a quilt pattern. Make sure the squares are in story sequence.
3. When students are pleased with their layout and agree that all events are in story order, have them glue the squares to the mural paper.
4. Write the title and author across the top of the paper.
5. For a finished look, you might scallop the edges of your quilt. Display your quilt for all to see.

The Writing Process

Brainstorm with students answers to these questions.
- *Who* was in the story?
- *Where* did the story take place?
- *Why* is there a story at all? (To share the history of the quilt and of the author's family; to show the importance of knowing your heritage.)

On the chalkboard, list with students the sequence of story events. Keep the list short, simple, and to the point, using students' own words. Below are suggested events, numbered in order.

1. Great-Gramma Anna arrived as a child in America, wearing the babushka.
2. Anna danced as she played with the babushka.
3. The ladies used the babushka and other pieces of clothing from family members to make the quilt.
4. The quilt was used as a tablecloth.
5. Anna and Great-Grandpa Sasha were engaged as they sat on the quilt.
6. Anna and Sasha were married under the quilt, which was used as a chuppa.
7. Grandma Carle was born and wrapped in the quilt.
8. Carle married Grandpa George under the quilt used as a chuppa.
9. Mary Ellen was born and wrapped in the quilt.
10. Great-Gramma Anna used the quilt to keep her legs warm when she was very old and sick.
11. The quilt was used as a tablecloth on Great-Gramma Anna's ninety-eighth birthday.
12. The quilt covered Great-Gramma Anna as she died.
13. The quilt covered Mary Ellen as a chuppa on her wedding day.
14. Patricia was wrapped in the quilt when she was born.
15. The quilt was a tablecloth for Patricia's first birthday.
16. The quilt was a pretend cape for Patricia.
17. The quilt covered Patricia as a chuppa when she married Enzo-Mario.
18. Traci Denise was wrapped in the quilt when she was born.

Show students how to create a patchwork-square for the quilt. Working individually or in pairs, students can write or illustrate one story event on a square.

ACTIVITY 2
Family Traditions Cookbook

Food is an important aspect of family and religious traditions. In many of Polacco's books, she mentions traditional Jewish foods that were prepared on specific occasions. In *The Keeping Quilt* she describes the cake, kulich, to celebrate Great-Gramma Anna's ninety-eighth birthday. Invite students to bring in recipes from home that reflect their backgrounds or heritages to contribute to a class Family Traditions Cookbook.

Procedure

1. First send a letter home, explaining that your class is studying family traditions. Ask family members to send a recipe for a favorite family food, perhaps one that has been passed down. Also encourage family members to discuss the recipe with their child. Why is the recipe important to the family? Why is it a family favorite? Give a specific time when all recipes must be collected.

2. Have students share their recipes with the class, telling brief stories related to them. Invite students to write their stories as well.

3. Enlist the help of teacher aides to type up the recipes and stories. Make sure each student has his or her own special page.

4. Present students with their typed pages, and invite them to illustrate their recipes and stories. Let them autograph and date the recipes, too.

5. Invite volunteers to create a cover for the class cookbook.

6. Use the school copier to print and staple copies of the class cookbook, one for each student.

Extra! This makes a great gift any time of the year.

Dear Family,

Our class is doing an author study on Patricia Polacco. In her book *The Keeping Quilt,* she shares many family traditions that have been passed down through generations. In many of her books, she also shares specific foods that are special to her family and the many cultures she has been touched by throughout her life.

We are making a class recipe book that focuses on traditional family foods. Please discuss with your child a favorite recipe that is special to your family. If possible, explain the significance of the recipe or any special stories connected to it.

Please send the recipe to school with your child by _____. Thank you for your cooperation and help with this activity.

Sincerely,

ACTIVITY 3

Class Keeping Quilt

The Keeping Quilt centers around a quilt that displays pieces of fabric from the clothing of Patricia Polacco's family members. This activity encourages children to build their own memories as they make a quilt from pieces of their own clothing.

Supplies
- a full-size flat sheet, color or print not important
- fusible web
- a hot iron (adult supervision required)

Procedure

1. Send the letter below home with students, explaining that your class is studying *The Keeping Quilt* by Patricia Polacco. Encourage students to share the story with family members.
2. In class, have students show their fabric pieces and tell from where they originated.
3. Use the iron to adhere the fabric squares to fusible web, following the directions on the package. This step should only be completed by you or an adult helper!
4. Help students cut away the excess fusible web.
5. With the class, arrange the prepared fabric squares on the sheet.
6. Now iron on top of each square, and the fusible web will adhere the fabric to the sheet. This step should only be completed by you or an adult helper!
7. Use your class keeping quilt for a tablecloth during special occasions, as a blanket during storytime, or to decorate a classroom wall.

Dear Family,

Our class is doing an author study on Patricia Polacco. In her book *The Keeping Quilt*, she shares the story of a quilt created with pieces of fabric from the clothing of family members. In keeping with this theme, we would like to make a Class Keeping Quilt.

Please send a piece of fabric from an article of clothing your child has worn. The piece needs to be at least 6 inches x 6 inches (15 cm x 15 cm). Have your child bring the fabric square to school by _____.

You are welcome to come to school and view the quilt when it is finished. Thank you for your cooperation. We are excited about this project.

Sincerely,

ACTIVITY 4

Family History Museum

In her books, Patricia Polacco shares treasures that her family has passed down through the generations. This activity gives students opportunities to share special things that have been passed down in their families.

Procedure

1. As a homework assignment, ask students to discuss with their families objects that have been passed from generation to generation. If none is available, suggest that they select with their families a new family item that might one day be passed down to them.

2. Have students bring the article to class or draw a picture of it.

3. Explain that the class is going to set up a "museum day" to display their family "artifacts." Mention that an artifact is an object that has historical interest.

4. Tell each student to write on a note card a brief history of the artifact he or she brought in.

5. Choose an area in your classroom in which to create your class Family History Museum. Invite each student to present a short oral report as he or she displays the family artifact.

ACTIVITY 5

Artist Technique

Patricia Polacco is both the author and the illustrator of *The Keeping Quilt*. The illustrations are in black and white, except for the fabrics used in the quilt itself. This technique draws the reader closer to the theme. The following art activity lets students try Polacco's techniques.

Procedure

1. Discuss with students the illustrations in *The Keeping Quilt*. Look at each one individually, guiding students to discover the technique. Point out not only the color, but the vivid details in each picture.

2. Now let students try it. Have them each draw a detailed picture in pencil on white paper.

3. Then instruct them to color in the one thing that is the focus of the picture.

4. Help students mat the pictures on black posterboard to display around the room.

ACTIVITY 6

Creative Dramatics

The beginning of *The Keeping Quilt* describes how Patricia Polacco's Great-Gramma Anna played with her babushka, which later became part of the quilt. Patricia played with the quilt much as her great-gramma had. This activity will bring out the creativity in your students as they "play" with a quilt.

Procedure

1. Bring a quilt, blanket, or sheet to class.

2. Clear a large space in the classroom, or take the class to the gym. You might want to take them outside, if weather permits.

3. Have students sit in a large circle. Discuss how young Patricia played with the quilt.

4. Now place your quilt in the middle of the circle. Challenge children to imagine what the quilt could be.

5. As students silently come up with ideas, invite them to the middle of the circle, to pick up the quilt, and to act out what they have imagined the quilt to be.

6. Challenge the rest of the class to figure out what their classmate is acting out. Once the answer is guessed correctly, the student places the quilt in the middle of the circle and returns to his or her seat.

7. The next student with an idea then takes a turn. Continue the game as long as interest holds.

ACTIVITY 7

My Time Line

Life's special events are easily identified in *The Keeping Quilt*. Each of us has memorable events that have shaped our lives. This time-line activity invites students to visualize and share their own personal histories.

Procedure

1. Discuss with the class the important events in Patricia Polacco's life, revealed in *The Keeping Quilt*.

2. Have students discuss important events in their lives.

3. Give each student a time line (Appendix, page 263). Have them complete the time line by briefly describing five important events in their lives, in order. Events could include the day they were born, when they lost their first tooth, their first day of school, the birth of a sibling, and so on. Make sure they include dates, if possible. Allow students to draw pictures or to attach photographs to their time lines.

4. Let volunteers share their time lines with the class.

The Bee Tree

*In **The Bee Tree**, a young girl decides that she is tired of reading. Her wise and understanding grandfather has the perfect cure. After leading her on a bee chase to find honey, he helps her realize that reading is "as exciting as a wild chase . . . and as sweet as honey from a bee tree." This book is a great way to show your students how reading can be an adventure, not a chore.*

Points of Interest Not Mentioned in the Story

- As in most of Patricia Polacco's books, the main characters are members of her family. The young girl, Mary Ellen, is Patricia Polacco's mother. And Grampa is her great-grandfather.

- Mary Ellen, Patricia Polacco's mother, still lives in the same house that Patricia grew up in. In fact, Patricia still lives near her mother. They see each other almost every day. Mary Ellen was a classroom teacher for 38 years.

- Patricia Polacco's first book, *Meteor*, is about an event in her mother's childhood. In this story she tells about a meteor that landed in the front yard when Mary Ellen was young. The event greatly influenced her mother, who still collects geodes and rocks.

Memorable Story Quote

"Just like we ran after the bees to find their tree, so you must also chase these things through the pages of a book!"

Activities for *The Bee Tree*

ACTIVITY 1: Beehive Mobile Book Report

ACTIVITY 2: "The Chase" Mural

ACTIVITY 3: Red-Hot Readers

ACTIVITY 4: Book "Tea"

ACTIVITY 5: Writing Extension—Valuable Lessons

ACTIVITY 6: Guest Speaker—Beekeeper

ACTIVITY 1
Beehive Mobile Book Report

The focus of *The Bee Tree* is the wonder of books. As Grampa leads Mary Ellen on a chase to discover the natural activities of a bee, he is really teaching her that reading is also an adventure, waiting to be discovered. To retell the events of the story, invite students to make this beehive mobile. Begin the activity with the writing process.

The Writing Process

Brainstorm with students the answers to these questions.
- *Who* was in the story?
- *Where* did the story take place?
- *Why* is there a story at all? (Mary Ellen was tired of reading, which sparked Grampa to teach her a lifelong lesson.)

On the chalkboard, list with students the sequence of story events. Keep your list short, simple, and to the point, using students' own words. Below are suggested events, numbered in order.

1. Mary Ellen is tired of reading, so Grampa decides to take her on a bee chase.
2. Mary Ellen and Grampa trap a jar of bees and carefully let one out. They chase it to find its hive.
3. Mrs. Govlock and her baby, Sylvester, join the chase.
4. Einar Tundevold joins the chase.
5. Olav Lundheigen and the Hermann sisters join the chase.
6. "Klondike" Bertha Fitchworth joins the chase.
7. The bee disappears. Grampa lets another bee out of the jar.
8. Feduciary Longdrop and the three traveling musicians join the chase.
9. The second bee disappears. Mary Ellen lets the last bee out of the jar, and it flies to the bee tree.
10. A fire smokes out the bees. Grampa pulls out pieces of honeycomb, and everyone enjoys biscuits and honey.
11. Grampa pours a bit of honey on one of Mary Ellen's books. He says, "There is such sweetness inside of that book, too."
12. Mary Ellen discovers that the sweetness in books is adventure, knowledge, and wisdom.

Distribute to each student a bee pattern. Tell the students to trace the pattern 12 times and to cut out the tracings. Have students write or illustrate each story event on one bee cutout, numbering the bees as well. Both sides of the bees may need to be used.

Assembling the Mobile

1. Give each student a round paper plate. Instruct the students to draw 12 dots evenly spaced around the edge.

2. Help them use a hole punch to punch a hole on each dot. Also have them punch a hole on each bee wing.

3. Tell students to cut 12 pieces of yarn of varying lengths. (The mobile will be more interesting if lengths are not all the same.)

4. Starting with Bee #1, show students how to tie one end of a piece of yarn to the bee wing and the other end to a hole in the plate. Going counterclockwise, continue this step until all bees are dangling from the plate.

5. Have students cut one more piece of yarn from which to hang the mobile, attaching it to the top of the plate. Finish the mobiles by asking children to write their names, as well as the title and author of the book, on top of the plate.

6. Hang the mobiles around the room. The bees will look like they are on a chase as they dangle around the plates.

ACTIVITY 2

"The Chase" Mural

In *The Bee Tree* many exciting and colorful people join the journey to the hive. Encourage your class to create a mural depicting the bee chase.

Procedure

1. Arrange students into pairs or small groups and assign one character to each. Also assign the tree with the beehive.

2. Roll out a length of mural paper along the floor, positioning each group in story order. For example, from right to left the characters should be: the tree with the hive of bees, Grampa with a jar of bees, Mary Ellen, Mrs. Govlock and baby Sylvester, Einar Tundevold, Olav Lundheigen and the Hermann sisters, Bertha Fitchworth, Feduciary Longdrop, and the three traveling musicians.

3. Invite students to first sketch, then to draw in their characters, using paints, markers, or crayons.

4. Also suggest that students add background scenery. Paper cutouts can be attached to add dimension to your mural.

5. Write "The Chase from *The Bee Tree* by Patricia Polacco" across the top of the mural. Display the mural in the hallway for other classes to see.

ACTIVITY 3

Red-Hot Readers

In *The Bee Tree* Grampa shows Mary Ellen the importance of reading. This activity will challenge your students to read more.

Procedure

1. Have your students set a reading goal by filling out and signing the reading contract on page 264 of the Appendix.

2. Set aside time for students to read each day.

3. Invite students to fill out the book form on page 268 of the Appendix, writing a short comment or drawing a picture about one book they read.

4. At the end of the week, present reading awards to your students. (See Appendix, pages 265–267.)

ACTIVITY 4

Book "Tea"

Explain to students that book groups are a popular way for people to meet and discuss books they have read. Encourage students to share their favorite books by holding an informal "tea party," during which students can enjoy biscuits with honey, just like Mary Ellen and Grampa.

Supplies

- homemade biscuits
- honey
- lemonade
- paper plates, napkins, and cups

Procedure

1. Tell the class that they are to prepare for a Book Tea. Explain that students will share books they enjoyed that they think their classmates might also like.

2. Have students prepare for the Book Tea by completing the outline below. You might suggest that they elicit help from parents or other family members at home. Also encourage them to pass along your letter, asking family members for assistance.

3. For your Book Tea, place chairs in an informal, comfortable setting, preferably in a circle. As you serve biscuits with honey, allow students to share their favorite books.

Dear Family,

One of my primary goals this year is to foster the love of literature in my students. On _____, our class will be having a Book Tea. At this time your child will be asked to talk about a favorite book. Your child may need help choosing a book. Help your child to choose a book that he or she enjoys and will feel comfortable discussing.

Below is an outline your child can follow when sharing the book. Please help your child prepare for the presentation.

Thank you!

Sincerely,

Outline for Book Tea
(time limit: _____ minutes)

1. Tell us the title of your book.
2. Tell us the author of your book and any information you know about her or him. (Look on the book jacket.)
3. Tell about the setting of the book. Where does it take place?
4. Tell about the characters in the book. What are their names? What are they like?
5. Now tell us what the story is about.
6. Describe your favorite part.
7. Tell us why you like this book.
8. Invite your classmates to ask questions.

ACTIVITY 5

Writing Extension: Valuable Lessons

Some of the most valuable lessons in life are learned in childhood. This activity will give your students time to reflect on important lessons they have learned.

The Writing Process

Discuss with students the valuable lesson Mary Ellen learned from her grandfather. Then encourage students to think about a time when they learned a lesson. It can be a lesson someone taught them, or something they learned on their own through experience.

Challenge students to write a paragraph about the lesson they learned. Suggest that they use the following questions as a guide.

- *What* was the lesson I learned?
- *Who* taught me the lesson?
- *What* experience taught me the lesson?
- *How* did I learn the lesson?
- *How* has it made a difference in my life?

ACTIVITY 6

Guest Speaker–Beekeeper

The Bee Tree centers around the activities of bees. No one knows the life patterns of bees better than beekeepers. Invite a beekeeper to be a guest speaker in your class.

Procedure

1. Locate a beekeeper or someone knowledgeable about bees to speak to your class. Check with your community agriculture center for suggestions.

2. Check out books on bees for your students to enjoy prior to the visit. Generate appropriate questions for the students to ask the guest.

3. Following the presentation, have students write or illustrate new facts they learned about bees to display in your science center.

4. Conclude by having the class dictate a thank-you letter to send to your guest.

Robert Munsch

Robert Munsch is a storyteller extraordinaire. Many of his stories come from real-life experiences or observations he's made while traveling. Humorous twists and exaggeration are trademarks of his work. Robert Munsch develops his stories as he tells them to numerous audiences of children, changing the stories according to children's reactions. With such a tested method of crafting his work, your students will not only enjoy but also relate to each of his stories.

Interesting Facts About the Author

Birth: Robert Munsch was born June 11, 1945, in Pittsburgh, Pennsylvania.

Family: In 1983, Munsch became a naturalized citizen of Canada. Today, he lives in Guelph, Ontario, with his wife, Ann. He has two daughters, Julie and Tyya, and a son, Andrew.

Education: Robert Munsch never set out to be a writer. For seven years he studied to become a Roman Catholic priest with the hopes of being an anthropological missionary. During this time, he took a part-time job at a day-care center. Growing up in a household of nine, he was used to being around children. The day-care job led him to work in a nursery school and orphanage, and later he earned a degree in early childhood education.

Beginnings as an author:

When Robert did his student-teaching at a nursery school near Boston, he began to make up stories for the children during circle time. This quickly became the highlight of the day as the children requested the same stories over and over. Robert never thought of these stories "as things in themselves, but rather as little machines that kept kids happy and occupied." Even when encouraged to write the stories down, Robert was hesitant because he hated to write and could not spell. Eventually, he did put the stories on paper, and the rest, as they say, is history.

Pastimes: Robert loves storytelling, cycling, and geology.

Common threads to look for throughout his books:

- Notice the dedications. Often they are dedicated to the people who actually lived the story. Sometimes the notes on the back of the book give insight into the story's origin.

- Many of Robert's books are illustrated by Michael Martchenko. Martchenko was born in France and educated in Canada.

- Robert often uses onomatopoeia to provide the reader with full sound effects for his stories.

- Most of Robert's books are about children and their adventures in real life.

Books by Robert Munsch

- *Moira's Birthday*
- *Mortimer*
- *Angela's Airplane*
- *David's Father*
- *The Dark*
- *Mud Puddle*
- *The Paper Bag Princess*
- *The Boy and the Drawer*
- *Jonathan Cleaned Up, Then He Heard a Sound*
- *Murmel, Murmel, Murmel*
- *Millicent and the Wind*

- *The Fire Station*
- *Thomas' Snowsuit*
- *50 Below Zero*
- *I Have to Go!*
- *A Promise Is a Promise*
- *Pigs*
- *Something Good*
- *Show and Tell*
- *Purple, Green and Yellow*
- *Wait and See*
- *Where Is Gah-Ning?*
- *Love You Forever*

Moira's Birthday

Moira's Birthday will immediately hook your students to the books of Robert Munsch. In this book, Robert combines home life and school life when Moira decides to invite the entire school to her birthday party, against her parents wishes. All children love a birthday story, and this is the birthday story of them all!

Point of Interest Not Mentioned in the Story

- Occasionally, Robert Munsch goes on government-sponsored tours in Canada, staying in the home of a family with children. Many times these families are the origins of his stories, as in the case of *Moira's Birthday*. Munsch stayed with Moira's family in Hay River, in the Northwest Territory. She celebrated her birthday while he was there, and he wrote this story for her. Notice that the book is dedicated to Moira Green.

Memorable Story Quote

"For my birthday I want to invite grade 1, grade 2, grade 3, grade 4, grade 5, grade 6, aaaand kindergarten."

Extra! Many of Robert Munsch's books have been made into videos. Check out *Moira's Birthday,* produced by: CINAR Productions
Golden Book Video and Design
Western Publishing Company, Inc.
Racine, Wisconsin 53404

Activities for *Moira's Birthday*

ACTIVITY 1: Birthday-Cake-Shaped Book Report

ACTIVITY 2: Writing Extension 1—My Ideal Birthday Party

ACTIVITY 3: Writing Extension 2—Design an Invitation

ACTIVITY 4: Writing Extension 3—Thank-you Cards

ACTIVITY 5: Onomatopoeia

ACTIVITY 6: Create a Menu

ACTIVITY 7: Cake Decorating/Class Birthday Party

ACTIVITY 1

Birthday-Cake-Shaped Book Report

Invite students to create book reports in the shape of birthday cakes.

Assembling the Book

1. Reproduce the cake pattern on page 39, one for each student. If possible, use pastel card stock.

2. Then reproduce the writing pages on page 39, eight copies for each student. (You could also have students trace the original cake pattern onto lined paper eight times to be cut out.)

3. Instruct children to cut out and staple the cover and writing pages together.

The Writing Process

Brainstorm with students answers to these questions.

- *Who* was in the story?
- *Where* did the story take place?
- *Why* is there a story at all? What are the main problems? (For example, Moira wants to invite the entire school to her party.)
- *What* happens?

With the class, list on the chalkboard the sequence of story events. Keep the list short, simple, and to the point. Whenever possible, use students' own words. Below are some suggested events. Have students tell about each event on one page of their cake books.

1. Moira wanted to invite all the children in school to her birthday party.

2. Her parents said no.

3. Moira invited them all anyway, and everyone came.

4. Moira ordered 200 pizzas and 200 cakes, but only 10 pizzas and 10 cakes were delivered.

5. Children ran home for more food.

6. Kids and presents were everywhere. The house was a mess.

7. Moira explained that if everyone helped clean, they would each get a present.

8. The house was clean. The children left. One hundred and ninety pizzas and one hundred and ninety cakes were dumped in Moira's front yard.

ACTIVITY 1
Birthday-Cake-Shaped Book Patterns

ACTIVITY 2

Writing Extension 1—My Ideal Birthday Party

Children always dream of a once-in-a-lifetime birthday party. This activity encourages students to plan their own out-of-this-world party.

The Writing Process

Brainstorm with students ideas for birthday parties they'd like to have. What would their dream party be?

Encourage students to write and illustrate their ideas about the perfect party. Guide their writing with the following questions.

- What will be the theme of the party?
- Where will the party take place?
- Who will be invited? How many guests will you have?
- Which refreshments will you serve?
- Which games might you play? How about music?
- Which party favors will you give to your guests?

Extra! Collect the essays and make a class book of party ideas. Or, display them on a bulletin board.

ACTIVITY 3

Writing Extension 2—Design an Invitation

Birthday invitations are an important part of any birthday celebration. Challenge students to come up with their own unique invitation designs.

The Writing Process

Invite volunteers to share their essays from Activity 2. Inform them that they will now design and write invitations to their dream parties.

Bring to class a variety of invitations as examples, such as those for birthdays, weddings, and graduations, both formal and informal. Discuss important information that each invitation includes, such as time, place, and date of the party, and perhaps even the theme.

Using the invitations as examples, encourage students to write and design their own invitations. If your class has a computer, allow children to create their designs using computer graphics.

Extra! Students' party essays from Activity 2, along with these invitations, make a great bulletin-board display.

ACTIVITY 4

Writing Extension 3—Thank-you Cards

At some point in their lives, children will have to write thank-you notes. *Moira's Birthday* provides the perfect opportunity to teach this form of writing etiquette.

The Writing Process

If possible, bring to class examples of thank-you notes you've received or written. Explain to students that thank-you notes can be written not only for gifts, but also for nice things someone has done. What experiences have your students had with thank-you cards, either writing or receiving them? Invite them to share their experiences with the class.

Explain to students that they will each write a thank-you note to someone in school who has done something special for them. Brainstorm ideas for who that person could be, for example, the school nurse, custodian, librarian, cafeteria worker, even the principal.

Discuss the parts of a thank-you note. Point out the greeting; the body, or main part of the note; and the ending, or closing. Tell students to first write rough drafts of their letters on notebook paper.

Guide students in editing their letters. Then encourage students to copy their letters and paste them inside folded sheets of construction paper. This is the card. Encourage them to decorate their cards and deliver them in school.

ACTIVITY 5

Onomatopoeia

Robert Munsch uses various forms of language arts to enrich his stories. In *Moira's Birthday* he uses onomatopoeia to give the reader a true sense of action. Encourage students to make comic strips to show the sound words in the story.

Procedure

1. Write the word *onomatopoeia* on the chalkboard and challenge students to recall what it means. Confirm that onomatopoeia is a word or phrase that describes a sound. For example, *bang, crash, boom, zip*.

2. Reread *Moira's Birthday* with the class to look for and list the onomatopoeia used throughout the book. You might start a hanger chart (Appendix, p. 261) for students to contribute and refer to.

3. Encourage students to list the words in their Writing Journals.

4. Pass out drawing paper and ask students to draw a particularly noisy scene from the book. For each noise they illustrate, tell them to draw a speech balloon above it in which to write the word of onomatopoeia.

5. Display students' comic strips on a bulletin board titled "A Noisy Time Was Had by All."

Create a Menu

Fried goat. Old cheese. Boiled bats. These are just a few of the foods Moira's guests brought to her party. Using these colorful foods as a guide, encourage students to create fun menus of their own.

Procedure

1. Ahead of time, collect menus from local restaurants to share with your students. Discuss the different categories of foods, such as salads, appetizers, beverages, and desserts, as well as the format of the menus.

2. Reread *Moira's Birthday* and list with students the different foods. Discuss the humor the author used naming the foods.

3. Explain to students that they will create a silly menu to recall all the fun foods from the story, adding their own ridiculous food ideas, too.

4. Once students' menus are complete, encourage them to come up with a fun name for a restaurant that might serve such foods.

5. Provide students with an assortment of paper on which to create and design their menus. Have students decorate the covers of their menus with foods and the restaurant names.

6. Invite students to share their menus with the class.

ACTIVITY 7

Cake Decorating/Class Birthday Party

One of the most exciting parts of a birthday party is the birthday cake. Use this cake-decorating activity as a culmination for *Moira's Birthday*.

Procedure

1. Ahead of time, prepare to bring to class uniced cupcakes, one for each child. You might send a letter home, asking family members for assistance, or ask a local bakery or grocery story to donate the cupcakes. You will also need icing and other decorating items, such as sprinkles, nuts, or small candies.

2. Set up a cake-decorating table and provide each student with a cupcake. Invite students to the table to choose the icing and other decorations they'd like. Then at their desks, have them ice their cupcakes using plastic knives.

3. Culminate your reading of *Moira's Birthday* by having a class birthday party, complete with decorations. Let students use construction paper, glitter, and streamers to make hats, confetti, and banners. Honor all students' birthdays, including your own, of course!

Extra! This would be a great time to watch the video of *Moira's Birthday*, if available.

Mortimer

In Mortimer *a young boy refuses to go to sleep and everyone, even the police, get involved. All children can relate to this story in which Robert Munsch turns the bedtime blues into a hilarious, unforgettable tale.*

Points of Interest Not Mentioned in the Story

- Although *Mortimer* was not the first book Robert Munsch published, it was the first story he told. In 1972, while student-teaching at a nursery school, he was assigned to lead the children in circle time. After giving each child a small container full of corn, he told them a "story-song" he had made up about a young boy who did not want to go to bed. The boy kept singing

  "Clang, clang, rattle bing bang,
  Gonna make my noise all day.
  Clang, clang, rattle bing bang,
  Gonna make my noise all day."

  The children joined in and began to shake their containers of corn as they sang the jingle. They loved the story and asked him to tell it over and over again.

- Ten years later *Mortimer* was published. Because his sister had encouraged him to publish this story, Robert Munsch dedicated *Mortimer* to her three children, Billy, Sheila, and Kathleen Cronin.

- The jingle provides opportunities to reinforce *-ang* and *-ing* endings.

Memorable Story Quote

"Clang, clang, rattle bing bang,   Clang, clang rattle bing bang
Gonna make my noise all day.   Gonna make my noise all day."

Activities for *Mortimer*

ACTIVITY 1: Mortimer Story Cube

ACTIVITY 2: Children's Play

ACTIVITY 3: Mortimer Postage Stamp

ACTIVITY 4: The Science of Sound

ACTIVITY 5: Writing Extension 1—"How I Go to Sleep" Class Book

ACTIVITY 6: Writing Extension 2—Rhymes and Jingles

ACTIVITY 1

Mortimer Story Cube

All children share the common experience of bedtime. Although their individual rituals may vary, most students have lived the story of Mortimer in some way. Invite students to retell the sequence of events of *Mortimer* on a paper cube.

The Writing Process

Brainstorm with students answers to these questions.

- *Who* was in the story?
- *Where* did the story take place?
- *Why* is there a story at all? *What* was the main problem? (For example, Mortimer did not want to go to sleep.)
- *How* was it resolved?

With the class, list on the chalkboard the sequence of story events. Keep the list short, simple, and to the point. Whenever possible, use students' own words. Below are suggested events.

1. Mortimer's mother put him to bed and told him to be quiet. Mortimer sang.

2. Mortimer's father stormed upstairs and told him to be quiet. Mortimer sang.

3. Mortimer's seventeen brothers and sisters ran upstairs and told him to be quiet. Mortimer sang.

4. Two police officers stomped upstairs and told Mortimer to be quiet. Mortimer sang.

5. Everyone fussed downstairs.

6. Mortimer slept.

Reproduce for each student the cube pattern on page 45. Tell them to write or illustrate the story events, one on each side. Make sure they number the events in story order, too.

Assembling the Cube

1. Instruct children to first cut out the cube along the thick, dark lines.

2. Then model how to fold the cube along the dotted lines.

3. Show students how to tape or glue the tabs to the inside of the cube.

4. For display, give each student a long length of yarn. Help them tape it to one corner of the cube. Hang the cubes around your classroom.

Story Cube Pattern

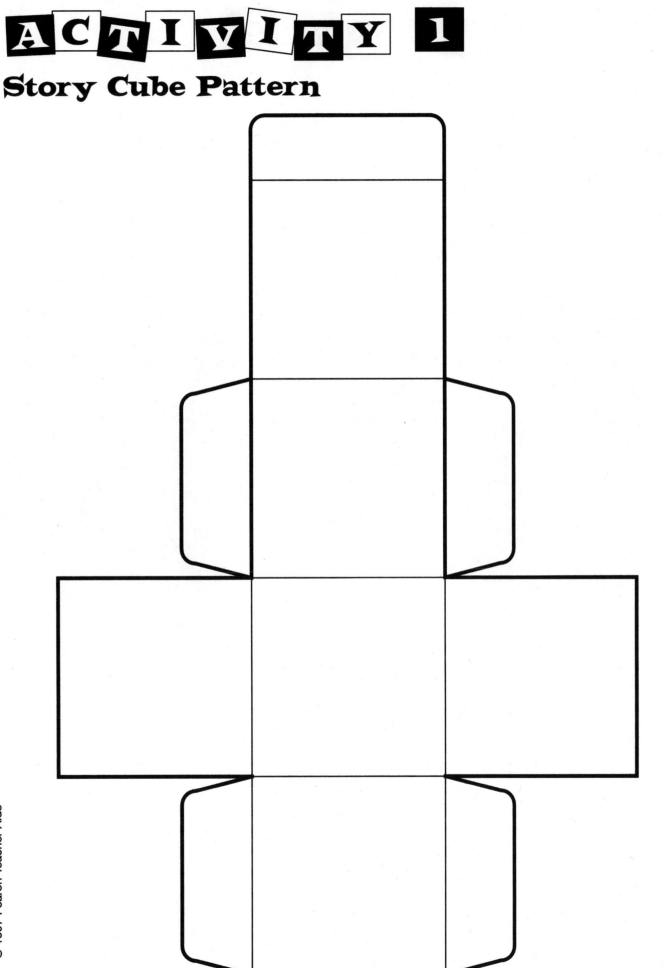

ACTIVITY 2

Children's Play

Because of the repetition and simplicity of this story, *Mortimer* makes a great play for children to act out. Cut off the top of this sheet, and reproduce the play script for students. You might assign groups of children to specific roles.

Mortimer

A Children's Play

Characters

- Mortimer
- his mother
- his father
- his 17 brothers and sisters
- two police officers

Costumes

- pajamas for Mortimer
- regular clothes for Mortimer's family
- modified police uniforms

Props

- a make-shift bed, perhaps of chairs pushed together, covered with blankets
- a stage or the classroom divided into upstairs and downstairs

Scene 1

(Mortimer is in his bed and his mother is standing over him, shaking her finger.)

Mother: Mortimer, be quiet and go to sleep!

(She leaves.)

Mortimer: Clang, clang, rattle bing bang.

               Gonna make my noise all day.

               Clang, clang, rattle bing bang.

               Gonna make my noise all day.

(Father enters Mortimer's room.)

Father: Mortimer, be quiet and go to sleep.

(He leaves.)

Mortimer: Clang, clang, rattle bing bang.

Gonna make my noise all day.

Clang, clang, rattle bing bang.

Gonna make my noise all day.

(17 brothers and sisters stomp into his room.)

Brothers and Sisters: Mortimer, be quiet and go to sleep.

(They exit.)

Mortimer: Clang, clang, rattle bing bang.

Gonna make my noise all day.

Clang, clang, rattle bing bang.

Gonna make my noise all day.

(Two police officers enter Mortimer's room.)

Two Police Officers: Mortimer, be quiet and go to sleep.

(They exit.)

Mortimer: Clang, clang, rattle bing bang.

Gonna make my noise all day.

Clang, clang, rattle bing bang.

Gonna make my noise all day.

(All the characters except Mortimer engage in an argument in the downstairs area of the stage. Meanwhile, Mortimer falls asleep in his bed.)

The End

ACTIVITY 3

Mortimer Postage Stamp

Mortimer's face is one your students will never forget. Why not put it on a postage stamp? Encourage students to have fun designing and drawing their own postage stamps to commemorate Mortimer.

Procedure

1. Ahead of time, invite students to search at home for stray postage stamps and to bring them to class. Invite any who collect stamps to share their collection. Point out that stamps are usually illustrated with significant people or objects.

2. Flip through the book and point out Mortimer's memorable face. Suggest that it might be the perfect face for a postage stamp. Allow students to practice drawing his face, perhaps inviting volunteers to show their drawings on the chalkboard.

3. Now give each student white drawing paper on which to draw Mortimer's face. Make sure they add a stamp price, too.

4. Have students glue the white paper onto black construction paper to create a border.

5. Help children create a ridged edge to the border with pinking sheers or scissors. Display the Mortimer postage stamps on a bulletin board.

ACTIVITY 4

The Science of Sound

As in many of his books, Munsch uses onomatopoeia to bring sounds to life. But how is sound really made? Let students explore with this simple science activity.

Extra! Ask children to add onomatopoetic words to your class hanger chart and to their Writing Journals.

Procedure

1. Invite students to say Mortimer's little rhyme in unison. Point out that as they speak, they are making sound. But how?

2. Have students say the rhyme again, only this time, tell them to lightly press two fingers to their throats. As they speak, what do they feel? They should feel the skin slightly vibrating at the sound of their voices.

3. Explain that sound occurs when something vibrates. In our throats we have vocal chords that vibrate as air passes over them, causing us to make sounds.

4. The same is true for musical instruments. Display a few, such as a drum, a tambourine, a guitar, and a triangle. Let children experiment with the instruments to make sound. Challenge them to point out the vibrating part on each that produces the sound.

5. Culminate by allowing students to come up with a musical accompaniment as they recite Mortimer's rhyme.

ACTIVITY 5

Writing Extension 1—"How I Go to Sleep" Class Book

Bedtime is usually a special time for most children. Which bedtime rituals do your students follow? Invite them to share their bedtime habits by completing this writing project.

The Writing Process

Discuss with students the things they do before they go to bed each night. For example, do they take baths? read stories? sing songs? How easily do they fall asleep? What helps them fall asleep? Invite students to write and illustrate a few sentences describing their bedtime rituals. Then assign a student to make a cover for a class bedtime book. Collect all the pages and bind them with the cover to keep in your Reading Center.

ACTIVITY 6

Writing Extension 2—Rhymes and Jingles

Rhyming and rapping are fun for children and often come naturally. Challenge students to write their own jingles and rhymes, using Robert Munsch's writing as examples.

The Writing Process

Start by reading and discussing the jingle in Mortimer. Encourage students to share other familiar jingles they know, for example, those heard in commercials.

Divide your class into cooperative learning groups. Tell the groups to first consider what a jingle might be about, for example, a food or game they enjoy, a favorite book character, and so on. Then challenge the groups to work together to write a jingle or rhyme.

Once groups are satisfied with their jingles, have them choose a recorder to write the finished product on a large chart or poster paper. Invite each group to present its jingle or rhyme to the class. During a second reading, invite the rest of the class to chime in as they read the group's rhyme from the poster. Display the posters in the hall for other classes to enjoy.

David's Father

When David moves to Julie's neighborhood, she couldn't be more thrilled. That is, until she sees the movers carrying in giant-size silverware. As the story unfolds, Julie discovers that David's father is a giant with a jumbo-size heart. This meaningful story ends with a touch of humor. David's Father is one your students will never forget.

Points of Interest Not Mentioned in the Story

- Robert Munsch intends for his books to have many meanings. However, he feels that the reader is the "arbiter of the meaning." In other words, he likes the readers to come up with their own meanings.

- Robert Munsch wrote *David's Father* with interracial adoption in mind. His daughter Julie, to whom it is dedicated, is half Jamaican. He realizes that many people will not get the meaning of adoption from the book. However, he respects whatever message they receive.

- Munsch's books have bright, vivid illustrations that capture the eyes of young children. Like many of Munsch's books, *David's Father* was illustrated by Michael Martchenko. Martchenko first creates pencil drawings of the major characters, allowing Munsch to edit them. Since many of the characters are based on real people, Munsch can guide Martchenko to make the illustrations resemble their namesakes.

- Six months before *David's Father* was due to be completed, a distributor requested the cover illustration for a catalog. Drawing in a rush, Martchenko didn't realize that the story was about Munsch's daughter Julie. Julie has curly hair and dark skin. Martchenko had drawn Julie with straight blond hair and fair skin. To fix the mistake, Martchenko put clear tape over the figure and changed the colors with markers. Even though the colors of Julie's hair and skin were changed, her hair could not be curled. An actual photograph of Julie appears on the back cover of *David's Father*.

Memorable Story Quote

Julie said, "Well, David, you do have a very nice father . . . but he is still kind of scary."

"You think he's scary?" said David. "Wait till you meet my grandmother."

Activities for *David's Father*

ACTIVITY 1: A "Giant" Book Report

ACTIVITY 2: David's Grandmother Class Book

ACTIVITY 3: Proper Introductions

ACTIVITY 4: Similes

ACTIVITY 5: "Dining With David's Father" Mural

ACTIVITY 6: Writing Extension 1—New Kid on the Block

ACTIVITY 7: Writing Extension 2—"Wait Till You Meet My _____" Class Book

ACTIVITY 1

A "Giant" Book Report

In *David's Father*, Julie discovers that her new friend's father is a giant, and she is very afraid of him. As Julie gets to know David's father, she learns that you "can't judge a book by its cover." Encourage students to record the humorous, often poignant, story events in a giant-size cutout.

Supplies

- 12-in x 18-in (30-cm x 45-cm) sheets of construction paper in the following colors: 2 peach or tan, 3 black, 1 green, 1 red, 2 brown
  - 10 brass fasteners or glue

The Writing Process

Brainstorm with students answers to these questions.

- *Who* was in the story?
- *Where* did the story take place?
- *Why* is there a story at all? *What* were the problems? (For example, Julie's fear of David's father.) *How* were they resolved?

With the class, list on the chalkboard the sequence of story events. Keep the list short, simple, and to the point. Whenever possible, use students' own words and ideas. Below are suggested events. Have students write the story events in their giant creations.

1. Julie saw a large moving van. Movers were carrying giant-size silverware into the house.

2. Julie got scared and ran home.

3. The next day she met her new neighbor, David. He didn't seem like a giant.

4. Julie played with David and stayed for dinner at his house.

5. Julie discovered that David's father was a giant!

6. David and Julie took a walk with David's father.

7. Everyone got out of their way, even the cars.

8. Julie slipped and scraped her elbow.

9. David's father put a special giant bandage on it.

10. Julie was not afraid of David's father anymore.

11. David says to Julie, "If you think he's scary, wait till you meet my grandmother."

Share *David's Father* with the rest of the school by displaying students' giant book reports in the hallway.

ACTIVITY 1

Assembling the Giant

1. Provide each student with the various sheets of colored construction paper from the Supplies list.

2. On the peach or tan paper, tell students to cut out a head shape, drawing in the face and using construction-paper scraps for hair.

3. Instruct students to glue writing paper to the green paper vertically. This is the giant's shirt. Show students how to attach it to the head with a brass fastener.

4. Have students fold the red paper in half lengthwise, then cut along the fold. These are the sleeves. Ask students to attach each sleeve to the shoulders with brass fasteners.

5. On peach or tan paper, invite students to draw and cut out the giant's hands, attaching them to the sleeves with brads.

6. Tell students to cut out a pair of pants from black construction paper. Point out where to attach them to the shirt with a brass fastener.

7. Have students fold another sheet of black paper lengthwise, cutting on the fold. These are the extensions of the pants and may need to be trimmed to fit at the "knees." Help students attach each to the legs with brass fasteners.

8. Finally, ask students to create two giant shoes, then to attach a shoe to the bottom of each leg with a brass fastener.

ACTIVITY 2

David's Grandmother Class Book

The ending of *David's Father* leaves much to the reader's imagination. This activity encourages students to let their imaginations fly as they consider what David's grandmother might look like.

Procedure

1. Talk with students about how the author wrote an ending that leaves the reader hanging. Do they think this allows their imaginations to work overtime? Why? What do they imagine David's grandmother might look like?

2. Ask students to pretend that they have been hired to illustrate Robert Munsch's next book, *David's Grandmother*. Pass out a large sheet of manila paper to each student and invite them to draw full-length portraits of David's grandmother.

3. At the bottom of the portrait, challenge students to write and complete the sentence, "David's grandmother is _____."

4. Collect the completed pages. Assign a volunteer to design a book cover. Staple the pages together and place the class book in your Reading Center.

5. If time and interest allow, let each child check out *David's Father* and your class book to take home to share with family.

ACTIVITY 3

Proper Introductions

In *David's Father* David introduces himself to Julie in a polite way. This is an essential social skill. Invite children to practice giving such introductions for new people they meet.

Procedure

1. Reread the passage in the book when Julie and David meet for the first time. Point out David's polite manner and words.

2. Then discuss with students their own experiences when introductions were required. Where were they? Whom did they meet?

3. Now role-play various situations in which you might meet someone, such as at a party, on the first day of school, or at a family wedding. Have students try it.

4. Also model the proper way to introduce an adult to a child. (Introduce the adult first.) Immediately have the students practice.

5. Model the proper way to introduce two children to each other. Let students try this one, too.

6. Culminate by inviting adults to drop by your classroom, allowing students to practice their new skill. Encourage students to practice introductions at home, too.

ACTIVITY 4

Similes

In *David's Father*, Robert Munsch uses similes to provide readers with vivid mental pictures. Invite students to explore these similes, listing them in their Writing Journals.

Extra! An example of onomatopoeia *(broum)* is found in *David's Father* and can be added to the appropriate page in students' Writing Journals.

Procedure

1. Create a coat-hanger chart for your classroom (see Appendix, p. 261). Write the word *simile* across the top. (If you have already started a simile chart, simply add to it.)

2. In their Writing Journals, have students title a page "Similes." If they've already begun a simile list, suggest that they add to it.

3. Discuss with students what a simile is. A simile is a literary device that compares two objects using the words *like* or *as*. "As hard as nails" and "brave like a lion" are both examples of similes.

4. With the class, reread *David's Father*. Have students listen for similes *(spoon as big as a shovel, fork as big as a pitchfork)*. List them on the coat-hanger chart while students list them in their Writing Journals. Add to the list as you read other books.

ACTIVITY 5

"Dining With David's Father" Mural

The food David's father ate was very unusual. Allow students to recreate David's father's interesting eating habits by making a dinnertime mural. Suggest that they use their imaginations to generate other foods that David's father might like.

Supplies

- mural-size sheet of white butcher paper
- construction paper of assorted colors and sizes
- markers or crayons
- glue
- other art scraps, such as yarn, glitter, fabric scraps, and so on

Procedure

1. Discuss and list with students the foods that David's father ate.

2. Using construction paper, markers or crayons, and art scraps, encourage students to create two food items: one food that David's father ate in the story, and a second food they think David's father would like.

3. While students work, draw the outline of a very long, very large table on the mural paper.

4. As students finish their foods, invite them to glue their art within the table outline, labeling the foods, too.

5. Ask a student to write the title "Dining With David's Father" across the top.

ACTIVITY 6

Writing Extension 1— New Kid on the Block

Moving to a new place can be a difficult experience. In *David's Father*, Julie helped David adjust to his new neighborhood. This activity challenges students to generate ideas for welcoming someone new to their town, neighborhood, or school.

The Writing Process

Invite students to share times when they have been in a new situation. How did they feel? What helped them adjust?

Brainstorm with students ways they could make people feel welcome in a new situation. Some ideas include writing a card, inviting them to play a game, helping to show them around, sharing a favorite book, and so on. List their ideas on the chalkboard.

Ask students to choose the one way that would make them feel most welcome and to write a few sentences about it, explaining why they like it. Let students illustrate their ideas, too. Have students write the title "New Kid on the Block" across the tops of their papers. Display students' work on a bulletin board with the same title.

ACTIVITY 7

Writing Extension 2— "Wait Till You Meet My _____" Class Book

The surprise ending in *David's Father* is both humorous and thought-provoking. What else would make a good ending? This writing activity challenges students to end the book in their own unique ways.

The Writing Process

Discuss with students how Robert Munsch used the element of surprise to end his book in a humorous way. Tell your students that they are to come up with their own ending for the book, using the prompt "Wait till you meet my _____."

Write the following story sentences on the chalkboard for children to copy on their papers.

> Julie said, "Well, David, you do have a very nice father after all, but he is still kind of scary."
>
> "You think he is scary?" said David. "Wait till you meet my _____."

Encourage creative responses. For example, "Wait till you meet my . . . pet whale, dinosaur, Martian friend," and so on. Let students illustrate their ideas, too.

Collect the completed pages. Invite a volunteer to create a cover, then combine and staple the pages together to make a class book. Place it in your reading center.

Angela's Airplane

In Angela's Airplane, *Angela's father gets "lost" at the airport, and her quest to find him becomes an interesting journey, to say the least. Your students will be thoroughly entertained as they share the excitement of Angela's adventure.*

Points of Interest Not Mentioned in the Story

- Robert Munsch made up *Angela's Airplane* in a day-care center in Coos Bay, Oregon.

- Note the onomatopoeia *Vroom! Vroom!* Have students add it to their Writing Journals.

- Many of Robert Munsch's books have been made into videos, including *Angela's Airplane*. Try to obtain a copy to share with your class.

Memorable Story Quote

"Angela didn't fly an airplane for a very long time. But when she grew up she didn't become a doctor, she didn't become a truck driver, she didn't become a secretary, and she didn't become a nurse. She became an airplane pilot."

Activities for *Angela's Airplane*

ACTIVITY 1: Airplane "Hanger" Mobile Book Report

ACTIVITY 2: A Day on a Plane

ACTIVITY 3: Writing Extension—Have You Ever Been Lost?

ACTIVITY 4: Career Day

ACTIVITY 5: Paper Airplane Science

ACTIVITY 6: Plan a Trip

ACTIVITY 1

Airplane "Hanger" Mobile Book Report

In *Angela's Airplane*, the events are both exciting and light-hearted. Creating this mobile provides students with opportunities to retell Angela's funny adventure.

Assembling the Mobile

1. Give each student a hanger and eight pieces of yarn of varying lengths.

2. Help students punch a hole in the top wing of each airplane.

3. Starting with the first airplane, have students tie the yarn through the hole, tying the other end to the hanger. Continue until all the airplanes are dangling from the hanger.

4. When displayed, the airplanes will look like they are flying around the room.

Supplies

- hangers, one for each student
- yarn
- airplane pattern, page 59
- hole punch

The Writing Process

Brainstorm with students answers to these questions.

- *Who* was in the story?
- *Where* did the story take place?
- *Why* is there a story at all? *What* were the problems? (For example, Angela's father got "lost.")
- *How* were they resolved?

With the class, list on the chalkboard the sequence of story events. Keep the list short, simple, and to the point. Whenever possible, use students' own words and ideas. Below are suggested events.

1. Angela's father took her to the airport, and he got "lost."
2. Angela looked for him everywhere, even in an empty airplane.
3. Angela sat in the pilot's seat and began pushing the buttons.
4. Soon she was flying!
5. Angela pushed a button, and the radio came on. Someone talked her down.
6. The airplane bounced on the runway and broke into little pieces, but Angela was okay.
7. Angela's father led a parade of fire trucks, buses, ambulances, and police cars to rescue her.
8. Angela did not fly an airplane for a very long time—until she grew up and became an airplane pilot.

Provide each student with an airplane pattern. Instruct students to trace the pattern onto colored construction paper eight times and cut them out. Have students write one story event on each airplane, numbering and illustrating them, too. Students may use the backs of their airplanes if they need to.

ACTIVITY 2

A Day on a Plane

Many children have never been near an airplane, much less ridden in one. Turn your classroom into an airplane to show students what it's like.

Extra! If possible, arrange a field trip to an airport.

Procedure

1. Ahead of time, contact a local airline, and invite a flight attendant to speak to your students. Ask the flight attendant to dress in uniform, explaining that you want to provide students with a true airplane experience. Inquire if they can bring such things as airline napkins, nuts, and cups.

2. The day of the visit, set up your classroom to resemble the inside of an airplane, with two vertical rows of two seats each. Place an index card on each desk, indicating the seat number. For example, Row 1, Seat A.

3. Assign students to seats by filling in the boarding passes and presenting one to each child.

4. Introduce your flight-attendant visitor, then have students line up outside the room with their boarding passes. As they file back into the "airplane," have the flight attendant show them to their seats.

5. Encourage the flight attendant to go through the preflight safety procedures and instructions, then describe what the actual flight is like. Allow students time to ask questions.

6. Tell students that on long flights, a movie is often shown. Now would be the perfect time to view the video for *Angela's Airplane.*

7. Afterward, be sure students send your airline guest and the airline thank-you notes.

ACTIVITY 3

Writing Extension—Have You Ever Been Lost?

Getting lost can happen to anyone—adults and children alike. Encourage students to write about such an experience.

Extra! Invite volunteers to read their essays out loud, or display them on a bulletin board.

The Writing Process

Discuss with students times they have been lost or a family member has been lost. How did they feel? How did they get "found"? Invite students to write about the experience, illustrating it, too. For students who have never gotten lost, suggest that they write a short story around a favorite book character who gets lost. Prompt students' writing with the following questions.

- *How* old were you when you got lost?
- *Where* did it happen?
- *How* did you feel?
- *Who* found you?
- *How* did you feel then?

ACTIVITY 2
Pattern for Airplane "Hanger" Mobile

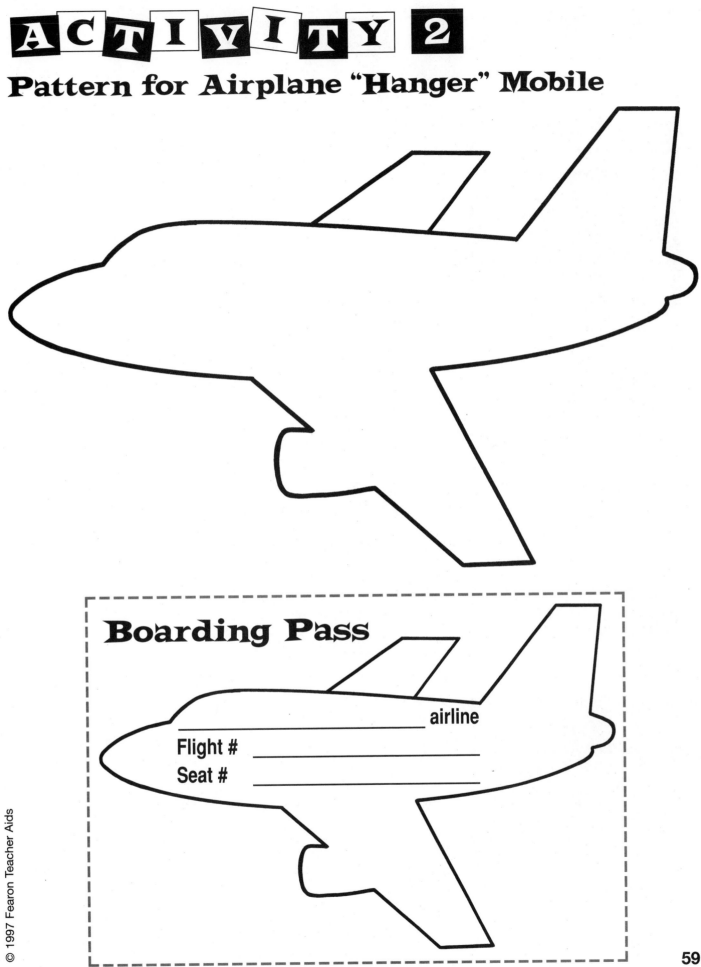

Boarding Pass

_____ **airline**

Flight # _____

Seat # _____

A C T I V I T Y 4

Career Day

Angela grew up to be a pilot. What do your students think they might like to be? Hold a Career Day to introduce students to different career possibilities.

Procedure

1. Set a date and invite people from your community to give a brief talk about what they do at their jobs. Invite students' parents as well. (Do not forget homemakers.)

2. Before the guests arrive, talk with students about what they would like to be when they grow up. Mention the occupations of the guests, and have students write a list of questions to ask.

3. Assign one student to "host" each guest. Ask the student to introduce the guest to the class and afterward show her or him around the school. Inviting your guests for lunch in your school cafeteria would be a treat for all.

4. Culminate by having students write and illustrate their own career aspirations, mentioning if any of the guests influenced their choices.

5. Follow up by asking students to send thank-you notes to each guest.

A C T I V I T Y 5

Paper Airplane Science

Have students construct paper airplanes as you explain the science behind why airplanes can fly.

Procedure

1. Pass out the paper airplane pattern on page 61 and demonstrate how to fold it along the lines. As in origami, solid lines are "hill" folds and dotted lines are "valley" folds.

2. Create a target in your classroom or outside. A large hoop is a good choice.

3. As one student holds the hoop or other target above his or her head, let students take turns trying to throw their planes through the target. You might hold a contest, eliminating those who miss until only the winner is left.

4. Back in class, ask students if they know how real airplanes fly. Explain that it has to do with the air moving over the plane's wings. Simply, the air moving under the flat bottom of the wing has more pressure than the air rushing over the curved top of the wing. So the air pressure beneath pushes upward on the wing and keeps the plane in the air. Planes must move very fast along the ground to get enough air moving along their wings and also enough force to break the pull of Earth's gravity.

Paper Airplane Pattern

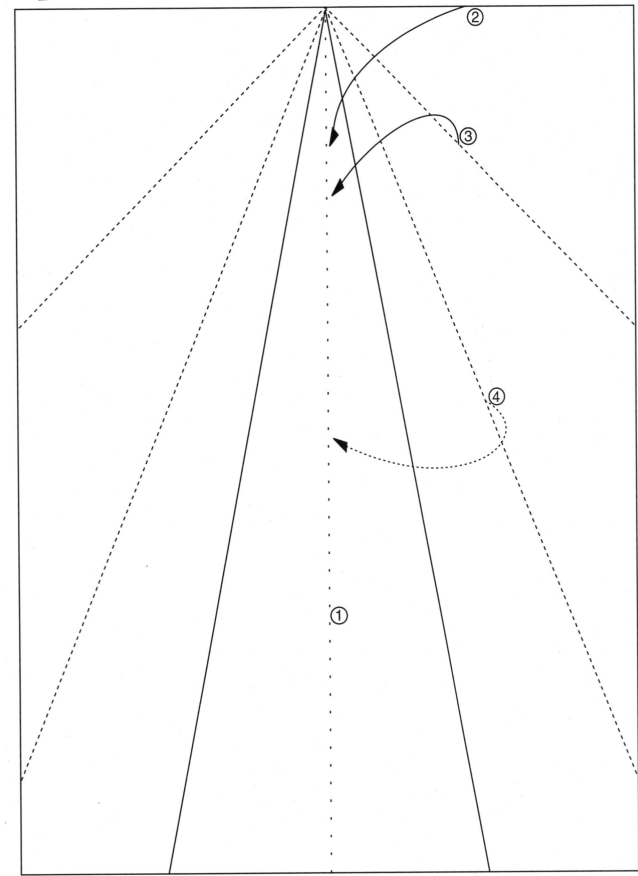

ACTIVITY 6

Plan a Trip

Remind students that most people fly in planes to take trips. Planning the trip can be just as much fun as taking it! Invite students to plan trips of their own.

Procedure

1. Brainstorm with students places they would like to visit. On a map of the United States, help children locate their choices, listing them on the chalkboard.

2. Ask each child to choose one place to visit. Keep a record so no two places are duplicated. Some suggestions include national parks, such as Yellowstone and Yosemite; natural wonders, such as the Grand Canyon and Niagara Falls; monuments, such as Mount Rushmore and the Statue of Liberty; exciting cities, such as Washington, D.C., and New York City; amusement parks, such as Disney World and Six Flags; historical memorials, such as Gettysburg and the Alamo; and scenic states such as Alaska and Hawaii.

3. Visit the public or school library and help students find the addresses of the Chambers of Commerce for their places.

4. Brainstorm the information that students will need to ask when they write their letters. List the information on the chalkboard or chart paper. For example, students should state that they would like to visit and that they are requesting information about the weather, transportation, hotel accommodations, and things to see and do there.

5. Have each student bring a stamped envelope to school. Older students will write their letters. Younger students may need to copy a form letter you have written, filling in the name and address. Be sure the return address is your school address.

6. Mail the letters and wait for the responses.

7. As the responses come in, have students plan their trips. Guide them with the following questions.

- When will you leave? How long will you stay?
- What kind of clothes will you need to take?
- What sights will you see?
- What kinds of foods will you eat?

8. Invite students to share the information they received, perhaps displaying it on posterboard.

9. As the presentations are given, challenge students to plot their trips on a map of the United States.

Judith Viorst

Judith Viorst is a favorite children's author, for her writing brings humor to everyday problems. Her unique insight into children's experiences and feelings often comes from meeting the needs of her own children. Viorst's keen use of language is inviting to both adults and children, as she explains, "the beauties and truths and delights they can offer to our children can meet the deepest needs of the heart and mind."

Interesting Facts About the Author

Birth: Judith Viorst was born on February 2, 1931, in Newark, New Jersey.

Family: Judith was born to Martin Leonard Stall, an accountant, and Ruth June Stall. On January 30, 1960, she married Milton Viorst, a writer. They have three children: Anthony Jacob, Nicholas Nathan, and Alexander Noah. Today, Judith lives in Washington, D.C., with her husband.

Education: Judith attended Rutgers University in New Jersey, from which she received her Bachelor of Arts degree, with honors, in 1952. She is also a graduate of the Washington Psychoanalytic Institute and a longtime columnist for *Redbook* magazine.

Beginnings as an author: Judith

Viorst began to write when she was very young. In fact, when she was seven or eight she wrote a poem to her dead parents—who were still very much alive! Naturally, her parents were a bit concerned. Upon completing college, Judith worked for several magazines as a secretary. In 1957 she became a children's book editor for William Morrow. Viorst never forgot her dream to become a writer. In the early 1960s she worked for the Science Service in Washington, D.C., editing and writing science books for children. In 1965 her first book of poetry for adults was published. And in 1968 she became a regular contributor to *Redbook* magazine. Also in 1968 her first children's book—*Sunday Morning*—was published. Judith went on to write many more books for children—several based on experiences with her own sons—for which she has won numerous awards.

Common Threads to Look For Throughout Her Books

- Judith's real-life sons—Alexander, Anthony, and Nicholas—play integral roles in many of her works of fiction.

- Many of the themes center around family issues—sibling rivalry, family pets, grandparents' visits, to name a few.

- Judith incorporates language that most children probably use.

Books by Judith Viorst

- *Sunday Morning*
- *I'll Fix Anthony*
- *Try It Again, Sam: Safety When You Walk*
- *The Tenth Good Thing About Barney*
- *Alexander and the Terrible, Horrible, No Good, Very Bad Day*
- *My Mama Says There Aren't Any Zombies, Ghosts, Vampires, Creatures, Demons, Monsters, Fiends, Goblins, or Things*
- *Rosie and Michael*
- *Alexander, Who Used to Be Rich Last Sunday*

- *The Good-Bye Book*
- *Earrings!*
- *Alexander, Who's Not (Do You Hear Me? I Mean It!) Going to Move*
- *If I Were in Charge of the World and Other Worries: Poems for Children and Their Parents*
- *Sad Underwear and other Complications: More Poems for Children and their Parents*

Alexander and the Terrible, Horrible, No Good, Very Bad Day

The day starts off bad when Alexander wakes up with chewing gum in his hair, and it continues to go downhill from there. In fact, so much goes wrong that Alexander thinks he'd be better off in Australia. Viorst brings humor to Alexander's mishaps, handling them in a sympathetic way. Students are certain to relate to Alexander's experiences.

Points of Interest Not Mentioned in the Story

- Judith Viorst uses her own children as subjects for many of her books. In fact, Alexander is the name of one of her sons.

- Many critics have proclaimed *Alexander and the Terrible, Horrible, No Good, Very Bad Day* as Viorst's most successful book. She has won lasting popularity in both the United States and England for Alexander and his troubles.

Memorable Story Quote

" . . . Nick took back the pillow he said I could keep and the Mickey Mouse night light burned out and I bit my tongue. The cat wants to sleep with Anthony, not me."

Activities for *Alexander and the Terrible, Horrible, No Good, Very Bad Day*

ACTIVITY 1: Newspaper-Style Book Report

ACTIVITY 2: Synonyms

ACTIVITY 3: Writing Extension 1—Descriptive Paragraphs

ACTIVITY 4: Solving and Preventing Alexander's Problems

ACTIVITY 5: Design a Shoe for Alexander

ACTIVITY 6: Writing Extension 2—What Was Your Most Terrible, Horrible, No Good, Very Bad Day?

ACTIVITY 7: Explore Australia's Animals

ACTIVITY 1
Newspaper-Style Book Report

In *Alexander and the Terrible, Horrible, No Good, Very Bad Day*, Alexander experienced a sequence of events that added up to a disastrous day. Your students will enjoy relating to many of his problems. This activity invites students to be reporters as they write about Alexander's crazy day.

Extra!

• Distribute to each student a large newspaper-size sheet of white butcher paper. Have students fold it in half to resemble a newspaper.

• Distribute the newspaper labels and have students fill in their school's name. Show them where to glue the label to the top of their newspapers.

• Now ask students to write and illustrate the events of Alexander's bad day. Students will probably need to use both sides of the butcher paper. Challenge older students to write more elaborate sentences to describe Alexander's day.

Supplies

• white butcher paper (1 large piece for each student)
• labels, page 67
• glue
• scissors

The Writing Process

Brainstorm with students answers to these questions.
• *Who* was in the story?
• *Where* did the story take place?
• *Why* is there a story at all? *What* is the main problem? (For example, Alexander's struggle with his mishaps.)
• *How* is it resolved?

With the class, list on the chalkboard the sequence of story events. Keep the list short, simple, and to the point. Whenever possible, use students' own words. Below are some suggested story events.

1. I slept with gum in my mouth, and now it is in my hair.
2. When I got out of bed, I tripped on my skateboard.
3. I dropped my sweater in the sink.
4. There was no prize in my cereal box.
5. I didn't get a seat by the window in car pool.
6. At school, Mrs. Dickens liked Paul's picture better than mine.
7. At singing time, Mrs. Dickens said I sang too loud.
8. At counting time she said I left out 16.
9. Paul said I was only his third best friend.
10. My mother forgot to put dessert in my lunch.
11. Dr. Fields found a cavity.
12. The elevator door closed on my foot.
13. Anthony made me fall in the mud, and Nick called me a cry baby.
14. Mother scolded me for being muddy and fighting.
15. I had to buy plain white sneakers.
16. I made a mess at Dad's office.
17. We had lima beans for dinner, and there was kissing on television.
18. My bath was too hot, and I got soap in my eyes.
19. I had to wear my railroad-train pajamas.
20. The cat wanted to sleep with Anthony.
21. It had been a terrible, horrible, no good, very bad day.

ACTIVITY 1

The _____ Express

A Bad Day Was Had by Alexander

ACTIVITY 2

Synonyms

Judith Viorst uses many words to describe Alexander's awful day. The title of the book is a perfect way to introduce students to synonyms. Encourage students to increase their vocabularies as they list synonyms in their Writings Journals for use in future writing projects.

Procedure

1. Write the word *synonym* on the chalkboard and challenge students to tell you what it means. Confirm that synonyms are words that have the same or similar meanings.

2. Now write the word *bad* on the chalkboard. Can students think of other words that mean bad? Ask a child to reread the title of the book. Point out that *terrible* and *horrible* can all mean "bad." List them on the chalkboard.

3. Challenge students to come up with other words as you list them on the chalkboard, too. For example, *awful, nasty, mean, lousy, crummy,* and so on.

4. Invite students to copy the words in their Writing Journals.

5. Then write these words across the chalkboard: *good, sad, happy*. Encourage students to come up with synonyms for these words to add to their Writing Journals. Suggest that students refer to their journals when looking for new words as they write.

ACTIVITY 3

Writing Extension 1—Descriptive Paragraphs

In *Alexander and the Terrible, Horrible, No Good Very Bad Day*, Alexander believes his problems will be solved if he moves to Australia. Encourage your students to express where they would move to if they had a day such as Alexander's.

The Writing Process

1. Recall with students that Alexander wanted to move to Australia to get away from his problems. Challenge a student to find Australia on a map. It's pretty far from the United States, isn't it?

2. Where would your students go if they could get away for just a day? Challenge them to come up with exciting, exotic locales that could be on this planet, out of this world, or even an imaginary setting from a favorite story.

3. Invite students to write paragraphs, describing their places. Ask them to explain why they would go there and what makes it special.

4. Invite volunteers to read their paragraphs to the class. Display students' work on a bulletin board titled "I'd Rather Be in . . ."

ACTIVITY 4

Solving and Preventing Alexander's Problems

Alexander's terrible day was due to an accumulation of many things gone wrong. Most of these problems could have been prevented or solved without moving to Australia. This activity challenges students to help Alexander prevent and solve his problems.

Procedure

1. Begin by inviting students to dictate to you the many problems Alexander faced on his very bad day. List them on chart paper.

2. Choose one problem and challenge students to come up with ways that Alexander could have solved or prevented it. For example, Alexander woke up with gum in his hair. How could he have prevented it? (By not falling asleep with gum in his mouth.)

3. Now ask students to each choose another problem and to write down a solution. After everyone has finished, let students read and compare their ideas.

Extra! You might choose to keep this an oral activity.

ACTIVITY 5

Design a Shoe for Alexander

Part of Alexander's horrible day was when he had to buy shoes. The red and blue ones he wanted were sold out, so he ended up with plain white ones. Shoes can be a "hot" item with children. Invite them to create their own spiffy shoe designs.

Procedure

1. Recall with students Alexander's experience in the shoe store. What other kind of shoe might Alexander have liked?

2. Reproduce and give each student a copy of the shoe pattern on page 70. Encourage them to decorate the shoe outline with markers, stickers, glitter, yarn, and fabric scraps to make their shoes as interesting as possible.

3. Hold a fashion showcase for students to present and display their shoe designs.

ACTIVITY 5
Alexander's New Shoe Pattern

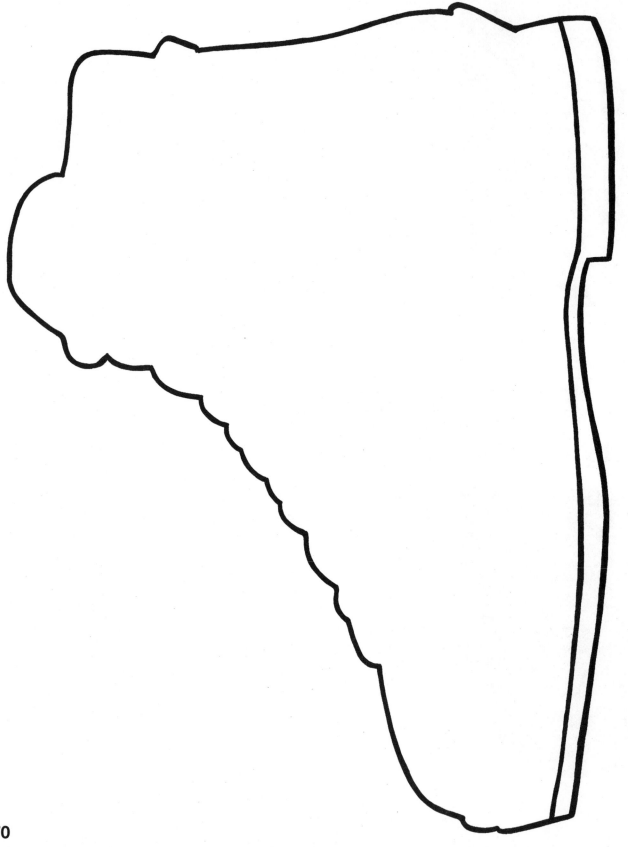

ACTIVITY 6

Writing Extension 2—What Was Your Most Terrible, Horrible, No Good, Very Bad Day?

Alexander's day was pretty horrible. But perhaps your students have had days that were just as bad. Encourage students to write about them.

The Writing Process

1. Start by discussing with children all the awful things that happened to Alexander. How would they feel if these things happened to them?

2. Then ask students to compare what happened to Alexander to a day they had that was truly terrible. What was their day like?

3. After a brief discussion, encourage students to write about their days, perhaps adding pictures, too.

4. Let children read their bad-day essays to the class. You might combine all the essays into a class book titled "Our Terrible, Horrible, No Good, Very Bad Days."

ACTIVITY 7

Explore Australia's Animals

Australia is an exciting country for many reasons, one being that many of the animals of Australia are not found anywhere else in the world. Invite students to research these animals to learn more about the world's only continent country.

Procedure

1. As you name each of these animals, invite students to share what they know about it: koala, kangaroo, wallaby, wombat, kookaburra, Tasmanian devil, thorny devil lizard, kowari, platypus, echidna, emu, dingo. Can students figure out what all these animals have in common? They all live in Australia!

2. Divide the class into small groups and assign one animal to each group to research. Provide animal encyclopedias and other children's references for students to investigate.

3. Encourage students to draw pictures of the animals, listing a few amazing facts about them on separate sheets of paper.

4. On a bulletin board, display students' work with the title "Animals of Australia—Like No Others on Earth."

Alexander, Who Used to Be Rich Last Sunday

For most children, receiving money is a special gift, a privilege. Children are now responsible for how they will spend that money or save it. Alexander wants to save his money very badly, but he can't. Judith Viorst tells a hilarious story that most students—and adults—can easily relate to.

Points of Interest Not Mentioned in the Story

- In real life, Alexander is the name of one of Judith Viorst's sons. Anthony and Nicholas are really his brothers.

- Judith Viorst has dedicated this book to her Grandma Betty and Grandpa Louie Viorst.

Memorable Story Quote

" . . . I used to have a dollar. I do not have a dollar any more. I've got this dopey deck of cards. I've got this one-eyed bear. I've got this melted candle. And . . . some bus tokens."

Activities for *Alexander, Who Used to Be Rich Last Sunday*

ACTIVITY 1: Piggy Bank Class Book Report

ACTIVITY 2: Make a Piggy Bank

ACTIVITY 3: Writing Extension 1—"If I Had a Hundred Dollars" Class Book

ACTIVITY 4: Disappearing Money Math

ACTIVITY 5: Writing Extension 2—Bus-Token Trips

ACTIVITY 6: Pearson's Store Role-play

ACTIVITY 1
Piggy Bank Class Book Report

Alexander was given a dollar by his grandparents. The money quickly "burned a hole in his pocket" as Alexander went on a spending frenzy. Finally, Alex has nothing left but bus tokens. Invite students to retell the story with this class project.

Supplies
- large sheet of pink butcher paper
- glue
- coin pattern, page 75
- scissors

The Writing Process

Brainstorm with students answers to these questions.
- *Who* was in the story?
- *Where* did the story take place?
- *Why* is there a story at all? *What* is the problem? (for example, how Alexander should spend his money)
- *How* is it resolved?

With the class, list on the chalkboard the sequence of story events. Keep the list short, simple, and to the point. Whenever possible, use students' own thoughts and ideas. Below are suggested story events in order.

1. My brother Anthony has two dollars, three quarters, one dime, seven nickels, and 18 pennies.

2. My brother Nicholas has one dollar, two quarters, five dimes, five nickels, and 13 pennies.

3. All I have are bus tokens.

4. Last Sunday my grandparents visited.

5. They brought my father lox and my mother a plant.

6. They brought a dollar for me, one for Nick, and one for Anthony.

7. My father told me to put the dollar away for college.

8. Anthony told me to buy a new face.

9. Nicky told me to bury it in the garden to grow a dollar tree.

10. Mother told me to save it for a walkie-talkie. (Saving money is hard.)

11. Last Sunday I bought bubble gum at Pearson's Drug Store. Goodbye 15 cents.

12. Last Sunday I bet Anthony that I could hold my breath till 300. I lost.

13. Then I bet Nicky that I could jump from the top of the stoop and land on my feet. I lost again.

14. I bet Mom I could hide a purple marble in my hand. Goodbye 15 cents.

15. I rented a snake for an hour. Goodbye 12 cents.

16. I said two words I shouldn't have. Dad fined me 5 cents for each. Goodbye dime.

17. I flushed 3 cents down the toilet by accident.

18. A nickel fell through a crack when I walked on my hands.

19. I ate Anthony's chocolate candy bar. I had to pay him 11 cents.

20. Nick did a magic trick that made my pennies disappear. Goodbye 4 cents.

21. Dad fined me a nickel for kicking.

22. At Cathy's garage sale, I bought a half-melted candle, a bear with one eye, and a deck of cards. Goodbye 20 cents.

23. I wanted to save more money! I tried to make a tooth fall out. No luck.

24. I looked in telephone booths for nickels and dimes.

25. I brought nonreturnable bottles to the market.

26. I have no money. Only bus tokens.

Assembling the Book Report

1. On the pink butcher paper, draw a large piggy bank (see illustration). Hang the piggy bank on a large bulletin board or wall.

2. Reproduce and give each student a coin pattern and assign each an event from the story. Tell students to write or illustrate their events on the coins.

3. After everyone has finished, have students place their coins on and around the bank in sequential order.

4. Write the book title and author across the top.

Coin Pattern

ACTIVITY 2
Make a Piggy Bank

Alexander did not know how to save money. Perhaps a piggy bank would have come in handy! Invite students to design and create their own piggy banks as an incentive to save money.

Extra! Make a class piggy bank to save for class field trips, parties, and supplies.

Supplies

- clean, empty pint-size milk cartons (perhaps you can obtain them from the school cafeteria)
  - assorted art materials, such as construction paper, glitter, paints, fabric scraps
    - glue
      - scissors

Procedure

1. Brainstorm with students ways that children can earn money. Invite students to share their own moneymaking experiences. For example, some students might have paper routes, pet-sit for neighbors, or even sell lemonade in the summer. What else might they do?

2. Then ask students to imagine that they've begun earning money at one of these jobs. What would be a good incentive to save their money? How about by making their own personal piggy banks?

3. Provide each student with a milk carton to serve as the base of the bank. Supply students with art scraps and encourage them to be creative as they decorate their cartons any way they wish.

4. Help students cut a coin slot. Have them take their banks home and start saving!

ACTIVITY 3

Writing Extension 1— "If I Had a Hundred Dollars" Class Book

Alexander was excited about receiving one dollar from his grandparents. If he had been given a hundred dollars, how might he have spent it? This activity encourages students to consider what they would do with a hundred dollars.

The Writing Process

Discuss with students how Alexander foolishly spent his money. What do they think he would have done had he been given a hundred dollars? Ask students to pretend that they have been given a hundred dollars to spend any way they like. Encourage them to write and illustrate what they would do with the money. Invite one student to create a cover with the title "If I Had a Hundred Dollars" by _____ Class. Collect students' papers, attach the cover, and staple together. Place your class book in your reading center.

ACTIVITY 4

Disappearing Money Math

Where, exactly, did Alexander's money go? Take this opportunity to have a mini math lesson for children to find out.

Procedure

1. At the top of a blank piece of paper, have students write $1.00. Explain that you will reread the story. Each time you say, "Goodbye (amount of money)," they are to subtract that amount from the dollar.
2. Reread the story, pausing for students to subtract each time an amount is mentioned. Have students raise their hands when they've spent all of Alexander's dollar.

Extra! Some students may need the teacher to subtract the amounts on the chalkboard or overhead along with them. Or use manipulatives. For example, each student begins with 100 beans, taking away beans each time Alexander spends his money.

ACTIVITY 5

Writing Extension 2—Bus-Token Trips

At the end of the story, all Alexander has left is a bunch of worthless bus tokens. But are bus tokens really worthless? If Alexander were to use the bus tokens, where might he go? What might he see? Invite students to brainstorm a new adventure for Alexander.

The Writing Process

Talk with children about the bus tokens that Alexander has at the end of the story. Invite students to share any bus rides they've taken. Where did they go? Who were they with? What did it feel like riding on the bus? Does your community have bus transportation? Where do these buses go?

Then speculate with children where Alexander might go with his bus tokens. Prompt children's ideas by posing the following questions.
• What sights might Alexander see outside the bus window?
• Which interesting people might Alexander meet on the bus?
• Where does the bus drop Alexander off? A park? Shopping mall? Museum? Zoo?
• Is Alexander having fun on his bus ride? Why or why not?

Pass out writing paper and encourage students to write down their ideas as if they were Alexander. You might review that when using *I*, students are writing in the first person. Provide students with drawing paper. Have them staple their papers to the top, then illustrate Alexander's adventures on the bottom. Invite students to share Alexander's new adventures with the class.

ACTIVITY 6

Pearson's Store Role-play

Buying items in a store and interacting with salespeople are part of our everyday lives. Invite students to become familiar with the experience—from both sides of the counter—by role-playing store scenes.

Procedure

1. Ahead of time, ask students to bring from home empty food containers, such as cereal and cracker boxes, yogurt and butter containers, milk cartons, juice bottles, soup cans, and so on.

2. Explain that they are going to set up a store, like Pearson's in the book. First they will need to affix price tags to the food containers they brought to class. Reproduce the label at the bottom of this page for students to write on.

3. Then clear an appropriate space in the classroom and invite students to arrange their cartons on shelves or tables.

4. Ask students to pretend that they have been given $1.00 to spend at Pearson's, just like Alexander. What would they buy? In small groups, let children go through the store while you, another child, or a teacher's aide serves as the cashier.

5. Afterward, discuss with children how easy or hard it was to keep their purchases under $1.00. Point out how honing their math skills will help when shopping on their own.

Rosie and Michael

In *Rosie and Michael,* Judith Viorst describes the friendship between a young boy and a young girl. The text portrays the friendship between the children as they take turns telling the reader what makes their relationship special. This book teaches students the value of having a friendship they can treasure.

Point of Interest Not Mentioned in the Story

- This book does not follow the typical story format. It is an ongoing list of events that continues to grow as Rosie and Michael's friendship grows. This will give you a chance to introduce a different form of writing to your students.

Memorable Story Quote

"I'd give her my last piece of chalk.

"I'd give him my last Chicklet.

"Rosie is

"Michael is

"My friend."

Activities for *Rosie and Michael*

ACTIVITY 1: Rosie and Michael's Tree Book Report

ACTIVITY 2: Writing Extension 1—Friendship Notes

ACTIVITY 3: Friendship Want Ads

ACTIVITY 4: Writing Extension 2—That's What Friends Are For

ACTIVITY 5: Friendship Bracelets

ACTIVITY 1
Rosie and Michael's Tree Book Report

Rosie and Michael is a book in which two children explain to the reader why they are special to each other. This activity gives students the opportunity to recount the events in the story, as well as events that have built their own friendships.

Extra! Upcoming books by Thomas Locker, Vera B. Williams, and Bill Martin, Jr., have activities that require class trees, too. You might reuse this tree for these activities.

Supplies

- brown butcher paper
- green construction paper
- pink construction paper
- leaf pattern, page 81
- markers
- scissors
- tape or glue

Procedure

1. Discuss with students why Rosie and Michael's friendship is special. Also talk about their own friendships and what makes them special.

2. Then reread the book. As you read, instruct students to mentally choose one event from the story that is their favorite.

3. Give each student a leaf pattern. Tell students to trace the pattern onto green construction paper twice and cut out the leaves.

4. On one leaf, invite students to write in their own words the part of the story they liked best.

5. On the second leaf, invite them to write something special about their own friendships. For example, favorite toys they share, games they play, secret codes they write, and so on.

6. As students work, create a large tree out of brown butcher paper. Also make a large pink heart with "Michael and Rosie" written inside. Glue the heart to the middle of the trunk.

7. Now invite students to tape or glue their leaves to the bare tree branches. Wow! What a great display!

Leaf Pattern

ACTIVITY 2

Writing Extension 1— Friendship Notes

Most children like to write notes to each other. Rosie and Michael probably wrote notes, too. Encourage students to sharpen their note-writing skills as they exchange friendship notes.

The Writing Process

1. Talk with students about the tradition of passing notes back and forth between friends. Of course, it is not usually acceptable behavior in school. But it will be for this activity. Ask students why they like to pass notes. What are the notes about? What do most notes have in common? (They are short and reflect something about the friendship.)

2. Assign students to partners. Suggest that they pretend they are Rosie and Michael. If these children were to pass notes to each other, what would the notes say? On small slips of paper, invite pairs to write their notes.

3. Set up a time for partners to exchange their notes and write notes in response. Make sure students use the time constructively to hone their writing skills.

ACTIVITY 3

Friendship Want Ads

Rosie and Michael both exhibited characteristics of good friends. Challenge students to think about which characteristics make a good friend by writing ads.

Procedure

1. Elicit from students the characteristics, or personality traits, that make someone a good friend. Answers might include: they are nice, they share, they are funny, they have good ideas, and so on.

2. Explain to students that they will be writing want ads advertising for a friend. Bring in want ads from newspapers to show as examples. Discuss the information and style of the ads. In their own ads, stress that students should include what kind of friend they want along with what kind of friend they will be in return.

3. Have students write a rough draft first. Then give each student a half sheet of posterboard on which to create their ads.

4. Display students' ads on a bulletin board.

A C T I V I T Y 4

Writing Extension 2—That's What Friends Are For

Rosie and Michael are very special to each other. Invite students to write about why friends are special to them.

The Writing Process

Encourage students to share what makes a friendship special. Explain that they will be writing and illustrating about a special friendship they have. It could be someone in class, someone in their neighborhoods, or even a member of their families.

Pass out the activity sheet on page 84. Tell students to write a few sentences about their friends on the lines. You might pose the following questions to prompt their writing.
• How long have you known your friend?
• What makes him or her special?
• What do you do together?

Have students finish up by drawing pictures of their friends in the picture frames. Invite students to take their work home to share with family.

A C T I V I T Y 5

Friendship Bracelets

Rosie and Michael carved their names in a tree to honor their friendship. Most children like to acknowledge their friendships in special ways. Giving friendship bracelets is one such way. Show students how to make friendship bracelets to trade with each other.

Supplies

• scissors
  • masking tape
    • ruler or tape measure
      • three 20-inch strands of colored yarn for each student

Procedure

1. Give each student three pieces of yarn. Demonstrate how to form a knot at one end, tying the three pieces together.
2. Help students tape the knot to a flat surface, such as the top of a desk.
3. Now demonstrate how to braid the three strings. Monitor students' work to make sure they are braiding correctly.
4. Model for students how to knot the end of the bracelet.
5. Help students tie the bracelets around each other's wrists.
6. Have students make more bracelets as interest holds. Encourage them to swap bracelets with their friends.

ACTIVITY 4

That's What Friends Are For

If I Were in Charge of the World and Other Worries

Judith Viorst adds a twist of humor to everyday circumstances and well-known fairy tales through this collection of poetry for children. The poems are short, easy to connect with, and simple. You will find yourself laughing along with your students as you share with them this delightful set of poems.

Points of Interest Not Mentioned in the Story

- Viorst began writing poetry when she was very young. Before she wrote poetry for children, she had already published several books of poetry for adults.

- Read with students the names of three of the consultants for this book: Alexander, Nicholas, and Anthony Viorst, Judith's sons.

- Another consultant, Elizabeth Pitofsky, has a poem in the book specially written for her. Can your students find it? ("The Lizzie Pitofsky Poem," on page 13.)

Extra! As with all authors and books we present, the types of activities you choose for your class depend on your class's personality. This is also true with the poems in *If I Were in Charge of the World and Other Worries*. You might want to read the book in its entirety, allowing students to choose the poems that are appropriate for your class. We have included suggested activities for several poems. However, do not let this limit you. Freely explore other poems in this fun collection with other activities your students will enjoy.

Memorable Story Quote

"And a person who sometimes forgot to brush,

"And sometimes forgot to flush,

"Would still be allowed to be

"In charge of the world."

Activities for *If I Were in Charge of the World and Other Worries*

ACTIVITY 1: What If You Were in Charge of the World? Class Poem

ACTIVITY 2: Scary Creatures Class Collage

ACTIVITY 3: Pet Poems

ACTIVITY 4: Before-and-After Springtime Bulletin Board

ACTIVITY 5: Reasons for Seasons Science Activity

ACTIVITY 6: Writing Extension—Updated Fairy Tales

ACTIVITY 7: Shape Poems

ACTIVITY 1

What If You Were in Charge of the World? Class Poem

In the title poem for this collection, Judith Viorst poses the idea "What if I were in charge of the world?" What an intriguing idea! What would your students do if they were in charge of the world? Invite them to contribute lines to a class poem to share their ideas.

Supplies

- pencils
  - yellow construction paper
    - mural paper
      - crown pattern on page 87
        - scissors
          - tape or glue

Procedure

1. Start by reading the poem with the class. You might invite volunteers to read each separate line or have different sections of the class read the various verses.

2. Then discuss with students the things the poet would do if she were in charge of the world. Which do students think is a good idea? Why do they think that?

3. Then challenge students to think of the things they would do. Brainstorm ideas.

4. Now tell students that they are going to write a class poem about being in charge of the world. Each student will get to contribute one line. Point out to students that the lines in Judith Viorst's poem don't rhyme. Their class poem doesn't have to rhyme, either.

5. Reproduce and pass out the crown pattern on page 87, one for each student. Instruct students to trace the pattern onto yellow construction paper and cut it out.

6. On their crown cutouts, encourage students to write one thing they would do if they were in charge of the world.

7. Hang a long length of mural paper on a blank wall, vertically.

8. Collect students' crowns and glue them down the length of the mural paper.

9. Read the class poem with your students.

Crown Pattern

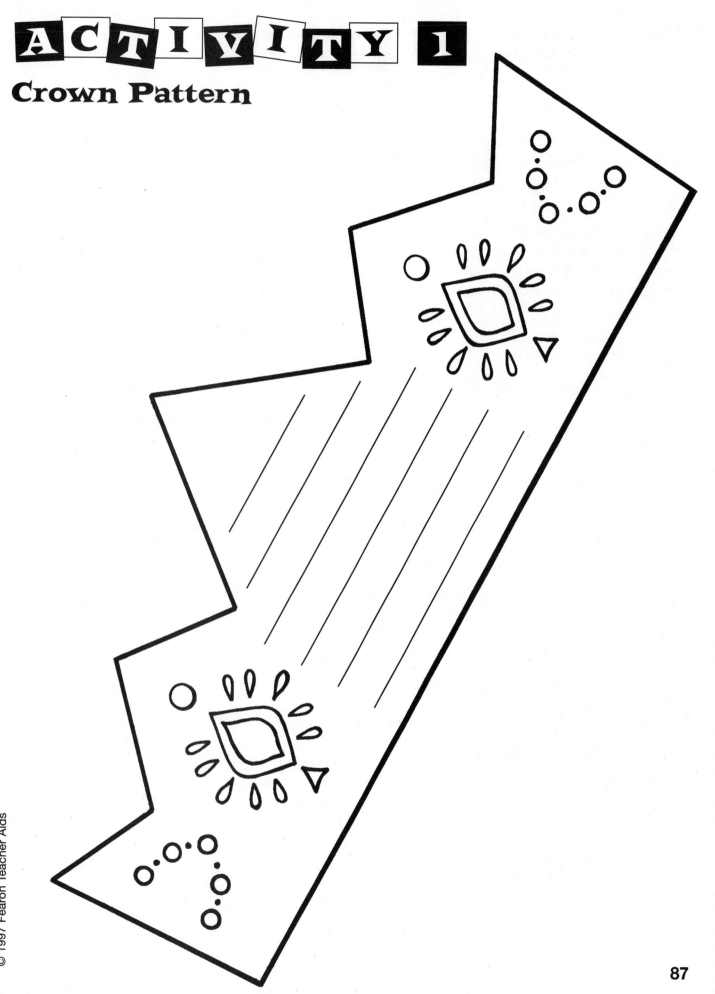

ACTIVITY 2

Scary Creatures Class Collage

In the poem "I Wouldn't Be Afraid," the poet lists some pretty scary monsters that would not scare her or him. However, the one creature that is frightening is a worm! Which animals might scare your students? Encourage them to draw pictures of the creatures to make a class collage.

Supplies

- drawing paper
- mural paper
- markers or crayons
- tape or glue

Procedure

1. Invite children to read with you the poem, "I Wouldn't Be Afraid." Point out the scary creatures the poet lists. Invite students to share their impressions of these different mythical beings.

2. Then help students notice that what makes the poem so funny is that, although these scary things don't frighten the poet, a little worm does. Have students compare worms with the other fantastic creatures in the poem. Which would be more scary to them?

3. Now have students think about other common creatures that they might find scary. For example, spiders, bees, snakes, cats, dogs, and so on. Which other animals might be a bit frightening?

4. Pass out drawing paper. Encourage students to draw their scary creatures using markers or crayons.

5. Lay out a sheet of mural paper. Invite students to the paper to arrange their scary-creature drawings.

6. Glue the pictures down to make a collage.

7. Display the collage in the school hallway.

Extra! This might make a great Halloween project.

ACTIVITY 3

Pet Poems

In "My Cat," Judith Viorst explains what is so wonderful about a pet cat. Invite students to write their own pet poems.

Procedure

1. Read the poem "My Cat." Talk with students about the things Viorst enjoys about her cat. Invite students who have pets to share the silly, lovable things their pets do.

2. Invite students to write acrostic poems about their pets. Encourage students who don't have pets to choose an animal they'd like to have. Explain that for these poems they will need to write the name of the pet down the left side of the paper.

3. For each letter of the pet's name, students begin a line of the poem, telling about the pet or why the animal would make a good pet. Make sure children realize that, just like Judith Viorst's, their poems can rhyme, but they don't have to. Invite volunteers to share their poems with the class.

ACTIVITY 4

Before-and-After Springtime Bulletin Board

Spring is a time of amazing change! Trees turn green, flowers bloom, and animals that slept throughout the winter reappear. "Just Before Springtime" is a celebration of the days before spring, when the world is getting ready to bloom again. Invite students to create before-and-after posters to illustrate the poem.

Procedure

1. Invite students to read "Just Before Springtime" with you. Elicit their impressions of spring. If you live in an area that does not experience seasonal changes, guide students to share what they know about springtime in other states.

2. Provide students with drawing paper and crayons or markers. Instruct them to draw a horizontal line across the center, splitting the paper in half.

3. Above the line, ask them to illustrate the last days of winter, using the descriptions in the poem as reference. Below the line, invite students to draw the same scene, but during springtime.

4. Write the poem in large letters on a bulletin board. Display students' artwork around the poem.

ACTIVITY 5

Reasons for Seasons Science Activity

Why do we have seasons? Some might think it's because the earth is closer to the sun. But it actually has to do with the earth's tilt. Invite students to participate in this simple activity to understand the reasons for seasons.

Supplies

- orange
- pencil
- lamp with the bulb exposed

Procedure

1. Present the orange to the class, explaining that it represents the earth.

2. Jab a pencil through the center of the orange, vertically, to be the earth's axis. Explain that our earth spins like a top around this imaginary line. That is why we have night and day.

3. Our earth also moves around the sun, slightly tilted. Tilt the orange on its axis.

4. Turn on the light. This represents the sun. Hold the tilted orange near it. Have students notice which area of the orange is closest to the bulb. If this were the earth, this part would be having summer! Put a pushpin in the orange where it is "summer."

5. Now, while keeping the orange at the same tilt and rotation, move the orange halfway around the bulb, reminding students that it takes one year for the earth to move once around the sun. Which part of the orange is closest to the bulb now? If this were the earth, this part would be having summer! What season would it be where the pushpin is?

ACTIVITY 6

Writing Extension—Updated Fairy Tales

Judith Viorst devotes an entire section in her book to taking a fresh look at some classic fairy tales. Invite your students to do the same to put together a class book of updated fairy tales.

The Writing Process

Invite volunteers to take turns reading the different fairy-tale poems in the book. Talk with students about the new view the poet presents about each fairy tale. You might mention that most fairy tales have been around for a very long time. How could some of the fairy tales that students know be updated? Brainstorm with students some fairy tales that need a modern-day approach. Write their ideas on the chalkboard.

Invite each student to choose one fairy tale and rewrite it with a fresh twist. You might prompt children's writing with such questions as

- If this poem was set in your neighborhood, how would it be different?
- If you were the hero or heroine, what would you do?
- What clothes would your updated fairy-tale characters wear?
- What modern games, appliances, or sports might be a part of your updated fairy tale?

Encourage students to write their new fairy tales, keeping them short and simple. After students read their updated fairy tales to the class, combine all the stories into a class book. Place the book in your reading center for students to read on their own.

ACTIVITY 7

Shape Poems

Judith Viorst dabbles a bit with shape poems for her title "Sometimes Poems." Challenge students to choose an object about which to model their own shape poems.

Procedure

1. Read "Sometimes Poems" with the class. Have students notice how the poet uses the words of the poem to express shape, in this instance, short and fat and tall and thin.

2. What other shapes can students think of? List their ideas on the chalkboard. For example, round, square, triangular, curly, star-shaped, wavy.

3. Challenge students to use a shape in which to write a few poetic lines. Suggest that their shapes and the subjects of their poems relate. For example, they might write a few lines about baseball in the shape of a circle.

4. After students share their poems, display the poems around the room.

Jerry
Pinkney

Andrea Davis
Pinkney

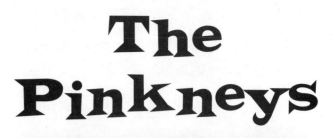
The Pinkneys

J. Brian
Pinkney

Gloria Jean
Pinkney

What a group! Mother, father, son, and daughter-in-law— this unusually gifted family shares their talents through writing and illustrating captivating children's books that offer hope and encouragement. Their stories celebrate the importance of family ties and hard work, while downplaying the disadvantages life might offer.

Interesting Facts About the Authors

Jerry Pinkney

Born on December 22, 1939, in Philadelphia, Pennsylvania, Jerry is the son of James H. and Williemae Pinkney. His father was a carpenter and his mother was a housewife. Jerry began drawing at a very early age, and he was rewarded for his artistic abilities at school. He attended the Philadelphia Museum College of Art (now the University of Arts) from 1957 to 1959. In 1960 he married Gloria Maultsby, and they had four children.

Jerry went on to have an extensive career that includes designing and illustrating greeting cards, opening his own art studio, and teaching classes at various universities. His artistic works have been exhibited extensively.

Gloria Jean Pinkney

Gloria Jean was born on September 5, 1941, in Lumberton, North Carolina. She is the daughter of Teed Daughtery, an insurance agent, and Ernestine Powell Maultsby, a seamstress. As a child, Gloria was surrounded by books and learned to read at an early age. She grew up as an only child in her great-aunt's boarding house in Philadelphia. Receiving much encouragement from the adults around her, Gloria dreamed big dreams. Her first book, *Back Home*, was published in 1992. Her husband, Jerry, was the illustrator. Along with collaborating with her husband, Gloria designs hats and jewelry for her personal boutique in Croton-on-Hudson, New York. She serves on several committees in her church and belongs to the Society of Children's Book Writers and Illustrators.

J. Brian Pinkney and Andrea Davis Pinkney

The son of Jerry and Gloria, Brian Pinkney was born on August 28, 1961, in Boston, Massachusetts. He graduated from the Philadelphia College of Art with a Bachelor of Fine Arts degree in 1983, and received a Master's degree in 1990 from the School of Visual Arts in New York. Brian taught at the Children's Art Carnival, in the heart of New York City, and also at the School of Visual Arts. He has illustrated several children's books as well as writing and illustrating *Max Found Two Sticks*. In 1993 he collaborated with his wife, Andrea, to publish the biography *Alvin Ailey*. Andrea Davis married Brian on October 12, 1991. Andrea is an editor in the Simon & Schuster Children's Publishing division. Along with writing children's books, she has also written feature articles for *The New York Times* and other publications.

Books illustrated by Jerry Pinkney*

- *Babushka and the Pig* by Ann Trofimuk
- *Song of the Trees* by Mildred D. Taylor
- *Roll of Thunder, Hear My Cry* by Mildred D. Taylor
- *Tonweya and the Eagles, and Other Lakota Indian Tales* by Rosebud Yellow Robe
- *Count on Your Fingers African Style* by Claudia Zaslavsky
- *The Patchwork Quilt* by Valerie Flournoy
- *Minty: A Story of Young Harriet Tubman* by Alan Schroeder
- *Mirandy and Brother Wind* by Patricia McKissack
- *The Talking Eggs* by Robert D. San Souci
- *Home Place* by Crescent Dragonwagon
- *Back Home* by Gloria Jean Pinckney
- *Sunday Outing* by Gloria Jean Pinckney
- *Drylongso* by Virginia Hamilton
- *Their Eyes Were Watching God* by Zora Neale Hurston
- *In for Winter, Out for Spring* by Arnold Adoff
- *Further Tales of Uncle Remus: The Misadventures of Brer Rabbit, Brer Fox, Brer Wolf, the Doodang, and All the Other Creatures* by Julius Lester
- *Pretend You're a Cat* by Jean Marzollo

* Jerry Pinkney has illustrated books too numerous to mention. Consult your library for a more extensive list.

Books written by Gloria Jean Pinkney

- *Back Home*
- *Sunday Outing*

Books written & illustrated by J. Brian Pinkney

- *Max Found Two Sticks*

Books illustrated by J. Brian Pinkney

- *The Boy and the Ghost*
- *The Ballad of Belle Dorcus*
- *Where Does This Trail Lead?*
- *A Wave in Her Pocket*
- *Sukey and the Mermaid*
- *Shipwrecked on Mystery Island*
- *Julie Brown: Racing With the World*
- *Harriet Tubman and Black History Month*
- *The Lost Zoo*
- *Alvin Ailey*
- *The Dark-Thirty: Southern Tales of the Supernatural*

Books written by Andrea Davis Pinkney

- *Alvin Ailey*
- *Seven Candles for Kwanzaa*
- *Dear Benjamin Banneker*

The Sunday Outing

Written by Gloria Jean Pinkney
Illustrated by Jerry Pinkney

The Sunday Outing *is the story of a girl's dream to ride the train to visit her family in the country. With the help of her family and the sacrifices they make, her dream comes true. This is a feel-good story that encourages family values. With the intrigue of journeying to a new place, your students will not only enjoy this story but also learn about the importance of family.*

Points of Interest Not Mentioned in the Story

- *The Sunday Outing* is actually a prequel to Gloria Pinkney's *Back Home*. This might be a good time to introduce children to the concept of prequels and sequels.

- This story's origin actually comes from an experience Gloria had as a child. (See *Back Home*.)

- If you have a new paperback edition of *The Sunday Outing*, notice that Myles Carter Pinkney is credited for Gloria and Jerry's photograph. He is their son.

Memorable Story Quote

"'All aboard,' the conductor yelled. Ernestine looked about the great train, too excited to feel scared anymore . . . as the Silver Star began the long journey south."

Activities for *The Sunday Outing*

ACTIVITY 1: Train Book Report

ACTIVITY 2: Writing Extension 1—Where Do You Dream About Going?

ACTIVITY 3: Writing Extension 2—Traveling Alone

ACTIVITY 4: Train-Station Field Trip

ACTIVITY 5: Train-Schedule Math

ACTIVITY 6: Family-Picture Posters

ACTIVITY 1

Train Book Report

Riding a train can be an exciting adventure for children as well as adults. Encourage students to retell Ernestine's expectations and experiences as they create their own paper trains.

Assembling the Train

1. Reproduce and give each student one engine and ten train-car patterns.

2. Instruct students to cut them out.

3. In their own words, encourage students to write one story event on each car.

4. Then give each student a sheet of butcher paper. Have students arrange their trains in order in an interesting way on the paper, then glue them down.

5. Encourage students to draw in scenery and tracks with crayons or markers.

6. Display your train book reports in the hallway.

Supplies

- train-engine pattern, page 96
- train-car pattern, page 96
- butcher paper
- glue
- scissors
- crayons

The Writing Process

Brainstorm with students the answers to these questions

- *Who* was in the story?
- *Where* did the story take place?
- *Why* was there a story at all? *What* was the main problem? (For example, Ernestine's desire to travel to the place where she was born.)
- *How* was it resolved?

With the class, list on the chalkboard the sequence of story events. Keep the list short, simple, and to the point. Whenever possible, use students' own words. Below are some suggested events in story order.

1. Ernestine waited for Aunt Odessa to take her to the train station to watch the trains. Her friends teased her.

2. Ernestine sat with Aunt Odessa on the trolley, pretending she was on the Silver Star.

3. Ernestine tells Aunt Odessa that her mother's family invited her to visit their farm. Her parents said they could not afford the trip.

4. Aunt Odessa suggested that Ernestine find a way to save her parents' money.

5. Ernestine heard her mother talk about buying material to make new school clothes. Ernestine says she can do without new clothes.

6. Ernestine's mother decided she could do without an electric sewing machine.

7. Ernestine's father thought he could do without a new tool set.

8. The next morning, Ernestine's father announced, "You are going to Lumberton."

9. Ernestine's mother showed pictures of her family.

10. Ernestine was scared but excited. She waved to her family from the Silver Star as she began her journey south.

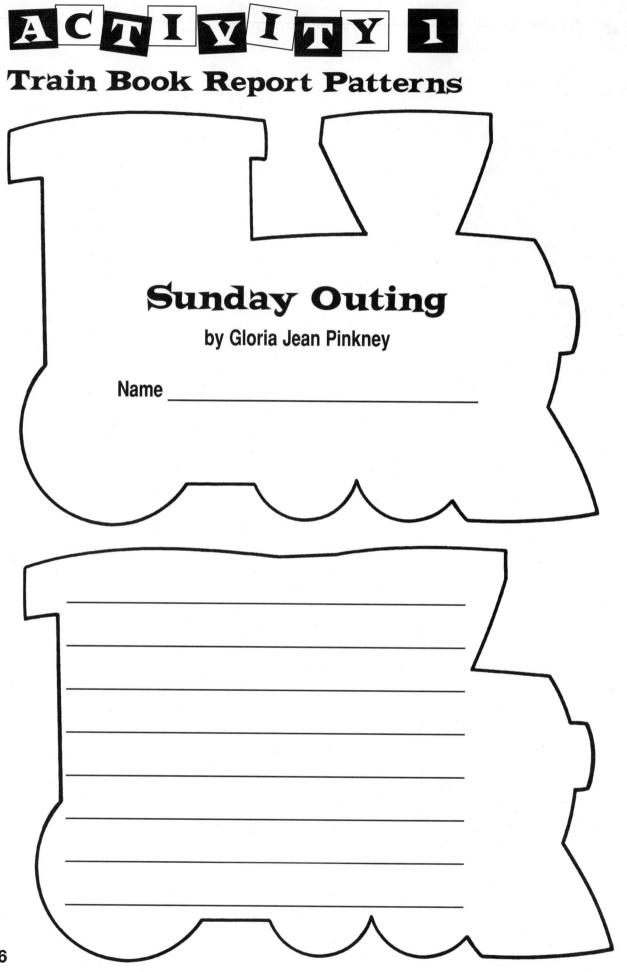

Sunday Outing
by Gloria Jean Pinkney

Name _____

ACTIVITY 2

Writing Extension 1— Where Do You Dream About Going?

Ernestine spent many hours dreaming about riding the train. Train travel is particularly exciting because of the incredible scenery that can be viewed as you zoom along. Where might your students like to travel to on a train? Invite them to write and illustrate their own train adventures.

The Writing Process

1. Recall with students that Ernestine imagined traveling south on the Silver Star to see her family. Let students share places they dream of going.

2. Suggest to students that they have been given a train ticket to anywhere in the country. Pass out writing paper, and invite students to explain where they would go and why. Guide their writing with the following questions.

- *Where* do you want to go?
- *Why* do you want to go there?
- *Whom* or *what* do you want to see?
- *What* will you do when you get there?
- *What* will you pack in your suitcase?
- *What* do you imagine this place is like?

3. After volunteers share their work, display their papers on a bulletin board titled "All Aboard!"

ACTIVITY 3

Writing Extension 2— Traveling Alone

Ernestine was a bit nervous about traveling alone on the Silver Star. Have your students ever traveled alone? How did they feel? How do they imagine it might feel? Invite students to write about such an experience.

The Writing Process

1. Discuss with students how Ernestine felt on the day of her trip. Why do they think she was nervous? With the class, reread this part of the book.

2. Invite students who have traveled alone to share their experiences. This could also be a time when students have been with friends' families or on school field trips.

3. Provide students with writing paper. Challenge them to describe a time when they had to travel alone or without members of their families or to imagine how they might feel. Prompt students' writing with the following questions.

- *Where* were you going?
- *Who,* if anyone, was with you?
- *How* did you feel without other members of your family?
- *What* made you feel better?

4. Select a few essays to read aloud. Then combine the papers in a class book titled "Traveling Alone" for your reading center.

ACTIVITY 4

Train-Station Field Trip

Every Sunday, Ernestine enjoyed going to the train station with her Aunt Odessa. They would watch the trains come and go and the people get on and off. This is a great time to arrange a field trip to a train station in your area.

Procedure

1. Ahead of time, contact the train station and inquire about school field trips. Perhaps a guide could be available to show students the station and the inside of the train.

2. Before the trip, brainstorm a list of questions for students to ask the guide. If possible, bring along a video or still camera to record your field trip.

3. Afterward, encourage students to draw pictures and write a few sentences about their favorite parts. Also have students dictate to you a thank-you letter to send the train station and guide.

Extra! If a train station is not convenient, check out the many books and videos on trains.

Extra! An even more extensive field trip could involve riding the train to a neighboring town! Have parents or a school bus pick you up to bring you back to school.

ACTIVITY 5

Train-Schedule Math

Figuring out the length of train rides and learning how to read train schedules is great for tying real-life skills into your reading curriculum. Challenge students to hone their math and reading skills as they try to decipher a train schedule.

Procedure

1. Ahead of time, contact a large train company and tell them you need train schedule information. Most likely they will send you free train schedules through the mail rather promptly.

2. Cluster children around the schedules in small groups. Go over the information they see. Where can they find the names of the train stations or the places where the trains stop? What do the numbers in the columns represent?

3. Using the schedules, pose some problems for children to solve. Choose a city of origin and the time of departure. Inform students to where the train is traveling. When will the train arrive there? Based on the departure and arrival times, challenge students to tell you how long the train ride will be.

4. Culminate your train-schedule study by finding the departure and arrival locations on a map. If possible, you might ask students to tell you the distances between various cities.

ACTIVITY 6
Family-Picture Posters

Ernestine's mother showed pictures of her family in Lumberton. Many children may have relatives that live in different towns. Invite students to learn more about these faraway relatives.

Procedure

1. Recall with students the pictures Ernestine's mother showed of her family. Lead students to talk about relatives they have in other towns. Who are they? Where do they live? How often do they visit?

2. Invite students to research these family members. Send a letter home, explaining the project. Invite family at home to help their child gather information and pictures about relatives who live in other places. Ask families to assist in arranging their findings on posterboard.

3. In class, let students share their posters and families. Invite classmates to ask questions.

Dear Parents,

We have been studying the books of Gloria and Jerry Pinkney. In their book *The Sunday Outing*, a young girl named Ernestine takes a train ride to visit relatives she has not seen since she was quite young. Before she travels south, her mother shows pictures of the relatives Ernestine will be visiting.

I would like for you to share with your child pictures of relatives who live in other places. Give your child any information about them that your child can share with the class. Help your child mount the pictures on posterboard to bring to school to share with the class. I will be sure that the pictures are returned to you safely and promptly.

Thank you for your help!

Sincerely,

Back Home

Written by Gloria Jean Pinkney
Illustrated by Jerry Pinkney

Back Home starts with the train ride Ernestine began in The Sunday Outing. It shares the memorable visit she had with her family in Lumberton. After reaching Lumberton, Ernestine experiences various feelings as she struggles to develop a friendship with her cousin, Jack. This story of relationships and family ties is one your students will enjoy as they find out what happens on Ernestine's visit.

Points of Interest Not Mentioned in the Story

- *Back Home* was Gloria Pinkney's first children's book. Gloria, herself, is from Lumberton, North Carolina. After attending a family reunion there, she was reminded of old family memories. She realized how special those memories were and wanted to write a book about them.

- This story is based on an actual trip Gloria took to Lumberton when she was eight years old.

- Gloria named the main character in the story Ernestine, after her mother. She also dedicated the book to her mother's memory.

Memorable Story Quote

"Ernestine put the scrapbook back on the shelf. Then she took one last look at Mama's room and pulled the door shut."

Activities for *Back Home*

ACTIVITY 1: Trip Back Home Journal Book Reports
ACTIVITY 2: Overalls for Ernestine
ACTIVITY 3: Writing Extension—Write to a Relative
ACTIVITY 4: Country/City Venn Diagram
ACTIVITY 5: Crayon-Wash Paintings
ACTIVITY 6: Ernestine's Birthplace

ACTIVITY 1

Trip Back Home Journal Book Reports

The events in *Back Home* reflect family relationships and values. What would Ernestine write about her trip if she kept a journal? Encourage students to retell the story in diary form.

Supplies

- journal-cover pattern, page 102
- writing paper
- stapler

Assembling the Journal

1. Give each student 15 sheets of writing paper. Also reproduce one journal cover for each student.

2. Help students staple the cover and pages together. Then have them number the journal pages.

The Writing Process

Begin by listing with the class the sequence of story events. Keep the list short, simple, and to the point. Use students' own words whenever possible. Below are suggested events in story order.

1. After a long train ride, Ernestine arrived in Lumberton.

2. Her great uncle June was waiting. They drove home in his old pickup truck.

3. Ernestine met Aunt Beula and cousin Jack.

4. Ernestine slept in her mother's old room.

5. Ernestine woke early and helped with the kitchen chores before going outside.

6. Aunt Beula told Ernestine to change into overalls. She wore an old pair of her mother's.

7. Ernestine wanted to see Jack's new baby goat. Jack commented about Ernestine's citified ways.

8. Ernestine felt embarrassed. She spent the afternoon canning peaches.

9. The next day, Jack showed Ernestine the barn. Ernestine couldn't roll in the grain like Jack.

10. Then Ernestine tried to ride Jack's goat. She fell.

11. Uncle June took everyone to Sandy Bottom, where Ernestine saw the house where she was born.

12. On Sunday everyone went to church.

13. Afterward the family took flowers to Grandmama's grave.

14. Jack named the new goat Princess, just as Ernestine had suggested.

15. Ernestine put the overalls in a drawer to wear on her next visit.

Talk with students about the purpose of keeping a journal. Confirm that people keep journals, or diaries, to record special moments they don't want to forget. Then review with students the story events listed on the board. If Ernestine wrote in a journal, how would she describe these events?

On each journal page, encourage students to write and illustrate one story event from Ernestine's point of view. Let students take the journals home to share the story with their families.

ACTIVITY 1

Journal-Cover Pattern

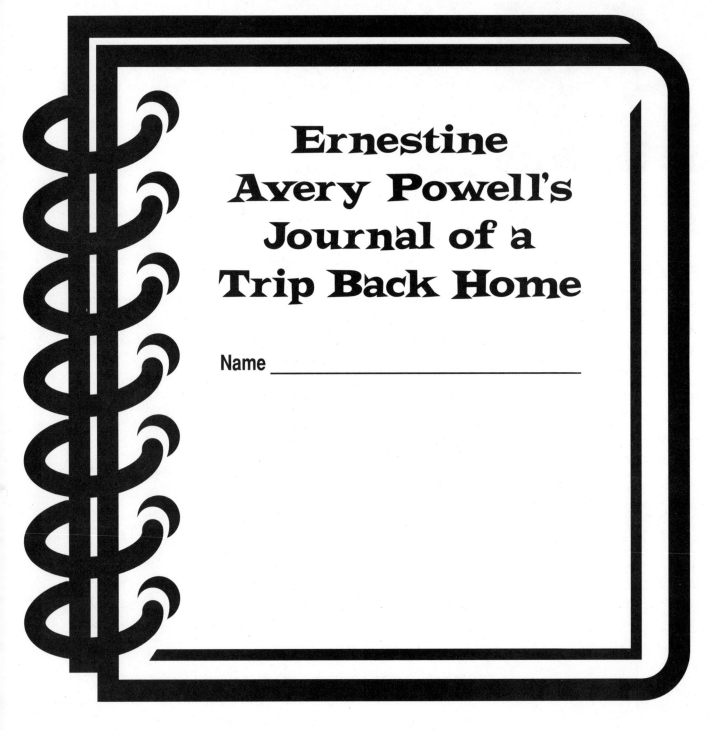

Ernestine
Avery Powell's
Journal of a
Trip Back Home

Name _____

ACTIVITY 2

Overalls for Ernestine

When Ernestine arrived in Lumberton, she was dressed in her Sunday best. She quickly realized that life in the country required more casual clothes. Invite students to design overalls for Ernestine's stay in the country.

Supplies

- Ernestine-figure pattern, page 104
- scraps of fabric, wallpaper, wrapping paper, rickrack
- crayons or markers

Procedure

1. Flip through the book with the class, and ask students to compare the clothes Ernestine wears at the beginning of the book with those she wears at the farm. How have they changed? Why have they changed?

2. Give each student an Ernestine pattern. Instruct the students to trace the pattern onto oak tag and cut out. Explain that they are going to design some new overalls for Ernestine to wear in the country. Encourage students to use the assorted fabric scraps you provide as well as crayons and markers. Suggest that they also include appropriate shoes and a farm hat.

3. Display the Ernestine figures on a bulletin board with the title "Ernestine—Dressed for the Country."

ACTIVITY 3

Writing Extension— Write to a Relative

Aunt Beula wrote Ernestine's family and invited Ernestine to visit. It is important to keep in touch with relatives near and far when possible. Invite students to keep in touch with relatives with this writing activity.

The Writing Process

Discuss with students how Ernestine enjoyed meeting her relatives in Lumberton. Talk about how letters kept the families in touch with each other's lives. For example, Ernestine knew about Jack and his goats from Aunt Beula's letters. Conclude that even though we may not be able to visit our families, we can stay in touch through letter writing.

This is a perfect time for a lesson on writing friendly letters. Have students choose a relative or family friend who lives in another city or town, perhaps someone they do not see often. In a friendly letter, invite students to describe how they are and what they are doing.

Have students share the letters in small groups to peer edit. Encourage students to take their letters home and mail them to their friends and relatives. In upcoming weeks, remember to ask about any responses that students might have received.

Ernestine-Figure Pattern

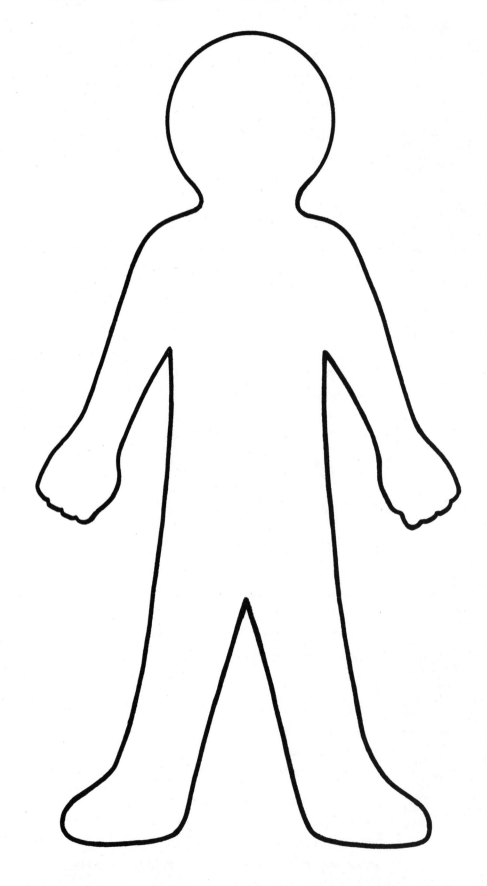

ACTIVITY 4
Country-City Venn Diagram

Ernestine learned a lot about country life while visiting Lumberton, North Carolina. In many ways, life in Lumberton was a contrast to her life in the city. Challenge students to compare and contrast country and city life, using a Venn diagram.

Procedure

1. Discuss with students how Ernestine's home in the city differed from her relatives' home in the country. Elicit what students know about these different lifestyles, and list their ideas on the chalkboard.

2. Give students a blank Venn diagram (Appendix, page 262). Explain that in a Venn diagram one can compare two things, noticing the similarities and differences at a glance.

3. Draw a large Venn diagram on the chalkboard or overhead, labeling the circles *Country Life* and *City Life*. Drawing on prior knowledge and information gained from the book, help students list characteristics for each circle as well as shared characteristics for the center.

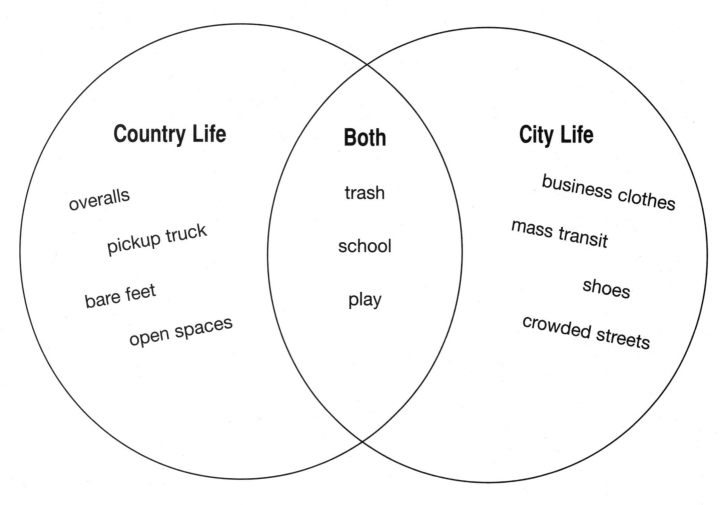

Country Life

overalls

pickup truck

bare feet

open spaces

Both

trash

school

play

City Life

business clothes

mass transit

shoes

crowded streets

ACTIVITY 5

Crayon-Wash Paintings

The illustrations in *Back Home* and *The Sunday Outing* are absolutely beautiful. The detail and dreamlike qualities of the illustrations make readers feel they are part of the story. Pinkney uses pencils, colored pencils, and watercolors to create these illustrations of reality. Your students will enjoy creating a piece of art with a "washed" appearance, too.

Supplies
- white drawing paper
- crayons
- newspapers to protect surfaces
- large paint brushes
- diluted yellow tempera

Procedure

1. Share with students the beauty of the illustrations in *Back Home* and *The Sunday Outing*. Point out the details of each picture. Display the illustration of the flowers Uncle June gave Ernestine for students to replicate.

2. Have students draw the bouquet in pencil on white paper. Emphasize that the bouquet should cover most of the paper.

3. Have students color their drawings with crayons. (Note: Markers or colored pencils will not work for this activity.) Instruct students to color hard and fill in all spaces.

4. Help students brush over the entire paper in broad, even strokes with diluted yellow paint. The crayon will resist the paint, and the paper will have a washed appearance.

5. When dry, mount the bouquets on posterboard for display. Title your display "Bouquets for Ernestine."

ACTIVITY 6

Ernestine's Birthplace

One of the most exciting things Ernestine did on her trip to Lumberton was to visit a small abandoned farmhouse where she was born. The house was no longer in good shape. She promised that one day she would come back to fix it. Speculate with students what her house might look like when Ernestine finishes with it.

Supplies
- drawing paper
- crayons and colored pencils

Procedure

1. Reread with students the page in the book where she visits the house where she was born. Have students look at the illustrations and talk about the condition the house is in. What do students think Ernestine will do to fix up the house?

2. Provide students with drawing paper. Instruct them to first draw an outline of the house, then to draw in the improvements that Ernestine might make.

3. Line up students' drawings on a chalkboard ledge to compare each other's work. Which improvements did most students make? Do they see a house a classmate has drawn that they would like to live in?

Alvin Ailey

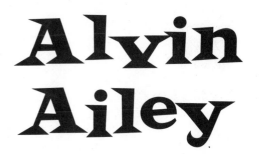

Written by Andrea Davis Pinkney
Illustrated by J. Brian Pinkney

Alvin Ailey is a biography about the life of dancer-choreographer Alvin Ailey. Separated into four areas of his life, Ailey's story is an inspiration to all.

Points of Interest Not Mentioned in the Story

• To accurately write and illustrate the author's life, Andrea and Brian studied the Dunham modern dance technique with Ella Thompson Moore, one of the original Alvin Ailey dancers.

• The last page of the book shows a photograph of Alvin Ailey and provides more facts about his life.

Memorable Story Quote

"Taking a bow, Alvin let out a breath. He raised his eyes toward heaven, satisfied and proud."

Activities for *Alvin Ailey*

ACTIVITY 1: Alvin Ailey's Life Book Report

ACTIVITY 2: Adjectives—Colorful Language

ACTIVITY 3: Creative Movement

ACTIVITY 4: Dancing Flip Books

ACTIVITY 5: Writing Extension—Biographies

ACTIVITY 1

Alvin Ailey's Life Book Report

This biography should be easy for students to understand and should leave them with a message of hope and inspiration. This activity encourages students to compile a book of reflections on the four periods of Alvin Ailey's life.

Supplies

- cover pattern, page 109
- crayons
- stage pattern, page 110
- stapler

Assembling the Book

1. Reproduce for each student one cover page and four stage pages.

2. Instruct the students to staple the cover and pages together, numbering the stage pages inside.

The Writing Process

Review with students that a biography is the story of someone's life written by another person. Point out that this biography is divided into four different periods of Alvin Ailey's life. Talk with students about each one.

Help students summarize these four phases of his life. Write their ideas on the chalkboard, the overhead, or on chart paper. Use students' own words and ideas whenever possible. Below are suggested summaries listed by time period. Have students summarize each period of Ailey's life in their own words on one page of their books.

1942: True Vine Baptist Church
Alvin Ailey learned to appreciate music and rhythm at the True Vine Baptist Church in Navasota, Texas. Ailey began to treasure the fulfillment he felt through music.

1945–1947: Los Angeles
After moving to Los Angeles, Alvin Ailey was exposed to theater and dance. Watching a famous African American dancer, he was inspired by her moves.

1949–1953: Los Angeles
At 18, Alvin Ailey began taking dance lessons. After hours of practice he quickly rose to the top of his class, choreographing as well.

1958–1960: New York
Alvin Ailey premiered with *Blues Suite*—dances set in a honky-tonk dance hall—which he choreographed. He produced *Revelations*, a suite of dances that celebrated the traditions of True Vine Baptist Church. Ailey was a great success.

Reflections on Alvin Ailey's Life

Los Angeles, California

New York, New York

Navasota, Texas

Name _____

ACTIVITY 1

ACTIVITY 2

Adjectives—Colorful Language

Andrea Davis Pinkney uses rich describing words to provide readers with vivid pictures of the characters and actions in the story. Suggest that students add these adjectives to their Writing Journals.

Procedure

1. Review with students what an adjective is: an adjective is a word that describes a noun. Emphasize that adjectives bring life to sentences and phrases.

2. Reread *Alvin Ailey* and have students listen for all the interesting adjectives.

3. With the class, list the adjectives on a chart. (See list below.)

4. Invite students to copy the words in their Writing Journals under the heading *Adjectives*. Advise students to consult their Writing Journals when looking for adjectives to liven up their writing.

thundering sermons
sweet sopranos
blue-black flies
joyful noise
small, dusty town

creaky locomotive
powdered babies
flashy town
distinguished suits
swinging music

wide-brimmed hats
blinking marquee
Texas heat
beautiful dancer
spindly legs

fluid moves
old wooden stage
moody shadows
weepy sadness
sleek moves

ACTIVITY 3

Creative Movement

Moving to music was essential in Alvin Ailey's life. Most children also enjoy moving to music. This activity allows students to move freely as you play a variety of music.

Extra! This activity may bring out special talents in some of your students.

Supplies

- assortment of musical selections, such as classical, jazz, rock, spiritual, and country
  - tape recorder or CD or record player for your music

Procedure

1. Review with students how dancing made Alvin Ailey feel and how important it was in his life. Ask your students if they like moving to music. What do they like about it? How does it make them feel?

2. Inform students that they will have a chance to move to music themselves. Remind them that dance and movement are a form of expression.

3. Play a variety of music for students to dance to. As they dance, stress that they should think about how the music makes them feel, moving accordingly. As the music changes, make sure children change their movements, too.

ACTIVITY 4

Dancing Flip Books

Dancing incorporates many intricate movements, combined to evoke a feeling or even a story. Many dances have been captured on film. Invite students to make their own dance movies by creating flip books.

Supplies

- index cards
- pencils

Procedure

1. Point out to students the fluid movements Brian Pinkney shows in his illustrations. If all these movements were put together, what would they look like?

2. Pass out six large index cards to each student. Explain that they will be making flip books of dance movements.

3. Begin by asking students if they know how traditional cartoons are made. Confirm that a sequence of actions is drawn, one action at a time. When the pictures move quickly, one after the other, the cartoon appears to come to life!

4. Let students try it. On each index card, ask students to draw one dance movement.

5. Placing the cards in order, show children how to flip the cards to make the dancing figure move.

ACTIVITY 5

Writing Extension— Biographies

Writing a biography is different than writing a fictional story. It takes time and research. Nonfiction writing is important for students to learn. Take this opportunity to have students write simple biographies about an adult family member or another important adult in their lives.

The Writing Process

Discuss with students the research Andrea Pinkney must have done to write this biography. Talk about the different resources she might have used. Then invite students to try writing biographies, too. Instruct them to choose an important adult in their lives to write about.

Provide students with a biographical information sheet (Appendix, page 269) to guide their writing. Some students will be able to transfer this information into paragraph form. Others may draw pictures about the information they learned. Encourage students to present their biographies to the people about whom they are written.

Max Found Two Sticks

Written and Illustrated by
J. Brian Pinkney

Max Found Two Sticks is about a young boy who finds two heavy twigs and uses them as drumsticks. Rhythm takes over his body and soul as he begins to tap out sounds on everything he can find. Students will enjoy his creativity and imagination. This is a story you may never "hear" the end of!

Point of Interest Not Mentioned in the Story

• At eight years old, Brian Pinkney began to play the drums. He still loves to play. To this day, Brian Pinkney keeps a set of drumsticks in his studio, where he still taps out a beat.

Memorable Story Quote

"Max watched the drummers with amazement as they passed, copying their rhythms. The last drummer . . . tossed Max his spare set of sticks."

Activities for *Max Found Two Sticks*

ACTIVITY 1: Tappin' Out the Rhythm Book Report

ACTIVITY 2: Illustrating the Wind

ACTIVITY 3: Guest Drummer

ACTIVITY 4: Creative Dramatics With Two Sticks

ACTIVITY 5: Onomatopoeia

ACTIVITY 6: Know the Code!

ACTIVITY 1

Tappin' Out the Rhythm Book Report

Music is Music is one of the few things that nearly everyone on the planet enjoys and responds to. Children especially love music. This story flows smoothly as a young boy taps his way though an afternoon with a couple of sticks, a washing bucket, hatboxes, soda bottles, a trash can, and finally real drumsticks. Invite students to recount Max's afternoon.

Supplies

- drum pattern, page 115
  - drum pattern with writing lines, page 116
    - scissors
      - crayons
        - stapler

Assembling the Book

1. Reproduce and pass out one cover and eight lined writing pages to each student.

2. Instruct students to staple the cover and writing pages together, then number the pages inside.

The Writing Process

Brainstorm with students answers to these questions.

- *Who* was in the story?
- *Where* did the story take place?
- *Why* was there a story at all?
- *What* was the main problem? (For example, Max's desire to keep drumming.)
- *How* was it resolved?

With the class, list on the chalkboard the sequence of story events. Keep the list short, simple, and to the point. Whenever possible, use students' own words and ideas. Below are suggested events. Have students write about each event in their own words on the lined drum pages.

1. Max picked up two heavy twigs.

2. He tapped his thighs with the sticks, imitating the sounds of pigeons.

3. He tapped on his grandfather's bucket, making the sound of rain.

4. He tapped on his sisters' hatboxes, creating the beat of tom-toms in the marching band.

5. He tapped on his friend's soda bottles, making the chimes of church bells.

6. He tapped on a garbage can, making the sound of train wheels.

7. A drummer in a marching band threw his spare drumsticks to Max.

8. Max didn't miss a beat.

Drum Pattern

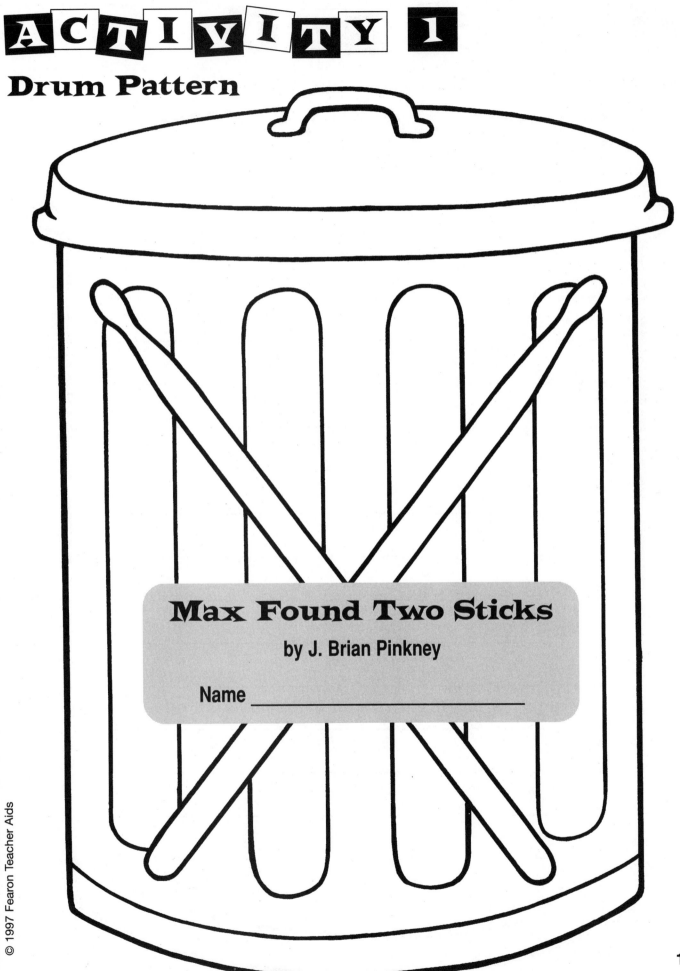

Max Found Two Sticks

by J. Brian Pinkney

Name _____

ACTIVITY 1

Drum Writing
Pages

ACTIVITY 2

Illustrating the Wind

It is obvious in the illustrations that the blowing wind made the sticks fall to the ground near Max. Invite students to make illustrations that show the wind blowing.

Supplies

- drawing paper
- drawing pencils

Procedure

1. Display for students the illustration of Max sitting on the front steps. How can they tell the wind is blowing? Talk about the techniques Brian Pinkney uses. (For example, white swirls in the sky, leaves falling to the ground, sticks falling to the ground.)

2. Brainstorm with students other ways an illustrator might show the wind blowing.

3. Give each student a sheet of drawing paper and challenge everyone to draw pictures in which the viewer can tell the wind is blowing.

4. Let students share their pictures with the class. Mount the pictures on a bulletin board titled ". . . And the Wind Blew, and Blew, and Blew!"

ACTIVITY 3

Guest Drummer

You've heard of a guest speaker. How about a guest drummer? Invite a drummer to visit your class for a demonstration.

Procedure

1. Locate a drummer to visit your class. Check with your school music teacher for ideas. Or contact a local high school or college for student volunteers.

2. Invite the drummer to visit to demonstrate his or her talents as well as to talk to students about how he or she learned to play.

3. The day before the visit, inform students about the visit. Generate with students appropriate questions to ask the guest.

4. During the visit, invite your guest to show the class a few simple drum techniques that students might be able to do themselves.

5. After the presentation, make sure students write thank-you notes to the drummer.

Extra! Due to the noise, you may need to set up another room in which your drummer can perform, such as the cafeteria.

ACTIVITY 4
Creative Dramatics With Two Sticks

Max found two sticks and had a wonderful afternoon. Challenge students to have fun, too, using only two simple sticks.

Procedure

1. Take the class outside and ask students or partners to find two sticks.

2. Back in class, invite a volunteer to beat out a rhythm on a desk.

3. Challenge the rest of the class to mimic the rhythm.

4. Repeat until everyone has had a chance to create a new rhythm for their classmates to try.

ACTIVITY 5
Onomatopoeia

Brian Pinkney uses onomatopoeia throughout *Max Found Two Sticks*. This is a fun writing form for children to learn. Encourage students to discover the onomatopoetic words in the book to include in their Writing Journals.

Procedure

1. Review with students that onomatopoeia is the use of words or phrases to mimic a sound. For example, *bang, crash, boom, zip*.

2. Reread *Max Found Two Sticks*. Ask students to raise their hands when they hear a word of onomatopoeia. List the words on the chalkboard, asking students to record the words in their journals as well.

3. Encourage students to use the words or phrases when writing on their own.

pat . . . pat-tat

putter-putter . . . pat-tat

tap-tap-tap

tippy-tip . . . tat-tat

dum . . . dum-dee-dum

di-di-di-di. Dum-dum.

dong . . . dang . . . dung

ding . . . dong . . . ding

cling . . . clang . . . da-bang

Vera B. Williams

> *Vera B. Williams tells stories of hope. Her themes are easy for young children to relate to and understand, and they also have deep implications that appeal to older children as well as adults. Her simple use of language and childlike illustrations encourage hard work, discipline, and patience.*

Interesting Facts About the Author

Birth: Vera B. Williams was born on January 28, 1927, in Hollywood, California.

Family: Vera grew up in New York City. She is a first generation American, her parents having emigrated from Russia and Poland. They met in America and married. Vera met and married her husband, Paul Williams, while in college. She has three children: Sara, Jennifer, and Merce.

Education: Vera attended high school for music and art, where she wrote, illustrated, and bound her first book about an enormous banana that feeds an entire family. She went on to graduate from Black Mountain College in Black Mountain, North Carolina in 1949.

Beginnings as an author and illustrator:

Vera's parents struggled greatly during the Great Depression, trying to make ends meet. Even so, they were very concerned about their daughter's education and were constantly looking for new opportunities. She was put into a school for gifted children, where she began to take art lessons. The lessons continued for eight to nine years.

When Vera was young, the Works Progress Administration—a government agency during the 1930s and 1940s that undertook improvement projects—held an exhibit of art created by adults and children at the Museum of Art in New York City. Vera's painting, *Yentas*, was displayed. Vera stood by the painting to talk with those who viewed it. One interested viewer was Eleanor Roosevelt, the President's wife. Mrs. Roosevelt, Vera, and the painting were featured in a Movietone newsreel at the local cinemas. In 1986, *Yentas* was again exhibited at the Bronx Museum's "Jewish Life in the First 50 Years of the Century" exhibit.

Books by Vera B. Williams

- *It's a Gingerbread House: Bake It, Build It, Eat It*
- *The Great Watermelon Birthday*
- *Three Days on a River in a Red Canoe*
- *A Chair for My Mother*
- *Something Special for Me*
- *Music, Music for Everyone*
- *Cherries and Cherry Pits*
- *My Mother, Leah, and George Sand*
- *Stringbean's Trip to the Shining Sea*

Other Interests:

Vera enjoys teaching, nature, and social issues.

Awards Highlights

- *Three Days on a River in a Red Canoe* was a Parents' Choice Book for illustrations in 1981.
- *A Chair for My Mother* received a Caldecott Honor in 1983 as well as being voted by the *School Library Journal* as a Best Children's Book for 1982.
- *Cherries and Cherry Pits* won numerous awards, including the Boston Globe-Horn Book Award Honor Book for illustration, 1987. It was also named by *The New York Times* as one of the Best Illustrated Books of the Year for 1986.

Common Threads to Look For Throughout Her Books

- Vera B. Williams's illustrations are much like those a child would draw, therefore capturing children's attention.
- Notice the vibrant colors used throughout her books.
- Many of Vera's themes show how to make happiness during times of hardship.

Cherries and Cherry Pits

Cherries and Cherry Pits is full of a child's active imagination. As a young girl enjoys drawing with her markers, she cleverly makes up stories. Interestingly enough, her stories always include cherries and cherry pits.

Point of Interest Not Mentioned in the Story

- Many times young children focus on an object or idea for a long period of time. This object or idea is often evident in their writings and drawings, just as cherries and cherry pits fill the illustrations and stories of Bidemmi.

Memorable Story Quote

"THIS cherry pit and THIS cherry pit and all the cherry pits start to grow until there is a whole forest of cherry trees right on our block."

Activities for *Cherries and Cherry Pits*

ACTIVITY 1: Cherry Orchard Book Reports

ACTIVITY 2: Cherry Research Tree

ACTIVITY 3: Draw as You Go

ACTIVITY 4: Writing Extension 1—Poetry and Illustration

ACTIVITY 5: Writing Extension 2—A Very Cherry Story

ACTIVITY 6: Cherry Math Manipulatives

ACTIVITY 7: Cooking With Fruit Cookbook

ACTIVITY 1

Cherry Orchard Book Reports

Invite students to "plant" a class cherry orchard as they retell *Cherries and Cherry Pits*.

Assembling the Cherry Tree

1. Distribute brown construction paper to each student. Tell the students to draw and cut out a tree trunk with branches.

2. Distribute green construction paper to each student. Tell them to draw and cut out the top of the tree.

3. Have students glue the cherries to the tree top in story order.

4. Show students how to glue the trunk of the tree to the tree top.

5. Ask students to write the title of the book, the author, and their names on the trunks of their trees.

6. On a blank wall or in the hallway, arrange all the trees to create a class cherry orchard.

Supplies

- brown construction paper, 12" x 18" (30 cm x 45 cm)
- green construction paper, 12" x 18" (30 cm x 45 cm)
- scissors
- cherry pattern sheet, page 124
- glue
- pencils

The Writing Process

Brainstorm with students answers to these questions.

- *Who* was in the story?
- *Where* did the story take place?
- *Why* was there a story at all? *Why* was it entertaining?

With the class, list on the chalkboard the sequence of story events. Keep the list short, simple, and to the point. Whenever possible, use students' own words. Below are some suggested story events.

1. Often I take a new marker to my friend, Bidemmi, who lives above me. She uses it to draw pictures as she makes up stories.

2. One story was about a man in the subway who had a white bag of cherries. He took the cherries home to his four children.

3. Another was about an elderly woman who also had a bag of cherries. She took them home to share with her parrot.

4. The next story was about a boy who brought a cherry home to his sister, reminding her, "Don't forget to spit out the pit.

5. The last story is about herself. She bought cherries from a man who sold them from the back of his truck. She ate them as she walked home.

6. She planted the cherry pits in her yard, hoping they would grow.

7. Bidemmi explained how a cherry tree grows and how a whole forest of cherry trees would be right on her block.

Distribute a cherry pattern sheet to each student. Have students number each cherry, one through seven. Guide students to write or illustrate one story event on each cherry.

ACTIVITY 2

Cherry Research Tree

Not only are cherries good to eat, but the rich color makes them beautiful to see. Encourage students to learn more about this delicious fruit.

Supplies
- brown butcher paper
- green construction paper
- cherry pattern sheet, page 124
- scissors
- pencils
- glue or tape

Procedure

1. Make the trunk and branches of a large tree by using brown butcher paper. Tape it to a wall in your classroom.

2. Make the leaves by using green construction paper. Tape them to the branches.

3. Invite students to share what they know about cherries. Do they like cherries? Have they ever eaten cherries in pies or pastries? What do cherries taste like?

4. Tell students they are going to learn more about this fruit. Take a class trip to the school library to find materials. Ask your school librarian for help.

5. Back in class, list on chart paper the cherry facts that students learned.

6. Give each student a cherry pattern to cut out. (You might reproduce the cherries on red paper for effect.)

7. Let each student choose a cherry fact to write on the cutout.

8. After students share their cherry facts, let them attach their cherries to the tree.

ACTIVITY 2

Cherry Patterns

ACTIVITY 3

Draw as You Go

In *Cherries and Cherry Pits*, Bidemmi tells stories as she illustrates them. Invite students to tell their own stories while drawing pictures as a partner listens.

Procedure

1. Discuss with students how Bidemmi told a story while drawing pictures at the same time. The picture evolved as the story did. Let students try it.

2. Divide students into pairs. Give each a piece of drawing paper and markers.

3. Instruct one student to tell a story while drawing accompanying pictures. Ask the other partner to listen attentively to his or her classmate's story.

4. After the first child has had a chance to tell and draw a story, invite partners to switch roles.

5. If time allows, culminate by inviting partners to share each other's stories with the class.

Extra! This makes a great listening activity.

ACTIVITY 4

Writing Extension 1—Poetry and Illustration

In *Cherries and Cherry Pits*, most of the pages with text have interesting borders. Encourage students to create attractive borders for their own poems.

The Writing Process

1. Reread *Cherries and Cherry Pits* to students. Pause on each page with a border and point out how the border stems from the text.

2. Invite students to write an acrostic poem to decorate. Explain that an acrostic poem uses one letter of a word to start each line. Here is an example.

> Cats are silly.
> Always playful.
> Teeth are sharp.
> So much fun.

3. Give students the poetry sheet on page 126. For each line, or for each letter of the word *cherries*, challenge students to write a sentence describing cherries.

4. Then ask students to decorate the poem by creating an interesting, appropriate border around it.

5. Mount students' work on a bulletin board titled "Cherries . . . Cherries . . . Cherries."

Cherries . . . Cherries . . . Cherries

C _____

H _____

E _____

R _____

R _____

I _____

E _____

S _____

ACTIVITY 5

Writing Extension 2 — A Very Cherry Story

As a common thread, cherries and cherry pits seem like improbable story elements. But Vera B. Williams found unusual and interesting stories for her character to tell. Challenge students to come up with their own cherry stories.

The Writing Process

1. Start by reviewing with students the various stories Bidemmi wrote around cherries and cherry pits.

2. Then brainstorm with students another story for Bidemmi to write. How else could cherries and cherry pits fit into a story? Encourage students to suggest ideas.

3. Provide students with writing paper. Encourage them to write their own stories that include cherries and cherry pits. Explain that they can use an idea suggested by their classmates or a new one they think up. Let students illustrate their stories, too.

4. Invite volunteers to share their cherry stories with the class. Display students' stories on a bulletin board titled "A Very Cherry Story."

ACTIVITY 6

Cherry Math Manipulatives

The cherry patterns on page 124 are perfect for math manipulatives. Invite students to help you color in and cut out several sheets of cherries to help solve math problems.

Extra! You might also use the cherries in conjunction with your cherry trees.
For example, if this tree has 8 cherries and I pick 2, how many are left? Which tree has more? And so on.

Procedure

1. Give students two or three cherry pattern sheets. Instruct students to color in the cherries and cut them out.

2. Working in groups, invite students to pool their cherries together. Also give each group several small brown-paper lunch bags.

3. Explain that using their cherries, children are going to solve some simple math problems. Then pose such problems as

- Bidemmi has 10 cherries in her bag. (Have students place 10 cherry cutouts in their bags.) She gives 3 to her friend. How many cherries does Bidemmi have left?

- The man who gave the cherries to his children had 12 cherries in his bag. The woman who shared the cherries with her parrot had 9 cherries in her bag. Who had more cherries? (Have students count out the numbers, then write on a separate sheet of paper the equation $12 > 9$.)

4. Continue with other problems, allowing groups to come up with their own problems to solve as well.

ACTIVITY 7
Cooking With Fruit Cookbook

Reading *Cherries and Cherry Pits* makes one hungry for a slice of cherry pie! Cherries are used in many dishes, as are other fruits. Encourage students to bring in recipes from home featuring cherries or another fruit.

Procedure

1. Brainstorm with students foods that contain cherries or other fruits, such as salads, pies, cakes, jams, breads, milkshakes, cereals, and ice cream. List their ideas on the board.

2. Ask students to bring in a fruit recipe to contribute to a class fruit cookbook. Send home the parent letter at the bottom of this page explaining the activity.

3. In class, invite students to share their fruit recipes. With the help of a parent, older student, or teacher's aide, type up each recipe on a separate sheet of paper.

4. Present students with their recipes. Invite them to decorate the pages.

5. Ask a volunteer to create a cover for your class fruit cookbook. Make sure she or he includes the year and class name on the cover.

6. Photocopy the cover and all pages and bind them together. Let students take their cookbooks home to share with their families.

Extra! These fruit cookbooks make great Mother's Day, Father's Day, or holiday gifts.

Dear Family,

Our class has been studying children's author Vera B. Williams. After reading her book *Cherries and Cherry Pits*, we have grown hungry for dishes made with cherries and other fruits. We would like to put together a class cookbook of tasty, healthy fruit dishes. Please contribute a fruit recipe that is a family favorite. We will need your recipe by _____ .

Thank you for your cooperation!

Sincerely,

A Chair for My Mother

A Chair for My Mother is the sentimental story of a young girl who helps save money to buy her hard-working mother a comfortable chair. This story promotes hard work and discipline as well as cherishes family moments.

Points of Interest Not Mentioned in the Story

- This book reflects some of the hard times Vera B. Williams's own family endured during the Great Depression. Using the struggles of her past, she writes a story of hope for a better life.

- The chair in this story serves as a symbol of comfort during troubled times.

- *A Chair for My Mother* is dedicated to the memory of Vera's mother, Rebecca Poringer Baker.

- The sequel to *A Chair for My Mother* is *Something Special for Me*.

- *A Chair for My Mother* is a Reading Rainbow selection.

Memorable Story Quote

"We set the chair right beside the window with the red and white curtains. Grandma and Mama and I all sat in it while Aunt Ida took our picture."

Activities for *A Chair for My Mother*

ACTIVITY 1: Money-Jar Book Report

ACTIVITY 2: Writing Extension—My Special Place to Be

ACTIVITY 3: A Chair for Us

ACTIVITY 4: Money Wrap Math

ACTIVITY 5: Guest Speaker—The Red Cross

ACTIVITY 1
Money-Jar Book Report

The events that lead up to the girl's mother receiving a new chair are poignant, touching, and inspiring. Encourage students to recall these story events with this money-jar book report.

Supplies
- jar pattern, page 131
- glue
- construction paper
- crayons or markers
- scissors
- pencils

Assembling the Jar

1. Reproduce for each students two copies of the jar pattern to cut out.

2. Show students how to glue the jars together, back to back, around the edges, leaving the top and center of the jar open.

3. Have students write the title "A Chair for My Mother" on the jar.

The Writing Process

Brainstorm with students answers to these questions.
- *Who* was in the story?
- *Where* did the story take place?
- *Why* was there a story at all?
- *What* were the problems? (For example, the girl's desire to buy a chair for her mother.)
- *How* were they resolved?

With the class, list on the chalkboard the sequence of story events. Keep the list short, simple, and to the point. Whenever possible, use students' own thoughts and ideas. Below are suggested story events in order.

1. My mother is a waitress. She comes home very tired and has nowhere comfortable to rest.

2. Last year, there was a fire. We lost everything.

3. Neighbors brought food, furniture, and clothes to help us.

4. For a year we have been saving money in a big jar, and now it is full.

5. We counted and wrapped the coins and took them to the bank to change to dollar bills.

6. We bought a big, beautiful chair with big pink flowers.

7. My mom, grandma, and I sat in the chair while my aunt took our picture.

Tell students that they are going to "save" this story in their paper jars. Pass out light-colored construction paper. (A light gray or brown would be perfect, but white paper is fine, too.) Instruct students to cut out seven equal circles to represent seven coins. Ask students to write one story event on each coin, numbering them in order. As students retell the story to friends or family, have them deposit each coin in the paper jar.

ACTIVITY 1

Jar Pattern

ACTIVITY 2

Writing Extension— My Special Place to Be

In *A Chair for My Mother*, a young girl longs for a special place for her mother to find comfort. Most of us have special places where we feel particularly comfortable. Ask students to write about and possibly share their favorite places.

The Writing Process

1. Elicit from students how the chair serves as a place of peace and comfort after a hard day's work.

2. Then discuss places that are special to them. Where do they find comfort? Is it inside or outdoors? What is their favorite room or piece of furniture? Why?

3. Challenge students to write about their places, describing where they are and why they find comfort there.

4. Culminate by letting students draw pictures of their places. You might read children's essays to the class, being sensitive to any that seem too personal.

ACTIVITY 3

A Chair for Us

After the girl, her mother, and her grandmother saved enough money, they went to a furniture store to find the chair of their dreams. What would your students' ideal chair look like? Invite them to design one.

Procedure

1. Show students the page of the furniture store in the book. Talk about the different chairs and why students think the girl and her family chose the big one with pink flowers.

2. Suggest to students that they redesign your classroom. Just like the girl's mother, they work very hard in school, and just like her, they sit in stiff wooden chairs each day. If they could design a new, comfy chair for school, what would it be like?

3. Give each student a photocopy of the chair on page 133. Encourage them to decorate it, adding special features. (Some students may want to design the shape of their chair without using the pattern. Encourage them to.)

4. Now tell students that they need to convince the school principal about why the school should have their chairs. Challenge them to write a few sentences describing the chair and why the school should buy it.

5. Display the chairs on a bulletin board to represent a furniture showroom. Title the bulletin board "A Chair for Us."

Chair Pattern

ACTIVITY 4

Money Wrap Math

In *A Chair for My Mother,* the girl wrapped the coins her family had saved before taking them to the bank. This is a great time to tie in math with the story.

Supplies

- several dollars in pennies
- penny wrappers (check with your local bank)

Procedure

1. Reread with students the part of the book where the young girl wraps coins to take to the bank. Discuss with students how this process organizes loose change, making it much easier to count.

2. Show students the penny wrappers and help them read the money value. (50 cents) How many pennies equal 50 cents? (50) That's a lot of pennies!

3. What do students think would be an easier method to count the pennies? Help students place the pennies in stacks. For example, a stack of 5 or 10 pennies is easier to count and keep track of than one stack of 50. How many stacks would they need? (5 pennies X 10 stacks = 50 pennies; 10 pennies x 5 stacks = 50 pennies.)

4. After students make the appropriate stacks, demonstrate how to place the pennies in the wrappers. Let several students try.

5. Set up a money center in your room for students to practice counting and wrapping pennies.

Extra! You might bring in blank bank-deposit slips for students to fill out to role-play depositing their pennies.

ACTIVITY 5

Guest Speaker–The Red Cross

Many neighbors and friends helped the family in *A Chair for My Mother* after they lost everything in a fire. This activity teaches students how to help disaster victims.

Procedure

1. Contact your local Red Cross. Explain the book you are reading and invite someone from the center to speak to your class about aiding disaster victims.

2. Before the speaker arrives, discuss with students how neighbors and friends helped the family in the book. Announce that you have invited a Red Cross worker to talk to the class. Brainstorm questions for students to ask the Red Cross volunteer.

3. Afterward, draw from students what they learned. On poster paper, list the ideas for helping disaster victims and display the list in school for others to learn from. Also make sure students write thank-you notes to your class visitor, perhaps summarizing some of the things they learned.

Extra! Follow up the activity by collecting food, clothing, or toys to be donated to a local charity.

Music, Music for Everyone

Music, Music for Everyone *involves the same main characters as in* A Chair for My Mother—*the young girl, her mother, and her grandmother. In this story the girl brings joy to her sick grandmother through music. The music also helps her earn extra money her family needs.*

Points of Interest Not Mentioned in the Story

• The chair at the beginning of the story is the same chair that was purchased in *A Chair for My Mother*. It is obvious in this story that the chair has been enjoyed by all.

• Before drawing the pictures for this story, Vera B. Williams rented an accordion, got a book on how to play it, then tried it. This helped her know how it feels to hold an accordion, and it gave her insight into how to draw a child holding this often cumbersome instrument.

Memorable Story Quote

"After that we played and played. We made mistakes, but we played like a real band. The little lanterns came on. Everyone danced."

Activities for *Music, Music for Everyone*

ACTIVITY 1: Music-Note Book Report

ACTIVITY 2: Music Art

ACTIVITY 3: Creative Dramatics: Musical Instrument Charades

ACTIVITY 4: Guest Speaker—Musician

ACTIVITY 5: Rhythm Band

ACTIVITY 1
Music-Note Book Report

Music might really make the world go 'round. It certainly did in this story. In *Music, Music for Everyone*, a young girl forms her own band with her friends, bringing pleasure to others and making money for her family. Invite students to retell the story in this entertaining way.

Supplies
- music-note book cover pattern, page 137
  - music-note writing page, page 138
    - stapler

Assembling the Book
1. Reproduce for each student one book cover and 11 writing pages. Have students cut them out.
2. Help students staple the cover and pages together to form a book.

The Writing Process
Brainstorm with students answers to these questions.
- *Who* was in the story?
- *Where* did the story take place?
- *Why* was there a story at all?
- *What* was the main problem? (For example, the girl's desire to help her family.)
- *How* was it resolved?

With the class, list on the chalkboard the sequence of story events. Keep the list short, simple, and to the point. Whenever possible, use students' own thoughts and ideas. Below are suggested story events in order.

1. Grandmother used to sit in the big chair and listen to me practice my accordion.
2. Grandmother got very sick and was moved upstairs. I talk to her each evening.
3. One day my friends and I played our musical instruments for my grandmother. She liked it.
4. My friends and I sat in the big chair and remembered how my family had saved money to buy it and my accordion. The jar is empty now because my grandmother is sick.
5. I had an idea that we could play our instruments to earn money.
6. Our music teachers helped us, and we practiced and practiced.
7. Leora's mother gave us our first job to play at a party for Leora's great-grandmother and great-grandfather.
8. Although we were scared, we played and everyone danced.
9. Leora's mother paid us for playing.
10. We divided the money into four equal shares.
11. I put mine into the big jar.

Instruct students to write each story event, in order, on one page of their music-note books. Students may take the books home to share the story with their families.

Music, Music for Everyone

by Vera B. Williams

Name _____

ACTIVITY 1
Music-Note Writing Page

ACTIVITY 2

Music Art

In *Music, Music for Everyone*, music was therapy for Grandmother. Some music makes people want to dance, while another type of music soothes them. This activity gives students an opportunity to find out how they react to different types of music.

Supplies
- a variety of music—country, classical, jazz, rock, and so on
- tape recorder or other playing device
- manila paper
- crayons, markers, or colored chalk

Procedure

1. Discuss with students how music made the grandmother feel better in this story. How do different types of music make them feel? Let students share their favorite songs and music styles.

2. Play short clips of different types of music. How does each make students feel?

3. Provide each student with four sheets of manila paper. Select four clips of music, approximately 15 minutes each.

4. Tell students that as they listen to each selection, they are to draw a picture that expresses the mood or feeling the music evokes. For example, does the music make them feel happy? sad? scared? excited? Can they show that, artistically? Tell them the name of the piece to write across the top of the page.

5. Divide a bulletin board into four sections, one for each type of music, on which to display students' drawings. Compare students work, looking at how each reflects the mood and feeling of the musical selection. Title the bulletin board "Music Moves Us."

ACTIVITY 3

Creative Dramatics: Musical Instrument Charades

Leora, Mae, Jenny, and the storyteller played different instruments in their Oak Street Band. Trying musical instruments is always fun—and so is pretending to play them. Students "play" imaginary instruments in this activity.

Procedure

1. Provide space in your classroom for students to sit in a large circle. Take them outside if weather permits.

2. Discuss the instruments that students saw in the book and brainstorm other instruments that students are familiar with.

3. Place a yardstick in the middle of the circle. Have students silently imagine an instrument the yardstick could be, such as a guitar, a saxophone, or a flute.

4. Going around the circle, invite students to pick up the yardstick and pretend to use it as a musical instrument. Challenge students to guess the instrument their classmate is playing.

5. Once they have guessed correctly, encourage the students to imitate the sound that instrument makes.

ACTIVITY 4

Guest Speaker—Musician

Whether they studied for years or have a natural gift, musicians inspire others with their special talents. This would be a great time to invite a musician to speak to your class.

Procedure

1. Contact a musician. Check with your school music teacher for ideas or with an area college or community arts center.

2. Tell the musician about the book your class is reading. Explain that you would like a real musician to speak to your class about his or her music and how he or she learned to play the instrument. Ask him or her to bring the instrument, if possible, to play for the class.

3. Announce to the class that they are going to have a very special guest. Generate appropriate questions for students to ask the musician.

4. During the presentation, encourage students to ask their questions, perhaps sharing their own musical aspirations. Instruct students to listen quietly as the musician performs.

5. Afterward, talk with students about what they learned. Do they think the instrument they heard is one they would like to learn? Why or why not? Might they like to be a musician someday? Ask students to write or dictate to you a thank-you letter to send the musician, expressing what they enjoyed most about the visit.

ACTIVITY 5

Rhythm Band

The four girls in *Music, Music for Everyone* called themselves The Oak Street Band. They enjoyed making music and performing. Invite students to work in groups to form their own bands, using rhythm instruments.

Procedure

1. Describe for students that in a rhythm band, musicians use simple objects to beat out rhythms. Brainstorm items in the classroom and at home that students could use as rhythm instruments, for example, pencils, rulers, books, rubber bands, trash-can lids, pot lids, plastic bottles or jars, and so on.

2. Divide the class into groups of four to form rhythm bands. Challenge students to find objects to use as rhythm instruments.

3. Set aside time for students to come up with a rhythm or rap to perform for the class.

4. Encourage students to name their bands, then to perform their rhythm or rap for the class.

Extra! Videotape or tape-record students' performances to view again!

Stringbean's Trip to the Shining Sea

This story describes a boy's trip from Kansas to the Pacific Ocean with his older brother. The text is written like a travel diary, on postcards. Each page is different, building on the travelers' experiences. This story not only offers adventure, but introduces students to a fun creative-writing technique.

Point of Interest Not Mentioned in the Story

• Vera B. Williams's daughter, Jennifer, also drew pictures for this book. Mother and daughter have taken many trips together, thrilled by the scenery they see.

Memorable Story Quote

"Well I just want to tell you that I am not even one little bit disappointed."

Activities for *Stringbean's Trip to the Shining Sea*

ACTIVITY 1: Postcard Class Book Report

ACTIVITY 2: Community Postcards

ACTIVITY 3: Writing Extension—Postcards Home

ACTIVITY 4: Fish-of-the-Sea Mobile

ACTIVITY 5: House on Wheels

ACTIVITY 6: Guest Speaker—Postal Worker

ACTIVITY 7: Stringbean's Geography Lesson

A C T I V I T Y 1

Postcard Class Book Report

The events in this adventure story are told on postcards. Have students retell one story event on a postcard they create.

Supplies
- postcard writing page (page 270)
- string or twine
- clothespins
- pencils, markers, and crayons

The Writing Process
Brainstorm with students answers to these questions.
- *Who* was in the story?
- *Where* did the story take place?
- *Why* was there a story at all?
- *What* was the main goal? (for example, Stringbean's desire to see the shining sea)
- *How* was it achieved?

With the class, list on the chalkboard the sequence of story events. Keep the list short, simple, and to the point. Whenever possible, use students' own thoughts and ideas. Below are some suggested postcard summaries.

1. Fred and I had a rough start on our journey, but the truck is doing OK.

2. Mr. Moe gave me this postcard. He gave us directions to the Pacific Ocean.

3. Potato found us, and he is doing fine.

4. We stopped at a historical place and learned about midwives.

5. We stayed at the same place as a circus. I saw elephants and found a big shoe.

6. We met Mr. Harlee Hawkins. He is a Sioux Native American. He has a ranch with 200 buffaloes.

7. We saw really high mountains and bears swimming in a creek.

8. We explored the silver mines and picked flowers for the graves of Great-Grandmother Josefina and Great-Grandfather Frederick.

9. We saw a big canyon and waterfalls.

10. We saw the oldest living things in the world—the Bristlecone pine trees.

11. We stopped at a store to buy a new fishing lure. We were told that a circus clown had tried to buy one big shoe.

12. We ate in a cafe shaped like a boot. Tomorrow we will cross the desert.

Give each student a photocopy of the postcard-writing page. Working individually or in pairs, ask students to write about one of the book's postcard messages on the left side of the postcard. Be sure each student or pair chooses a different event to write about, numbering it, too.

On the right side, have students address the postcard to

Coe Family
Coe Springs Motel
Jeloway, Kansas
66708

On the back of the postcard page, invite students to illustrate the scene from the book. String a length of twine across the room, and attach the postcards with clothespins. Invite students to view the illustrations, then read the postcard messages.

ACTIVITY 2

Community Postcards

The postcards in *Stringbean's Trip to the Shining Sea* are unique to the places they represent. Invite students to design postcards about their own communities.

Extra! Your local Chamber of Commerce might enjoy displaying the postcards for others to enjoy.

Supplies
- 4" x 6" (10 cm x 15 cm) index cards
- markers or crayons
- actual postcards for examples
- pencils
- three-ring binder with clear plastic pouches

Procedure
1. Let students view the front of each postcard in the book, discovering the uniqueness of each. Also show students the postcards you collected.
2. Brainstorm local attractions that students think might make good postcards. List them on the chalkboard.
3. Give each student a blank index card. Tell them to draw the local attraction on the blank side. On the lined side, suggest that they write a few interesting facts about it.
4. Collect the postcards and arrange them in the three-ring binder. As students view the postcards, they'll also be able to read the facts provided by their classmates. Keep the three-ring binder in your community or social studies center.

ACTIVITY 3

Writing Extension— Postcards Home

The postcards in this story are a form of journal writing. Suggest that students also write postcards to record the events of one school week.

Supplies
- postcard-writing page (page 270)
- pencils

The Writing Process
1. Discuss with students the creative way this story is told. Instead of reading a "story" in the traditional sense, the reader reads postcards that convey the plot.
2. Invite students to try it. Near the close of school each day for one week, give each student one postcard-writing page. Instruct them to write about their day at school, addressing the postcards to their parents or other family members.
3. Encourage students to flip the cards over to illustrate their favorite event of that day.
4. At the end of the week, let students take the postcards home to share with family members.

ACTIVITY 4

Fish-of-the-Sea Mobile

Stringbean's desire was to visit the shining sea—the Pacific Ocean. Might Stringbean have seen any fish in the ocean? Invite students to research ocean animals to create mobiles.

Supplies

- nonfiction nature books
- construction paper
- markers or crayons
- scissors
- paper plates
- string
- tape

Procedure

1. Recall with students Stringbean's desire to see the Pacific Ocean. Once he got there, do students suppose he might have seen any fish?

2. Share with students that the world's oceans are teaming with animal life, from fish to mammals to other creatures unlike any on land. Provide students with nonfiction nature and science books to investigate the rich animal life of the ocean.

3. Invite students to choose four ocean animals that they particularly like. Ask them to draw the animals on construction paper and cut them out.

4. Now provide each student with a paper plate and five lengths of string. Tell students to tape one end of a string to each cutout.

5. Show students how to tape the other end of the strings around the edge of the paper plate.

6. Instruct students to tape the final length of string to the center of the plate, by which it can be hung.

7. Display the mobiles around the room. Encourage students to imagine that your classroom has been turned into Stringbean's shining sea.

ACTIVITY 5

House on Wheels

In *Stringbean's Trip to the Shining Sea*, Fred and Stringbean literally build a house on the back of their truck. Ask students to be creative as they design a home on wheels.

Supplies

- truck pattern, page 145
- crayons or markers

Procedure

1. Show students the picture of the pickup truck and its labeled compartments in the book. Talk about its originality and how it met Fred's and Stringbean's needs on their trip. Conclude that because of their limited space, Stringbean and Fred had to be inventive.

2. Reproduce for each student the pickup truck on page 145. Challenge them to come up with their own house-on-wheels design, drawing it in the back of the truck.

3. At the top of the page, ask students to name their new car contraption, just as Fred and Stringbean named their vehicle.

4. Invite students to share their designs with the class.

ACTIVITY 5

Pickup Truck Pattern

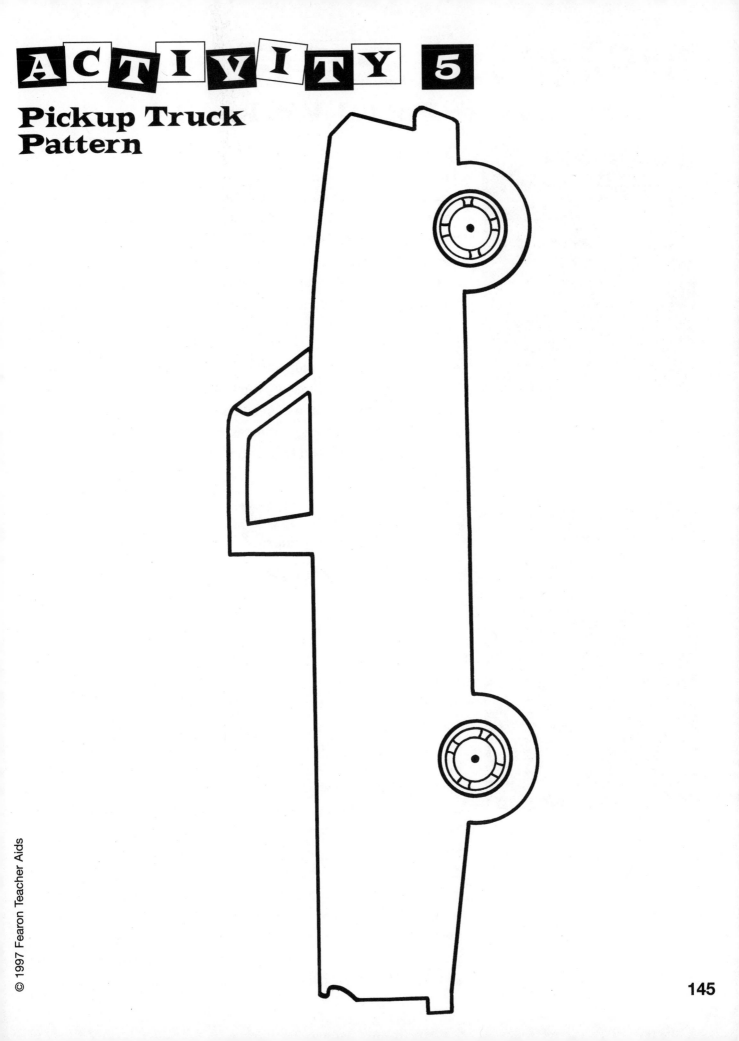

ACTIVITY 6
Guest Speaker–Postal Worker

Each stamp featured on the postcards in this book adds to the story. Many people collect postage stamps for their history and uniqueness. Invite students to learn more about the post office and postage stamps by listening to a guest speaker.

Procedure

1. Contact your local post office, inviting an employee to speak to your class. Suggest that the postal worker talk about postal rules and regulations as well as the history and interest of postage stamps. Ask the speaker to bring a display of stamps from both past and present.

2. Before the speaker arrives, brainstorm with students information they would like to know about the post office and postage stamps.

3. The day of the visit, encourage students to listen attentively and to politely pose their questions.

4. Afterward, talk with students about what they learned. Did they learn anything that surprised them? Do they think they might someday like to work at a post office?

5. Follow up by encouraging students to write or dictate to you thank-you letters to send to your post-office guest.

ACTIVITY 7
Stringbean's Geography Lesson

This book provides wonderful opportunities for students to discover the geography of our country. Challenge students to act as travel guides for Stringbean and Fred as they plot their trip on a map.

Supplies
• maps of the United States

Procedure

1. Recall with students that Stringbean and Fred journeyed great distances across the United States. Which roads might Fred and Stringbean have taken? Invite students to view maps to find out.

2. Divide the class into groups and provide each group with a road map of the United States.

3. Help students locate the state of Kansas, then the Pacific Ocean. Which states might Stringbean and Fred drive through? Which roads might they drive on?

4. Challenge students to plot a course for Fred and Stringbean's journey, jotting down the names or numbers of the highways and some of the towns they might pass through.

5. Help groups hang their maps on a bulletin board, then invite the groups to share with the class their suggested routes for Stringbean and Fred. How many different ideas did your class come up with?

Thomas Locker

Thomas Locker is a writer and illustrator whose books leave a lasting impression on the reader. His fabulous illustrations and flowing language are spell-binding. While they provide lessons in fine arts, Thomas Locker's books also tell beautiful stories.

Interesting Facts About the Author

Birth: Thomas Locker was born on June 26, 1937, in New York, New York.

Family: Thomas Locker has five sons: Anthony, from his first marriage, and Aaron, Josh, Jonathan, and Gregory from his second. Upon marrying Candace Christiansen, he enlarged his family to include nine children.

Education: Locker graduated from the University of Chicago with a Bachelor of Arts degree in 1960. In 1963 he received a Master of Arts degree from American University in Washington, D.C. He has studied and taught art in many places in the United States and Europe.

Beginnings as an author and an illustrator:

Thomas Locker had an extensive career in gallery painting before he became a writer. When reading picture books to his five sons, he realized that children's illustration was an art form that when combined with stories could be shared with young people. Thomas found joining painting and writing rewarding. His work was successful, and he now devotes most of his time to writing and illustrating children's books. His first book, *Where the River Begins*, was published in 1984.

Award Highlights

- **Where the River Begins** *has won much acclaim, including mention on* **The New York Times** *Ten Best Illustrated Books of the Year, 1984, and an Outstanding Science Trade Book for Children by the National Science Teacher's Association, 1985.*

- **Sailing With the Wind** *is a Reading Rainbow Selection.*

Common Threads to Look For Throughout His Books

- The illustrations in Locker's books are gallery quality. Be sure students have time to appreciate the art that accompanies his writing.

- Many of Locker's books deal with nature and the wonders of our earth. Your students will expand their knowledge and appreciation of the beauty of nature.

Books Written and Illustrated by
Thomas Locker

- *Where the River Begins*
- *The Mare on the Hill*
- *Sailing With the Wind*
- *Family Farm*
- *Rip Van Winkle*
- *The Young Artist*
- *Anna and the Bagpiper*
- *Sky Tree*

Books Illustrated by
Thomas Locker

- *The Ugly Duckling,* retold by Marianna Mayer
- *The Boy Who Held Back the Sea,* retold by Lenny Hort
- *The Ice Horse,* retold by Candace Christiansen

Sky Tree

Your students will never look at a tree or the sky the same way after they read Sky Tree. Locker has created exquisite paintings and used eloquent language to present one year in the life of a tree. As the seasons change, the tree adjusts yet still stands firm.

Points of Interest Not Mentioned in the Story

- Thomas Locker received his first award for art when he was seven years old, winning first prize in the children's division of the Washington, D.C., *Times Herald* art fair. His painting was of a giant tree.

- Even though we say a tree "changes" its colors in the fall, trees are actually revealing their true colors! Chlorophyll, which gives the leaves their green color, is made by sunlight. As the days grow shorter and cooler in autumn, the chlorophyll breaks down, and the green color fades, showing the leaves' true colors.

- The questions at the bottom of the pages are written by Candace Christiansen. Candace, Thomas's wife, is a science and math teacher at a school in Columbia County, New York. She is also an author of children's books. Further information about the questions is provided at the back of the book.

- The tree in this book stands on a hill near Thomas Locker's home in Connecticut. He observed the tree for a year, painting it as it changed with the seasons.

- Please notice the ever-changing sky in the illustrations. It is just as dramatic as the tree.

Memorable Story Quote

"Once a tree stood alone on a hill by the river. Through the long days its leaves fluttered in the soft summer breeze."

Activities for *Sky Tree*

ACTIVITY 1: Tree Book Report

ACTIVITY 2: Tree Research

ACTIVITY 3: Planting a Tree

ACTIVITY 4: Paper Recycling Drive

ACTIVITY 5: Tree Drawings

ACTIVITY 6: Adjectives—Colorful Language

ACTIVITY 1
Tree Book Report

Trees grow and change with the seasons, as illustrated in this beautiful book. Both the language and illustrations will enchant you and your students. Invite students to describe the changes the tree experiences with this book-report activity. (NOTE: Due to the time needed to properly complete this activity, the Writing Process may need to be completed over several days.)

Supplies

- manila paper, 9" x 12" (22.5 cm x 30 cm)
- stapler
- tree writing page, page 151
- markers or crayons

Assembling the Book

1. Give each student two pieces of manila paper and 14 copies of the tree writing page. Instruct students to place the manila paper on the front and back of the tree pages to serve as a book cover. Help students staple or bind the pages with yarn.

2. Ask students to write the book title and author on the cover. Allow time for students to decorate the cover with a tree motif.

The Writing Process

1. Ask students to open their tree-book-report books to the first page as you read to them the first page of *Sky Tree*, showing them the illustrations. Encourage students to write about the tree in their own words, describing what they see and hear.

2. Allow time for students to complete the tree and draw in the sky.

3. Continue until all 14 pages are complete. Your students will have a beautiful product to be proud of. Invite students to take the books home to share with their families.

ACTIVITY 2

Tree Research

Not only are trees beautiful plants to look at, but they are important to our earth in many ways. Invite students to research trees to find out all they do for us.

Supplies

- brown butcher paper
- green construction paper

Procedure

1. Make the trunk and branches of a tree by using brown butcher paper. Tape it to a wall in your classroom.

2. Discuss with your students what they know about trees. What tree names do they know? (maple, oak, cedar, etc.) Have they ever climbed a tree? Which tree parts can they name? (trunk, branches, leaves, buds, roots, bark, etc.) List students' tree knowledge on chart paper.

3. Invite students to learn more about these stately, important plants. Take the students to the library and help them locate children's nonfiction nature books. (For younger students, you might need to collect these materials.)

4. Hang up three sheets of chart paper. Label one *Tree Facts*, the second *Tree Uses*, and the third *Tree Conservation*.

5. Now invite students to explore the materials. Working in groups or in pairs, ask students to find information to add to each chart. (You might need to explain that *conservation* means "to save something.") Let students fill in the charts or dictate sentences to you.

6. Pass out green construction paper and invite students to cut out leaf shapes.

7. Have students write a tree fact, use, or conservation idea on their leaves.

8. As students attach their leaves to your butcher-paper tree trunk and branches, encourage them to read the information they jotted down.

Extra! Judith Viorst's *Rosie and Michael*, Bill Martin, Jr.'s *Ghost-Eye Tree*, and Vera B. Williams's *Cherries and Cherry Pits* also have activities that require a class tree. You might reuse this tree for those activities.

ACTIVITY 3

Planting a Tree

Trees are a natural resource that must be conserved and replenished. To serve this goal, invite students to plant a tree.

Supplies

- young tree or sapling
- area set aside for planting
- planting tools, such as a shovel or hoe

Procedure

1. Visit your local nursery. Explain that your class is studying trees and that students would like to plant a tree at school. Many nurseries will donate a tree. If not, ask each student to contribute a small amount, or you might raise money by having students collect cans to be recycled.

2. Find an appropriate spot on school grounds to plant your tree (with permission).

3. Set a date for your tree planting. You might invite your principal, the mayor, the school superintendent, or parents.

4. At the beginning of the ceremony, read or have a student read an excerpt from *Sky Tree*.

5. After the tree has been planted, invite each student to throw a handful of dirt around the base of the tree. Encourage students to care for the tree throughout the year.

Extra! Planting a tree makes a great Arbor Day activity.

ACTIVITY 4

Paper Recycling Drive

One of the ways we can conserve trees is by recycling paper. A large amount of paper is thrown away daily in school. This is a great time to start a paper-recycling project.

Procedure

1. Ask students if they realize that paper is made from trees. Have students look around the room and list all the paper products they see.

2. Share with students this fact: Experts estimate that we throw away 44 million newspapers a day. After one week, that's 500,000 trees! What can we do to conserve our trees? Write the word *recycle* on the board and discuss its meaning.

3. Encourage students to start a recycling drive. Obtain large boxes or bins for collecting paper and place them in central locations in your school. Label them *Paper Recycling Center*, and have students decorate them.

4. Invite a volunteer or assign to students the task of creating a schoolwide announcement explaining the recycling drive. Assign other students to make posters to advertise the recycling project. Suggest that students include slogans, such as "Save our trees."

5. Contact a local recycling center to pick up the collected paper on a regular basis. They may even supply you with recycling bins.

ACTIVITY 5

Tree Drawings

The tree in this story is one that actually stands near Thomas Locker's home. This was the model he used as the subject for his paintings and writings. Invite students to draw pictures of trees near their school.

Supplies

- drawing paper
- clipboards, if available
- pencils

Procedure

1. Mention to students that the tree in this book is based on an actual tree. The author modeled a tree near his home to serve as the subject for this story.

2. Take a walk with your class around your schoolyard. Invite students to choose a tree to draw. Set aside time for students to observe their trees, noticing special characteristics. Talk about the current season and how weather affects trees.

3. Then provide students with pencils and drawing paper attached to clipboards, if possible. Allow time for students to sketch the trees and the sky around them.

4. Mount children's tree art on posterboard and display.

ACTIVITY 6

Adjectives—Colorful Language

The language Thomas Locker uses in *Sky Tree* breathes life into his beautiful paintings. He describes nature with beautiful words, perfect for students to add to their Writing Journals.

Procedure

1. Talk with students about the power of adjectives. Emphasize that adjectives bring writing to life.

2. Reread *Sky Tree* and have students listen for the interesting adjectives. List the adjectives on a chart as you read them.

3. Invite students to copy the list into their Writing Journals. Encourage them to choose a few adjectives to include in sentences for examples.

Adjectives From *Sky Tree*

long days

tight buds

soft summer breeze

warm hillside

leaves turned *gold, orange,* and *red*

wet earth

thin, silver frost

fresh grass

old snappy turtles

golden light

bare branches

misty morning

empty branches

cold winter days

The Young Artist

In The Young Artist, Thomas Locker tells about a talented young man who strives to become a landscape artist. Instead he is granted the opportunity to become a famous portrait painter. In his new career he is asked to compromise his integrity by falsifying the appearances of his subjects. He remains true to his values, however, and it pays off in the end.

Points of Interest Not Mentioned in the Story

- Share with students that an apprentice is someone learning a trade or art by working with a skilled worker. In former times, apprentices worked for little or no pay.

- This book is told in the first person. Help students recognize this writing form, possibly using it in their own writing.

Memorable Story Quote

"The other day I met my former student out in the countryside. He was teaching his own apprentice how to paint the trees and the clouds, with the tower of the castle far, far in the distance."

Activities for *The Young Artist*

ACTIVITY 1: Artist's Palette Book Report

ACTIVITY 2: Drawing Live Models

ACTIVITY 3: The Oldest Art Form

ACTIVITY 4: Guest Speaker—Artist

ACTIVITY 5: Artist Research

ACTIVITY 6: Writing Extension 1—What I Want to Be

ACTIVITY 7: Writing Extension 2—A Picture Is Worth a Thousand Words

ACTIVITY 1
Artist's Palette Book Report

The story of *The Young Artist* has many twists and turns. Students should find the story, coupled with the illustrations, a compelling one. Let them retell the story with this book-report activity.

Supplies

- manila paper, 12" x 18" (30 cm x 45 cm)
  - pencils
    - palette pattern, page 157
      - markers or crayons
        - scissors
          - glue

Assembling the Palette

1. Reproduce a palette pattern for each student, enlarging the pattern if necessary. Instruct students to cut out the palette, including the finger hole. Have students trace the palette to manila paper twice, then cut out again.

2. Show students how to draw five large circles around each palette in which to write the story events. Have students number the circles one through ten.

3. Complete the palettes by asking students to write the book title and author in the center.

The Writing Process

Brainstorm with students answers to these questions.

- *Who* was in the story?
- *Where* did the story take place?
- *Why* was there a story at all?
- *What* were the main problems?
  (for example, the young artist's desire to stay true to his values.)
- *How* were they resolved?

With the class, list on the chalkboard the sequence of story events. Keep the list short, simple, and to the point. Below are some suggested story events. Then invite students to write their story events in story order in the numbered circles on their palettes. Encourage students to use their own words.

1. Adrian went to live with an artist because he wanted to become one himself. He was an excellent apprentice.

2. Adrian painted a portrait of the king's chef. The chef was not pleased, but Adrian refused to paint a lie. The chef bought the painting.

3. Adrian painted portraits of the king's tailor and baker.

4. Adrian was summoned to the castle to paint all of the king's court, including his daughter.

5. The nobles threatened Adrian to improve their appearances.

6. Adrian consulted his teacher, who encouraged him to paint their lies.

7. But Adrian couldn't do it. He quit painting for a long time.

8. One day he saw the princess, who inspired him to paint again.

9. Adrian painted many portraits of the princess. The king was so pleased that he gave the young artist permission to paint true pictures of his courtiers.

10. Adrian was rewarded with a piece of land and a fine house.

ACTIVITY 1

Palette Pattern

ACTIVITY 2

Drawing Live Models

The young artist drew portraits of live models. To better appreciate the artists' craft, let your students try it. Challenge them to sketch live subjects, using their classmates as models.

Supplies

- drawing paper
- pencils

Procedure

1. Discuss with students how the portraits the young artist drew were of live models. Speculate how the models and the artist might feel during these sessions.

2. Then arrange students into pairs, and give each student a sheet of large drawing paper. Explain that they will each sketch a portrait of their partners.

3. As one student poses, challenge the other to sketch the portrait. Remind the posers to remain as still as possible while their partners draw.

4. After about ten minutes, instruct partners to switch roles.

5. Give students time to color their portraits.

6. Mount the portraits on posterboard or a bulletin board to form your own class art gallery.

ACTIVITY 3

The Oldest Art Form

Painting as an art form has been around for a very long time. But which art form is the oldest? Sculpture! Invite your students to try this art, which has been around for thousands of years.

Supplies

- clay

Procedure

1. Share with students that the first art medium available to people was probably stone. From stone, people began to carve and mold figures. So, thousands of years ago the very first art form was born.

2. Supply children with balls of clay. Encourage them to mold the clay to represent common figures they see around the room or perhaps characters from the story.

3. Set the clay sculptures aside to dry. If time and materials allow, let students paint their sculptures.

4. Conclude by asking students which medium they enjoyed more—painting or sculpting. Why? Encourage them to explain their ideas.

ACTIVITY 4

Guest Speaker—Artist

The Young Artist portrays both the triumphs and trials of an artist's life. An artist's talent is special and unique. Students are especially intrigued by artists, for young children are just developing their own art skills. Inviting an artist to speak to your class will excite students and lend extra meaning to the study of this book.

Procedure

1. Ahead of time, check with your local community arts center, college, or library for a local artist who might be willing to talk to your class. Explain the book you are reading and that you would like to expose students to a real artist of today. Set a date and time for the visit.

2. Announce to your class that you have invited an artist to speak to them. Brainstorm appropriate questions to ask the artist.

3. During the artist's presentation, encourage students to politely pose their questions and view the artist's work.

4. Afterward, talk with students about the artist and his or her work. What did they like about it? Do they think being an artist is something they might like to do? Why or why not?

5. Follow up by asking students to write or dictate to you thank-you letters to send to your guest.

ACTIVITY 5

Artist Research

Developing an appreciation for art and artists opens students' minds to not only different art forms, but to life long ago. Invite students to research famous artists to enhance their appreciation of history and fine arts.

Procedure

1. Share with students that men and women from many countries are renowned for their art. Read the names of famous artists listed below.

2. Encourage students to choose an artist to learn more about. To guide students' research, reproduce page 160 for students to complete.

3. Set aside time for students to go to the library or provide research materials in class. For some students this activity may require assistance, This can also be a homework assignment, with which family members can lend a hand.

4. On the backs of their papers, encourage students to draw a picture of their artists.

5. Set a time for students to present oral reports about the artists. Encourage them to display pictures or prints of the artist's work.

List of Famous Artists

Pablo Picasso	Winslow Homer	Claude Monet	James McNeill Whistler
Vincent Van Gogh	Piet Mondrian	Georgia O'Keefe	Mary Cassatt
Edgar Degas	Maurice Pendergast	Grandma Moses	Rembrandt van Rijn
Leonardo da Vinci	Pierre-Auguste Renoir	Paul Cezanne	Salvador Dali
Georges Seurat	Francisco Goya	Andrew Wyeth	George Inness

Famous Artist Research

_____

My Artist

1. When and where was your artist born?

_____

2. Where did the artist receive his or her training, and how did his or her career begin?

_____

_____

_____

_____

_____

3. List several of the artist's masterpieces and where they are on display.

_____

_____

_____

_____

_____

_____

4. Is your artist still alive? If so, where does he or she live?

_____

_____

5. Describe your artist's style of painting. Do you like it? Why or why not?

_____

_____

_____

_____

ACTIVITY 6

Writing Extension 1— What I Want to Be

In *The Young Artist*, Adrian wanted to be an artist from the time he was a young boy. Most children have already begun to think about what they might do when they grow up. It is very important to foster these dreams. Invite students to write about and draw their dreams for a future career.

The Writing Process

1. Speculate with students the things they could be when they grow up. Discuss how Adrian pursued his dreams of becoming an artist. Although it took a lot of hard work, dedication, and many years, Adrian made his dream come true.

2. Provide students with writing paper and encourage them to write about their aspirations. You might prompt students' writing with such questions as these.

- *What* would you like to do?
- *What* do you like about this job?
- *What* do you think you would have to do at this job?

3. Display students' work on a bulletin board titled "Our Dreams for the Future."

ACTIVITY 7

Writing Extension 2— A Picture Is Worth a Thousand Words

Sometimes drawing and art can express things more aptly than the written word. Invite children to practice their creative-writing skills and use of adjectives as they write descriptive paragraphs about a piece of art.

The Writing Process

1. Say the expression "A picture is worth a thousand words." Speculate with children what they think it means. Help them realize that if they were to try to describe one picture, it might take them a thousand words to do it!

2. Have students choose a picture in the book to write about. Supply students with writing paper and challenge them to describe their pictures. Encourage them to refer to their Writing Journals to find appropriate adjectives.

3. Invite volunteers to show the pictures they described, then to read their paragraphs. Conclude with students that often it is hard to include all the images and impressions conveyed in one painting by merely using words.

Family Farm

Family Farm is the heartwarming story of a family working together to save their farm and heritage. When times were tough and money was short, the family took a risk and changed their crops, planting pumpkins and flowers instead of corn. The pumpkin crop not only saved their farm, but brought the family closer.

Points of Interest Not Mentioned in the Story

- Pumpkins are vegetables that belong to the gourd family, the same family as squash and cucumbers.

- Pumpkins need a lot of room to grow. Pumpkins grow on vines along the ground. Because pumpkins can grow to be very heavy, the vines cannot be trellised like vines for grapes.

- Pumpkins can be small enough to hold in the palm of your hand, or as large as 800 pounds!

Memorable Story Quote

"None of my friends sit with their sisters on the school bus, and neither do I. But the day we heard that our school was going to be closed, I did."

Activities for *Family Farm*

ACTIVITY 1: Pumpkin-Patch Book Report

ACTIVITY 2: Teamwork

ACTIVITY 3: Family Portraits

ACTIVITY 4: Guest Speaker—Farmer

ACTIVITY 5: Planting Pumpkin Seeds

ACTIVITY 6: Pumpkin Party

ACTIVITY 7: Class Fair

ACTIVITY 1
Pumpkin-Patch Book Report

The story line in *Family Farm* will touch your heart. Encourage students to retell the story with this activity.

Supplies

- manila paper
- glue
  - pumpkin patterns, page 164
    - scissors
      - markers or crayons

Assembling the Pumpkin Patch

1. Give each student two pieces of manila paper and two pumpkin pattern sheets.

2. Have students number the pumpkins one through nine, cut them out, and glue them to the manila paper in numerical order.

3. Allow time for the glue to dry.

4. Ask students to write the book title and author across the top of one page.

The Writing Process

Brainstorm with students answers to these questions.

- *Who* was in the story?
- *Where* did the story take place?
- *Why* was there a story at all?
- *What* was the main problem?
  (For example, the family's need to save their farm.)
- *How* was it resolved?

With the class, list on the chalkboard the sequence of story events. Keep the list short, simple, and to the point. Whenever possible, use students' own words. Below are some suggested story events.

1. Mike and Sarah's school is going to close because so many farmers are losing their farms and moving away.

2. Mike and Sarah's family is in jeopardy of losing their farm, too.

3. Their mom planted pumpkins and flowers to make extra money. They sold well.

4. Times got rougher, and Mike and Sarah's dad got an extra job. The children had to quit after-school activities and do extra chores.

5. Sarah and Michael had no time to groom their cow, Derinda, for the fair.

6. Their dad lost his job, and their family was about to lose the farm.

7. Sarah and Mike suggest that they plant pumpkins and flowers for their main crops. The family learned how to raise them.

8. The flowers and pumpkins were a success, and the family was able to keep the farm.

9. Derinda did not win a prize at the fair, but she gave birth to a calf that was sure to win next year.

Have students write one story event in each pumpkin on their papers, tape the pages together, and connect the pumpkins by drawing in vines and leaves.

ACTIVITY 1

Pumpkin Patterns

ACTIVITY 2

Teamwork

Saving the farm in *Family Farm* was not easy. It took sacrifice and cooperation from everyone. Elicit from students the things the family did and the sacrifices they made to save their farm.

Procedure

1. Discuss with students the importance of family values. Talk about how this family pulled together to save their farm.

2. Draw a large T-chart on butcher paper.

3. Brainstorm with students things the family did together to save the farm, such as taking on extra jobs, getting up earlier to do their father's chores, quitting after-school activities, encouraging each other. List these on the left side of the chart.

4. On the right side, have students list ways they can help their families to make life easier. For example, doing extra chores, doing homework without having to be reminded, keeping their rooms clean, and helping care for younger siblings and pets.

5. Compare with the class the items on the chart. Which things do they do that are comparable to things done in the story?

ACTIVITY 3

Family Portraits

All families are different and special in their own ways. The illustrations of the family members in *Family Farm* are beautiful. Encourage students to draw portraits of their own families.

Supplies

- drawing paper
- scissors
- markers or crayons
- glue
- brown construction paper

Procedure

1. Have students look at pictures of the family in the book. What do the pictures tell us about the individuals?

2. Provide students with drawing paper on which to draw portraits of their own families. Suggest that they draw the family working together, highlighting something they might do as a team.

3. Supply students with brown construction paper. Tell them to cut strips of paper and glue them to the edge of the portrait to create a picture frame.

4. Encourage students to take their portraits home.

ACTIVITY 4

Guest Speaker—Farmer

Family Farm tells the story of a farming family. What do your students know about life on a farm? Invite a local farmer to speak to your class to enhance their understanding and appreciation of farm life.

Procedure

1. Get in touch with a local farmer. You might invite a friend you know, or check with your county agriculture center for ideas. If your area has any farmer's markets, you might inquire there as well. Explain the story you are reading and why a visiting farmer would be beneficial to your studies.

2. Tell your class that you have invited a farmer to speak with them. Brainstorm appropriate questions to ask your guest.

3. During the visit, make sure students listen quietly, and encourage them to ask their questions at suitable times.

4. Afterward, talk about what they learned. Do students think they'd like to live on a farm? Why or why not?

5. Culminate by writing a class thank-you letter to your guest.

Extra! If possible, arrange a class field trip to a farm.

ACTIVITY 5

Planting Pumpkin Seeds

What better way to learn about story events firsthand than by trying something a character did? In this case, plant some pumpkin seeds!

Supplies

- packets of pumpkin seeds
- paper cups
- potting soil

Procedure

1. Obtain a variety of pumpkin seeds from your local hardware or garden store. Also gather potting soil and paper cups for planting.

2. Arrange the class into groups. Provide each with a packet of seeds and a paper cup filled with soil.

3. With students, read the planting instructions on the packets. Students will notice that pumpkins need a lot of room to grow. Room might be sparse in your area, so tell children that they are just going to see what baby pumpkin plants look like. (Of course, if possible, you might plant your pumpkins outdoors, but be aware that pumpkins need warm weather and time to grow. If you live in a warm climate, you might plant pumpkins in fall to pick in spring. Check with your garden store for more specific advice.)

4. Demonstrate how to place a few pumpkin seeds in the soil, about 1 to 1 1/2 inches deep.

5. Let students water their plants until the soil is moist, not soaked.

6. Instruct students to check their cups over the next few days, making sure the soil does not dry out. In six to ten days, students should see little pumpkin sprouts!

ACTIVITY 6

Pumpkin Party

Pumpkins are fun for everyone. During the fall, pumpkins are plentiful in grocery stores and at roadside stands. Pumpkins can be carved into many shapes. This activity will give your students opportunities to observe a carving while decorating their own pumpkins and eating pumpkin pie.

Supplies

- large pumpkin for carving
- smaller pumpkins for decorating
- paints or permanent markers
- pumpkin pie (optional)

Procedure

1. Invite students to share experiences they have had with carving or decorating pumpkins.

2. Then invite students to have a pumpkin party. Set a date and send home the family letter requesting pumpkins.

3. On the day of your party, bring a large pumpkin to carve as students observe. Let them feel the pulp inside and handle the seeds.

4. Now let students decorate their own pumpkins with paints and permanent markers. Display them around the room.

5. Culminate by serving pumpkin pie.

Extra! Clean the pumpkin seeds from your carved pumpkin. Roast them in an oven, add a little salt, and invite students to try this healthy snack.

Dear Family,

We are studying the author and illustrator Thomas Locker. In his book *Family Farm*, Locker tells about a family that saves its farm by planting pumpkins instead of corn. As a culminating activity, we would like to have a pumpkin party. Students will decorate pumpkins and enjoy pumpkin pie. Our party will be on _____ . Please have your child bring a pumpkin of any size to school. If you have a special pumpkin-pie recipe and would like to make it for our class, let me know.

Thank you for your cooperation!

Sincerely,

ACTIVITY 7

Class Fair

Sarah and Mike were excited about taking their cow, Derinda, to the county fair. County fairs are popular throughout the country. Invite students to experience a county fair by holding one in your classroom.

Procedure

1. Discuss the fair in *Family Farm*. Explain what a fair is, talking about the various contests. Mention that ribbons are awarded in many categories, including cooking, arts and crafts, animals, and vegetables. Invite students who have been to a county fair to share what it was like.

2. Explain to students that they will be having a class fair. As a homework assignment, encourage them to complete a craft project or to bake cookies, cakes, or another special dish with the help of their families.

3. Set a date for your fair and send the family letter home, explaining the project.

4. Make blank awards, enough for each child in the class. (See Appendix, page 267.)

5. On the day of your fair, invite students to display their crafts and dishes. Ask students to help you present awards to their classmates, coming up with original categories. For example: Most Original Artwork, Most Colorful, Neatness Award, Most Useful, Best Present for Mom/Dad, Most Inventive, Best Use of Recycled Materials, and so on. In this way each child will receive an award.

Dear Family,

We are studying author and illustrator Thomas Locker. In his book *Family Farm*, two young children are excited about entering their cow in the county fair. Our class will be holding its own fair to judge craft projects and foods. Please help your child complete a craft project or cook a food item, such as cookies, a cake, or any other special family dish. The entries will be judged and awarded ribbons.

I would really like each child to participate. Our class fair will be held on _____ .

Thank you for your cooperation!

Sincerely,

Where the River Begins

Where the River Begins *takes the reader on a journey through a beautiful countryside. Josh and Aaron are wondering where the river that flows near their home begins. Their grandfather satisfies their curiosity by taking them on a hike they will never forget.*

Points of Interest Not Mentioned in the Story

- Share with students that most rivers begin high in mountains or hills. The water source of a river might be a glacier, a spring, an overflowing lake, or even a melting snowfield. As a river flows, it receives more water from springs, other rivers, and rainfall. The river eventually empties into a larger river, a lake, or an ocean.

- Two of Thomas Locker's sons are named Aaron and Josh.

Memorable Story Quote

"But their grandfather paused for a moment and . . . watched the river, which continued on as it always had, flowing gently into the sea."

Activities for *Where the River Begins*

ACTIVITY 1: River Book Report

ACTIVITY 2: Adjectives—Colorful Language

ACTIVITY 3: River Research Geography

ACTIVITY 4: Writing Extension 1—Journal Entries

ACTIVITY 5: Writing Extension 2—Grandfather's Thoughts

ACTIVITY 6: Indoor Camp-out

ACTIVITY 1

River Book Report

Where the River Begins is not only exciting but educational as well. Let students retell the story on the "river" that flows through their book reports.

Supplies

- white paper
- stapler
- blue construction paper
- markers or crayons

Assembling the Book

1. Give each student ten sheets of white paper and two pieces of blue construction paper. Have students sandwich the white paper between the two sheets of blue paper and staple them together to form a book.

2. Tell students to turn the book so that it opens upward. Have them write the book title and author on the cover.

3. Now ask students to open their books to the first page. Instruct them to draw a river that flows through the pages of their books, drawing the river on each page. Tell them they will add scenery after they complete the Writing Process.

The Writing Process

Brainstorm with students answers to these questions.

- *Who* was in the story?
- *Where* did the story take place?
- *Why* was there a story at all?
- *What* was the main goal?
  (For example, the boys' desire to find where the river begins.)
- *How* was it achieved?

With the class, list on the chalkboard the sequence of story events. Keep the list short, simple, and to the point. Whenever possible, use students' own words. Below are some suggested story events.

1. Josh and Aaron wondered where the river began, and their grandfather agreed to take them on a camping trip to find out.

2. They reached the foothills of the mountains. The river became so narrow that they could jump across it.

3. They set up camp by the river.

4. They got up early, knowing they were close to the end of their search.

5. Finally, they found the small, peaceful place where the river began.

6. On the return trip a storm broke out, but they stayed dry and warm inside their small tent.

7. The second morning they woke to the sound of the river rising and roaring. It had overflowed and was flooding the fields around it.

8. During their return trip they recognized places and became excited about getting home.

9. The boys could not wait to tell their parents about their adventure.

10. Grandfather paused to meditate on the river and its passage before going home.

Have students write the events on each page of their river books. They will choose a place to write according to where they drew their rivers. After students finish writing, have them go back and add scenery along their rivers on each page.

ACTIVITY 2

Adjectives—Colorful Language

As in *Sky Tree*, Thomas Locker uses breathtaking language to help the reader visualize the scenes and feelings in *Where the River Begins*. His word choices entice us to want to be in the pictures that accompany the text. Invite students to add these adjectives to their Writing Journals.

Procedure

1. Review adjectives with students.

2. Reread *Where the River Begins* and have students listen for the colorful adjectives, perhaps raising their hands as they hear each one. List the adjectives on a chart.

3. Encourage students to list the words in their Writing Journals for future use.

Adjectives From *Where the River Begins*

golden wheat

morning mist

gentle, wide, deep river

white clouds

familiar road

peaceful river

flickering campfire

still pond

forest noises

small tent

thick mist

fading light

grassy knoll

ACTIVITY 3

River Research Geography

The young boys' curiosity about where the river began is not uncommon in most children. Challenge students to trace a river to its origin.

Procedure

1. Ask students if they have ever wondered where a river begins. Elicit from them rivers they know. Which rivers are in your area?

2. Photocopy a map of your state. Give a map to each student.

3. Display a large map of the United States. With students, trace the rivers in your state to find their origins and their mouths, or where they empty.

4. Have students highlight the river on their state maps.

5. Culminate by inviting students to write a new story for an adventure they might have on one of these local rivers.

ACTIVITY 4

Writing Extension 1— Journal Entries

Keeping a diary is a great way to remember cherished moments. Josh and Aaron's experiences are ones they should remember. Challenge students to write about Josh's and Aaron's experiences as journal entries.

The Writing Process

1. Discuss with students how finding the headwaters of the river was a once-in-a-lifetime experience for Aaron and Josh. Brainstorm emotions they might have had, including emotions for their grandfather, too. For example: excitement, enthusiasm, awe, fear, exhaustion. List them on the chalkboard.

2. Draw from students why some people keep journals. Explain that they will write a journal, pretending to be either Josh or Aaron. In this way they will tell about their trip.

3. Provide students with writing paper to write their journal entries.

4. Invite students to peer-edit each other's work.

5. Bind students' work between construction-paper covers. Write the book title across the top and leave the books in your reading center for students to read on their own.

ACTIVITY 5

Writing Extension 2— Grandfather's Thoughts

At the end of *Where the River Begins*, the grandfather pauses to look at the river. Sometimes we all need to pause and reflect about where we have been. Speculate with students what the grandfather might have been thinking as he paused to look at the river.

The Writing Process

Reread the last page of *Where the River Begins*. Speculate with children what the grandfather might be thinking before he walks home. Stimulate discussion with these questions.

- *Why* do you think the grandfather stopped to look at the river?
- *What* do you think this camping trip meant to him?
- *What* might he be thinking?
- *What* will he remember most about this time with his grandsons?
- *What* experiences might the grandfather have had as a young boy?

Provide students with writing paper to express their ideas about the grandfather's thoughts. Invite students to share their essays with the class.

ACTIVITY 6

Indoor Camp-out

Supplies

- at least one small tent that can be set up in the classroom
- several sleeping bags
- blankets
- flashlights
- sack lunches

To some students there is nothing more exciting than a camping trip. In *Where the River Begins*, Josh and Aaron relished the idea of camping and hiking with their grandfather. This activity will give students the opportunity to "camp" in the comfort of your own classroom.

Procedure

1. Explain to students that they will be taking a camping trip—without leaving the classroom. Brainstorm things they would need to bring on a camping trip and list their ideas on the chalkboard.

2. Set a date for your campout and tell students that they will need to bring books to read, blankets, sleeping bags, flashlights, and a sack lunch. Send a letter home to families, explaining your class campout and the supplies their children will need.

3. On the day of your campout, let students help you set up camp. Allow them to spread out blankets, possibly draping them over desks and chairs to form tents. Give them time to read their books, perhaps using the flashlights.

4. Often at campouts, campers sit around a fire and tell stories. Invite your class to sit in a circle too (minus the fire, of course!) and tell stories they like. You might also invite a guest to play the guitar while students sing traditional camp songs.

5. Culminate by rereading *Where the River Begins* as students eat their sack lunches around your "campfire."

Dear Family,

We have been studying author and illustrator Thomas Locker. One of his books is titled *Where the River Begins*. The story is about a camping trip that two young boys take with their grandfather.

As a culminating activity, we will be having a campout in our classroom. On _____ , your child will be allowed to bring to school a sleeping bag or blanket, a flashlight, a sack lunch, and books to read. Please help your child gather and remember to bring in these "camping supplies."

In addition, if you play the guitar and/or sing, we would love to have you come "sing around the campfire" with us.

Thank you for your cooperation!

Sincerely,

Eve Bunting

Eve Bunting is a compassionate author who addresses many social issues in ways that children can understand. Most of her stories come from current events or public concerns. Her eloquent writing style will capture you and your students while instilling hope for a better world. Eve Bunting once said, "Each of us has a choice of what we will do with our lives. I hope the children [in her books] will make the right choice, whatever it is, and in my books I try to help them make it."

Interesting Facts About the Author

Birth: Eve Bunting was born on December 19, 1928, in Maghera, Northern Ireland.

Early family: Eve grew up in the small Northern Ireland town of Maghera. Her father was the postmaster and a produce merchant.

Education: Eve began attending boarding school in Belfast at the age of nine. It was there that she developed her lifelong love of books and reading. She graduated from Methodist College in Belfast in 1945 and studied for two years at Queen's University, also in Belfast.

Present family: While attending Queen's University, Eve met her husband, Edward. They married in 1951 and moved to Scotland, where they lived for the next nine years. They had three children—Christine, Sloan, and Glenn. In 1960 they made the life-altering decision to move to California. Eventually Eve became a naturalized citizen of the United States. Today, Eve and her husband live in Los Angeles.

Beginnings as an author: Eve began to write when her children were all in school. She claims that she never set out to become an author. However, upon receiving through the mail a brochure advertising a "Writing for Publications" course at a local junior college, she signed up. As she explains, it "was the first step to the new career."

Eve's first book, *The Two Giants*, was published in 1972, when Eve was 43. The story was a well-known fable from her homeland, although little-known in the United States. She has been a prolific children's writer ever since. Eve feels she will never run out of ideas. "I couldn't possibly write about all the interesting thoughts that pop, unannounced, into my head. There aren't that many hours in a day or that many days in a year!"

Other Interests: Eve Bunting loves spending time with her grandchildren and enjoys keeping current with world events.

Common Threads to Look For Throughout Her Books

- Eve Bunting likes to put children in tempting situations. "But," she says, "whatever the tempting situation, kids will find a message, well-hidden I hope, that says, 'better not.'"

Books by Eve Bunting

- *The Once-a-Year Day*
- *The Wild One*
- *Barney the Beard*
- *Skateboard Four*
- *One More Flight*
- *The Big Cheese*
- *Market Day*
- *The Big Red Barn*
- *Blackbird Singing*

- *The Robot Birthday*
- *The Giant Squid*
- *The Valentine Bears*
- *The Mother's Day Mice*
- *No Nap*
- *The Wall*
- *A Day's Work*
- *Fly Away Home*
- *Sunshine Home*

Eve Bunting has also written a number of series.

- *Magic Circle Series*
- *Dinosaur Machine Series*
- *No Such Thing? Series*
- *Eve Bunting Science Fiction Series*

It is not possible to list all of Eve Bunting's books here.
Please consult your local library for a more extensive list.

A Day's Work

A Day's Work is a sensitive story that provides a meaningful message for everyone. Francisco and Abuelo, his grandfather, set out to find work. Because Abuelo does not speak English, Francisco must do all the talking. Francisco finds them a job gardening, but only after he lies about Abuelo's skills. Francisco soon learns the "price of his lie."

Point of Interest Mentioned in the Story

- Eve Bunting likes to create situations in which her characters are faced with tempting, often difficult choices. A message to the reader is usually hidden in the story. Challenge your students to find the temptation as well as the message.

Memorable Story Quote

"And tell your grandfather I can always use a good man—for more than just one day's work."

Activities for *A Day's Work*

ACTIVITY 1: Cap-Shaped Book

ACTIVITY 2: Learning About Want Ads

ACTIVITY 3: Guest Speaker—Gardener

ACTIVITY 4: Writing Extension—Sequels

ACTIVITY 5: Graphing: Our Favorite Sports

ACTIVITY 6: Plant Science

ACTIVITY 7: Social Studies—Say It in Spanish

ACTIVITY 1

Cap-Shaped Book

A Day's Work is a compassionate story about a boy who tries to help his grandfather. In the end he learns an invaluable lesson. As students read this story, they will gain an understanding of the consequences of not telling the truth.

Supplies

- cap cover pattern, page 179
- stapler
- cap writing paper, page 180
- purple and yellow crayons

Assembling the Book

1. Reproduce the cap pattern for each student to cut out. To resemble the cap Francisco wore, suggest that students add in yellow the Laker's team name, then color the rest of the hat purple.
2. Reproduce and pass out eight cap writing pages to each student. Tell students to cut out the hats.
3. Help students stack the cover and pages together, then staple along the left side.

The Writing Process

Brainstorm with students answers to these questions.

- *Who* was in the story?
- *Where* did the story take place?
- *Why* was there a story at all?
- *What* were the main problems?
  (For example, Francisco and his father's need to work.)
- *How* were they resolved?

With the class, list on the chalkboard the sequence of story events. Keep the list short, simple, and to the point. Whenever possible, use students' own words. Below are suggested events in story order. Invite students to write the events of the story in their cap books, one for each page.

1. Francisco and his grandfather, Abuelo, are looking for work. Abuelo speaks no English.
2. Francisco convinces Ben of Benjamin's Gardening to hire him and his grandfather. He tells Ben his grandfather is an experienced gardener.
3. Francisco and Abuelo work hard all day. However, because Abuelo is really a carpenter, they weed the plants and leave the flowering weeds, instead of the other way around.
4. Ben is very angry that all his plants have been pulled up.
5. Abuelo realizes what Francisco has done. He makes Francisco tell Ben that they will be back the next day to make it right.
6. Ben tries to pay them half their wages, but Abuelo refuses until the job is done right.
7. Abuelo and Francisco go home to return the next day.
8. Francisco has learned the "price of his lie."

Cap Cover Pattern

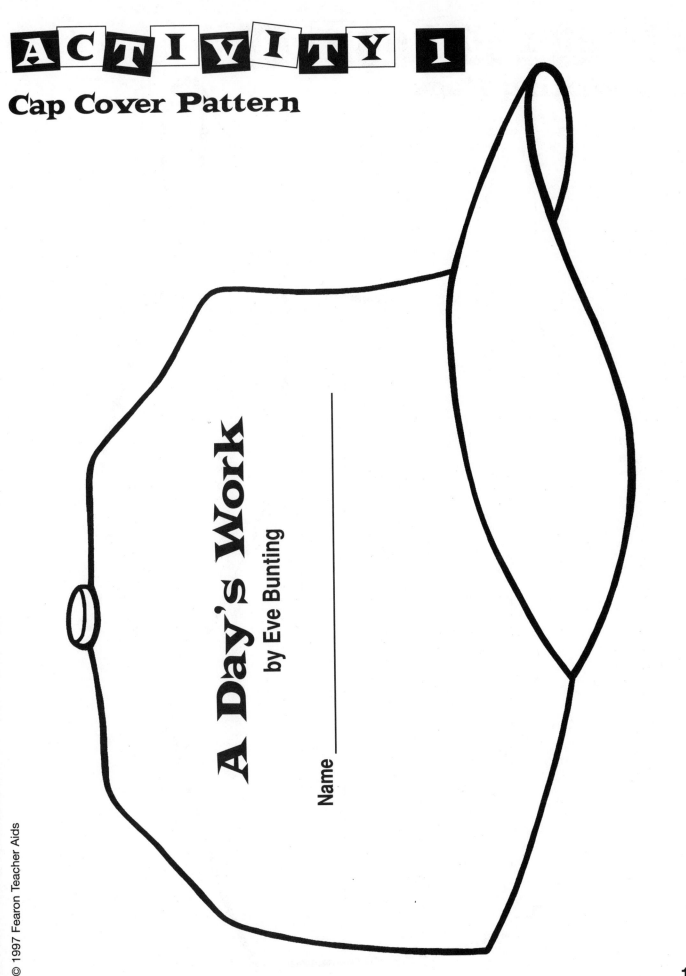

A Day's Work
by Eve Bunting

Name _____

ACTIVITY 1
Cap Writing Page

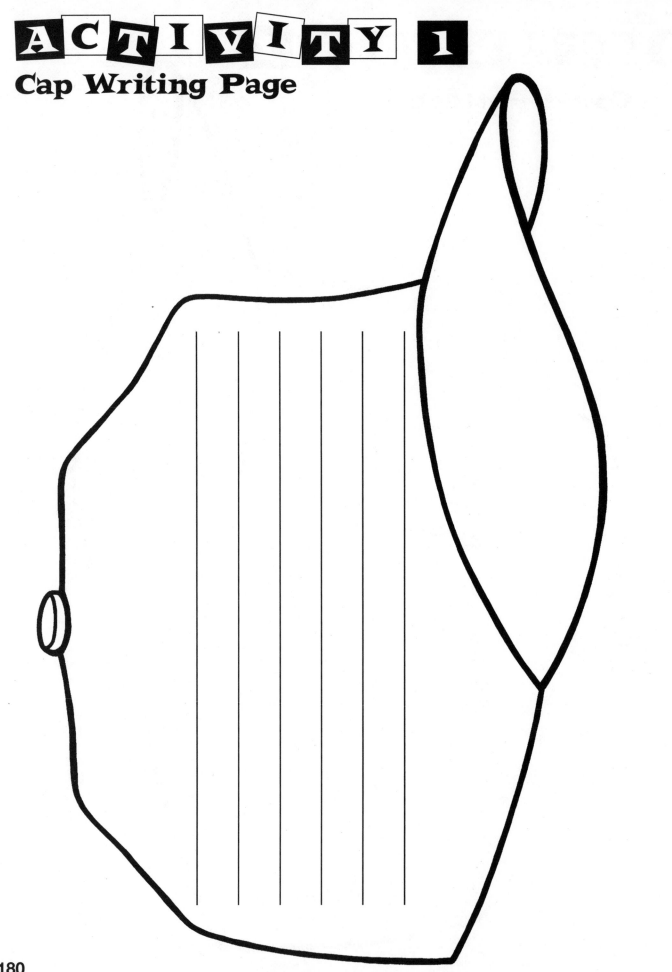

ACTIVITY 2
Learning About Want Ads

Francisco and his grandfather were looking for work. Share with students that sometimes people look for work by reading the want ads in the newspaper. Introduce students to want ads by helping them read the ads, then write some of their own.

Procedure

1. Bring in the want-ads section of your local paper. Reproduce and possibly enlarge a section to pass out to students.

2. Help students read the ads. Which positions are the want ads looking for? How much experience is necessary? Who should they contact? Ask students why Francisco and his grandfather didn't just pick up the paper. Do they think it might have been difficult to read the want ads, especially since Abuelo did not speak English?

3. Using their want ads as a model, challenge students to write an ad for Benjamin's Gardening. What type of worker is Ben looking for? How much experience must he or she have?

4. Encourage students to write a want ad about themselves. In their want ads, have students explain why someone should hire them. Which qualities do they have that would make them great workers? (hard-working, quick learner, enthusiastic, willing to learn something new, punctual, neat) Which special skills or talents do they have?

5. Invite children to mount their work on construction paper to display around the room.

ACTIVITY 3
Guest Speaker—Gardener

In *A Day's Work*, Francisco and Abuelo accidentally pulled out the wrong plants. Invite a gardener to speak to your class about proper planting and weeding practices.

Procedure

1. Ahead of time, contact a local garden shop to locate a gardener willing to speak to your class. Describe the book you are reading and how the characters didn't know the difference between a weed and a plant of value. Explain that you were hoping someone could talk to the class about planting and weeding.

2. Inform the class that you have invited a local gardener to speak to them about maintaining a garden. Brainstorm with students a list of questions to ask the gardener. Also assign one student to share with the gardener the story they have been reading.

3. During the visit, instruct children to listen attentively, posing their questions at the appropriate times.

4. Afterward, talk with children about what they learned. Did they discover which plants were weeds and which were ones we keep? Did anything surprise them? You might have children create a chart of flowers and weeds.

5. Follow up by asking children to write or dictate to you thank-you letters to your gardener guest.

ACTIVITY 4

Writing Extension— Sequels

At the end of *A Day's Work*, Francisco and Abuelo wearily return home. The reader is led to believe that they will return the next day to correct their mistakes. Speculate with students what might have happened next.

The Writing Process

1. Discuss with students how the author ends the story. What will Abuelo and Francisco be doing tomorrow? How do we know that?
2. What do students think Francisco and Abuelo's next day at work will be like? Encourage them to write a sequel to *A Day's Work*, describing their day and what they do.
3. Invite students to share their sequels with the class. Ask students to compare the events their classmates wrote about.

ACTIVITY 5

Graphing—Our Favorite Sports

Sports are important to many children. Invite students to share their favorite teams, athletic endeavors, or games to play.

Procedure

1. Ahead of time, create on chart paper the outline for a large bar graph.
2. Then hold a sports day. Invite students to bring to class a cap or shirt representing a favorite team. It could be a professional team or a team they play on. Students could also bring in sports objects, such as karate belts, bike helmets, ballet slippers, gymnastics leotards, horseback-riding ribbons, or other paraphernalia that represents the sports they play or enjoy.
3. In class, invite students to share their favorite sports, displaying their sports items and explaining what their items represent.
4. As students share, record their sports on your bar graph.
5. When everyone has finished, challenge students to interpret the bar graph. Which sport is the most popular? How can they tell?

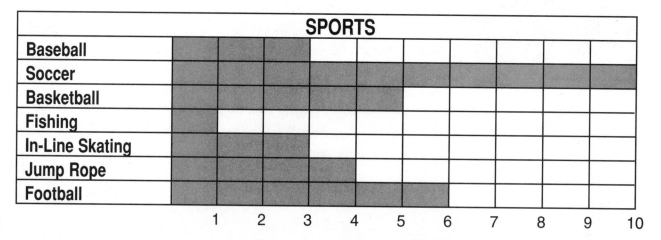

SPORTS	1	2	3	4	5	6	7	8	9	10
Baseball										
Soccer										
Basketball										
Fishing										
In-Line Skating										
Jump Rope										
Football										

ACTIVITY 6

Plant Science

If Francisco and Abuelo had been a little bit more familiar with plants, they might not have made the mistake they did. Invite students to become familiar with plants by planting some of their own.

Extra! Radishes grow very fast. Students should see seedlings by the third day. About three to four weeks later, their radishes might actually be ready to eat!

Supplies

- seeds for a fast-growing plant such as radishes
- potting soil
- paper cups
- Now You're Growing! sheet, page 184
- ruler

Procedure

1. Arrange the class into groups and provide each with a cup of soil and some seeds.

2. Demonstrate how to push the seeds about 1/2" below the soil.

3. Instruct students to water their plants but not "drown" them.

4. Arrange the cups on a sunny windowsill.

5. Now pass out the Now You're Growing! sheets on page 184, one to each student. Every few days, invite children to view their plants and to write down and draw the changes they see. Tell children to measure their plants too, to see how much they have grown.

ACTIVITY 7

Social Studies—Say It in Spanish

One of the problems Abuelo and Francisco faced was that Abuelo could only speak Spanish. How many Spanish words do your students know? Encourage your students to learn some.

Procedure

1. Review with students how Abuelo could only speak Spanish. In fact, abuelo means "grandfather" in Spanish. How do they think it might feel to be in a country where no one speaks your language? Tell children that they are going to pretend to make Abuelo feel right at home by learning some Spanish words.

2. On index cards, write some of the Spanish words listed below. Use the index cards to label objects around the room.

3. Help children pronounce each word, then try to use the word in conversation. For example, "I am going to check my plants next to the *ventana*." "We should close the *puerta*."

table	mesa	(MAY-sah)
chair	silla	(SEE-yah)
door	puerta	(PWAIR-tah)
book	libro	(LEE-bro)
school	escuela	(es-KWAY-lah)

ACTIVITY 6

Now You're Growing!

Group Members

_____   _____

_____   _____

Your plant will change and grow very fast. Record the changes by drawing them, measuring them, and writing about them.

My Plant

Day _____ Inches _____   Day _____ Inches _____

Day _____ Inches _____   Day _____ Inches _____

Day _____ Inches _____   Day _____ Inches _____

Fly Away Home

Eve Bunting addresses the subject of homelessness in *Fly Away Home*. *In this story a young boy and his father live in an airport, trying to save money for a home of their own. The difficulties and disappointments faced by homeless people are shown in a realistic, compassionate manner. This book gives readers insights into the feelings and struggles of the homeless.*

Point of Interest Not Mentioned in the Story

- When Eve Bunting first began writing, such topics as homelessness were not addressed in children's books. As time progressed, however, realism became an important aspect of children's literature. Eve Bunting enjoys helping children understand such sensitive and important social issues as homelessness.

Memorable Story Quote

"Then I remember the bird. It took a while, but a door opened. And when the bird left, when it flew free, I know it was singing."

Activities for *Fly Away Home*

ACTIVITY 1: Airport Mural—Cooperative-Group Book Report

ACTIVITY 2: Foreshadowing

ACTIVITY 3: A Home for Andrew

ACTIVITY 4: Writing Extension—Andrew's Journal

ACTIVITY 5: Class Project—Helping the Homeless

ACTIVITY 1
Airport Mural—Cooperative-Group Book Report

The setting of *Fly Away Home* is an airport, which is the home of a young boy and his father. Encourage students to work in cooperative groups to retell the story in this book-report mural.

Supplies

- mural paper
  - crayons, markers, or paints

The Writing Process

Brainstorm with students answers to these questions.

- *Who* was in the story?
- *Where* did the story take place?
- *Why* was there a story at all?
- *What* was the main problem?
  (for example, the boy and his father's need for a home)
- *How* was it resolved?

With the class, list on the chalkboard the sequence of story events. Keep the list short, simple, and to the point. Whenever possible, use students' own thoughts and ideas. Below are suggested story events in order.

1. Andrew and his father are homeless and live in an airport. They must be careful not to be noticed, or they will have to leave.

2. They move from terminal to terminal around the airport so they will blend in. Other homeless people live in the airport, too.

3. Andrew watches a bird, trapped in the main terminal. Finally the bird flies free, and Andrew is happy for it.

4. Andrew's dad works on the weekends as a janitor in the city. Andrew stays with another homeless family at the airport.

5. Andrew carries suitcases for tips and returns luggage carts for 50 cents each. He saves the money in his shoe.

6. Andrew and his father are saving money to get their own apartment.

7. Andrew gets discouraged when he sees happy people going to their homes.

8. Then he remembers the bird, and he knows that one day he too will fly free.

Divide the class into eight groups or however many events your class listed. Give each group a large sheet of butcher paper and assign each group one story event. Tell groups to first design and decorate the butcher paper as an airport terminal. Suggest that they look at the book for ideas. Make sure they leave space for writing.

Then ask them to write about their event. They might write their event on a separate sheet of writing paper to glue to their mural. Line the groups' murals on a wall in story order. Title your large wall mural "Fly Away Home."

ACTIVITY 2

Foreshadowing

In *Fly Away Home* the author uses a simple bird to give Andrew hope for his future. Use the opportunity to introduce foreshadowing to your students.

Procedure

1. Write the word *foreshadowing* on the chalkboard. Challenge children to tell you what it means. Confirm that foreshadowing is like a clue. It symbolizes something that will happen in the future.

2. Reread *Fly Away Home*, and have students discover that the bird is a foreshadowing. Guide students to draw connections between the bird finding freedom and the boy's freedom—leaving the airport to go to a home of his own.

3. Culminate by asking students to complete Andrew's tale. Encourage them to write about Andrew and his father finding freedom as they move from the airport to a new home.

ACTIVITY 3

A Home for Andrew

Andrew and his father needed a home. Invite students to design a home for them.

Supplies

- variety of art scraps (construction paper, boxes)
- variety of art supplies (glue, scissors, tape)
- markers and crayons

Procedure

1. Review with students the plot of the story and Andrew and his father's need of a home. What type of home might Andrew and his father like?

2. Invite students to act as architects to create a home for Andrew and his father. Pass out an assortment of art supplies, such as construction paper, glue, scissors, markers, and fabric scraps. To make 3-D homes, provide shoeboxes, craft sticks, and foam meat trays, thoroughly cleaned. Encourage students to be as creative as possible in building their homes.

3. Suggest that students finish their homes by drawing and arranging cutouts of Andrew and his father enjoying their new home.

ACTIVITY 4

Writing Extension— Andrew's Journal

Fly Away Home is told in the first person, as Andrew tells about his homeless life. Invite students to try this writing technique as they write a journal entry for Andrew.

The Writing Process

1. Read a line from the story and ask students what they notice about it. How is the story told? Is a narrator telling the story? No, Andrew is. We can tell this by the use of the word *I*. When the main character tells a story from his or her point of view, the story is being told in the first person.

2. With students, reread *Fly Away Home*. Point out the pronouns *I* and *we*. These are all indications that the story is being told in the first person.

3. Let students try it. Pass out writing paper. Suggest to students that Andrew keeps a journal. Journal writing is a form of first-person writing. Challenge students to write a journal entry as if they were Andrew, describing one day at the airport.

4. Invite students to peer-edit, making sure their classmates have correctly written in the first person.

5. After volunteers show their work, bind the essays into a class book titled "Andrew's Journal."

ACTIVITY 5

Class Project—Helping the Homeless

There are many homeless people, not only in the United States, but all over the world. Take the opportunity this book provides to invite students to help those in need.

Procedure

1. Conduct a serious discussion with the class about homelessness in the United States. Why might people become homeless? (loss of job, illness) How do students think it feels to be homeless? Do they think it would be fun to live in an airport, like Andrew, or possibly out on the streets? Why or why not?

2. Explain that many organizations, such as the Red Cross, the Salvation Army, and local food banks and clothes closets strive to help those less fortunate. If possible, you might have a representative from one of these organizations speak to your class.

3. Ask students for ways they think they could help the homeless. For example, they could start a food drive, a clothing collection, or a fund-raising project to donate money.

4. Involve students in one of their suggestions. Arrange a place and time to set up the activity. Alert a local help-for-the-homeless organization about what you are doing and invite a representative to be present. Afterward, talk with children about how they felt while helping the homeless.

The Wall

The Vietnam War is a sensitive part of American history, often difficult to discuss. Many lives were lost in this controversial war, and the effects are still felt today. In The Wall, *Even Bunting personalizes the individual sorrows of war as she writes about a boy and his father who travel many miles to visit the Vietnam Veterans Memorial in Washington, D.C. Your students' minds and hearts will be opened to this poignant story.*

Points of Interest Not Mentioned in the Story

- Most children have probably heard of Vietnam but aren't really sure where it is. Pull down your wall map to help students locate this country in Southeast Asia, bordered by southern China, Laos, Cambodia, and the South China Sea.

- Give children a brief history lesson to explain the Vietnam War. The war was fought to prevent communism from spreading. South Vietnam was a non-communist country, and North Vietnam was controlled by the Communists. It was thought that if North Vietnam took over South Vietnam, the other Southeast Asian countries would also become Communist. In 1965, President Johnson sent the first American combat troops to protect South Vietnam. After much controversy, tremendous loss, and many long years, a cease-fire was signed in 1973. At this time most U.S. troops were sent home. However, in April 1975, the North Vietnam army broke the cease-fire and took over South Vietnam. This officially ended the war. Today, North and South Vietnam are one country, called simply Vietnam.

- The results of this war were devastating to Americans. More than 58,000 service personnel were killed or missing in action. And at least 300,000 were wounded, many left severely disabled both physically and emotionally.

Memorable Story Quote

"The names are the names of the dead. But the wall belongs to all of us."

Activities for *The Wall*

ACTIVITY 1: American-Flag Shaped Book

ACTIVITY 2: Flag Research

ACTIVITY 3: The United States Constitution

ACTIVITY 4: Writing Extension—Letter Writing

ACTIVITY 5: Reporter Role-play

ACTIVITY 6: Crayon Resist Wall

ACTIVITY 7: Model Memorials

ACTIVITY 1
American-Flag Shaped Book

This touching story about the Vietnam Veterans Memorial will help students understand the feelings a family experiences when losing a loved one during wartime. Let students retell the poignant events as they create flag-shaped books.

Supplies

- flag cover pattern, page 191
- writing paper
- stapler

Assembling the Book

1. Reproduce the flag pattern on page 191, one for each student.
2. Distribute to students eight sheets of writing paper each.
3. Instruct students to place the cover on top of the writing paper, then staple the pages down the left side.

The Writing Process

Brainstorm with students answers to these questions.

- *Who* was in the story?
- *Where* did the story take place?
- *Why* was there a story at all?
- *What* is the main focus of the story?
  (for example, the wall and dealing with the loss of a loved one in a war)

With the class, list on the chalkboard the sequence of story events. Keep the list short, simple, and to the point. Whenever possible, use students' own thoughts and ideas. Below are suggested story events in order. Invite students to write each story event on a separate sheet of paper. Encourage them to use their own words. Let students take the books home to share the story with their families.

1. A boy and his father visit the Vietnam Veterans Memorial in Washington, D.C. They are looking for the boy's grandfather's name.
2. The boy sees sad people also looking for names. They place sentimental items against the wall.
3. His father finally finds the name of his father, George Munoz. He rubs his fingers across the letters.
4. Another boy and his grandfather pass by the wall on their way to the river. The grandfather tells the boy to button his jacket.
5. A group of school girls come by with flags, which they place in front of the wall.
6. The boy places his school picture on the grass below his grandfather's name.
7. The boy's father says he is proud that his father's name is on the wall.
8. The boy says that he is proud too, but he would rather have his grandfather walking with him to the river.

Flag Cover Pattern

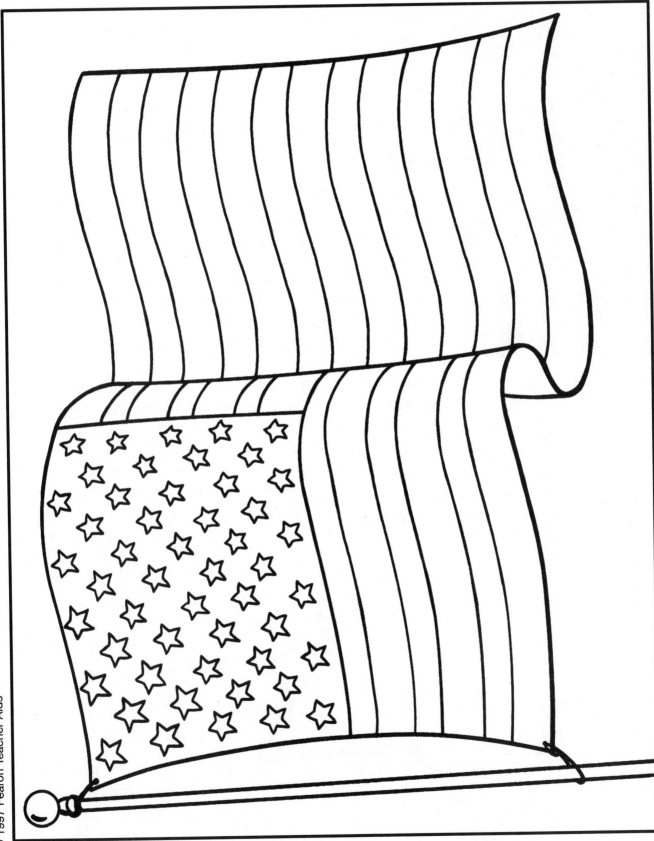

ACTIVITY 2
Flag Research

The Wall is a story that brings out feelings of patriotism. Our country is a wonderful one, and it is important to instill a sense of pride and to make children aware of the freedoms we often take for granted. Respect for and knowledge about our flag is an important means to that end. Encourage students to learn more about the flag in an effort to gain respect for its meaning.

Supplies

- white, blue, and red butcher paper to create a large flag
- star pattern
- pencils
- scissors
- glue

Procedure

1. On white butcher paper, have students make a large mural-sized flag. Suggest that they first draw the outline, then cut out red strips of paper to represent the red stripes and a blue square to represent the field for the stars. The white stripes of the flag can be the background created by the white paper.

2. Elicit from students what they know about our flag. Invite them to research the flag to learn more about it and the appropriate etiquette for handling the flag. Take the class to the library to obtain research materials.

3. Make a large chart in your classroom labeled *Flag Facts*.

4. Read the materials with your students. Invite them to list information they learn about the flag on your chart.

5. Give each student a star pattern to cut out.

6. Let students choose flag facts from the chart or other source to write on their stars.

7. Invite students to read their flag facts to the class. Let them attach the completed stars on the blue field to replicate the flag's own pattern.

8. Encourage students to continue writing facts on stars until all 50 stars are on the flag. Display proudly!

© 1997 Fearon Teacher Aids

ACTIVITY 3

The United States Constitution

The history of the United States is full of meaningful events and documents that are symbolic of our country. One of these documents is the Constitution. Encourage students to recite the Preamble to the Constitution, honing their memorization skills.

Procedure

1. Ask students if they know what the Constitution is. Explain that the United States Constitution is the document that describes the principles by which our country is governed. These principles are the basic rights and laws guaranteed to each citizen, for example, the right to vote and the right to a jury if standing trial. The Constitution was written in 1787 and accepted in 1788. It began to function in 1789. It is an important document, for it stands for the "law of our land," and it is well-respected in other countries as an example for setting up a government. The Preamble to the Constitution is the introduction. It contains phrases that students might be familiar with.

2. Share with students that knowing the Preamble by heart helps to not only make them proud of our country, but also to show them how special and meaningful our Constitution is. Reproduce and pass out the Preamble at the bottom of this page.

3. Read the Preamble with your students and discuss its meaning.

4. Set a date for students to recite the Preamble in class. You might let students recite in groups or pairs. You might also invite another class, parents, or school workers, such as librarians, the nurse, or the principal, to listen to the recitations.

THE PREAMBLE TO THE CONSTITUTION OF THE UNITED STATES OF AMERICA

We, the people of the United States, in order to form a more perfect union, establish justice, insure domestic tranquility, provide for the common defense, promote the general welfare, and secure the blessings of liberty to ourselves and our posterity, do ordain and establish this Constitution of the United States of America.

ACTIVITY 4

Writing Extension— Letter Writing

Many survivors of the Vietnam War were left disabled physically and mentally. Many feel that Vietnam veterans have been forgotten and their needs neglected. Encourage students to write letters of appreciation to a Vietnam veteran.

The Writing Process

1. Discuss with students that many of those who fought in the Vietnam War are still alive. Talk about how these veterans might feel upon visiting the Vietnam Memorial and remembering their lives during war.

2. Explain to students that they will be writing letters to Vietnam veterans or their families, thanking them for fighting for our country. Brainstorm issues that might be included. Review letter form if necessary.

3. Review students letters for appropriateness. Then if you wish, send the letters to

National League of POW and MIA Families
1001 Connecticut Avenue, NE Suite 919
Washington, D.C 20056

4. Use the school address as the return address. Some students may receive responses. Invite them to share their responses with the class.

ACTIVITY 5

Reporter Role-play

The Vietnam Veterans Memorial is often in the news, especially during Memorial Day or Veterans Day. Invite students to role-play being reporters, interviewing the boy and his father or characters they saw in the book who visited the memorial.

Procedure

1. Flip through the book with the class and point out all the people visiting the wall. Mention that during Memorial Day and Veterans Day, the wall is extremely significant. Often reporters visit the wall to interview people about their experiences and feelings.

2. Divide the class into small groups. Encourage students to pretend that they are a character they saw in the book, such as the boy and his father, the boy and his grandfather, or even the girls who lay flags against the wall. Another student can be a reporter.

3. What kinds of questions might the reporter ask? What might the visitors reply? Invite students to write questions and answers for their role-plays, keeping in mind what the wall represents.

4. After a brief rehearsal period, invite students to share their reporter role-plays with the class.

ACTIVITY 6

Crayon Resist Wall

Eve Bunting uses the Vietnam Veterans Memorial as the setting for a heartwarming story. This activity gives students an opportunity to make their own versions of the wall.

Supplies

- white construction paper
- black tempera paint
- white wax crayons
- paint brushes

Procedure

1. Review with students the importance of the wall in the story. Tell students that they will be making their own versions of the wall.

2. Give each student white construction paper. With a white crayon, have them copy from the chalkboard or overhead one of the following statements.

"This is the wall, my grandfather's wall. On it are the names of those killed in a war, long ago."

"The names are the names of the dead. But the wall is for all of us."

3. Mix black tempera paint so that it is very thin. Instruct students to use a paint brush to paint over the entire paper with broad, even, overlapping, strokes. The wax crayon will resist the paint and become visible.

4. After the paint has dried, use the papers to arrange a bricklike pattern on a large wall, taping the art in place. Title the display "*The Wall* by Eve Bunting."

ACTIVITY 7

Model Memorials

The Vietnam Veterans Memorial commemorates those who have died in battle during service to our country. Encourage students to design their own memorials for a special person.

Procedure

1. Reflect with students how the Vietnam Veterans Memorial was erected to honor those who died during this controversial war. Go on to explain that Washington D.C., where the wall is located, is full of memorials. You might show students pictures of the Washington Monument, the Lincoln Memorial, and the Jefferson Memorial, to name a few. Conclude with students that memorials are built to help us remember and honor people who are special and have made a contribution. If you have any memorials in your community, point them out the class.

2. Who do your students think is worthy of a memorial? Explain that the person doesn't need to be famous. It could be someone in the community who has made it a better place to live.

3. Pass out clay and encourage each student to mold his or her own memorial for that special person. Supply children with plastic knives to etch in details.

4. Invite each student to share the memorial, explaining who it is for and why that person deserves such an honor.

Sunshine Home

In Sunshine Home, Timmie, a young boy, is forced to deal with his grandmother living in a nursing home. As Timmie and his parents visit Sunshine Home for the first time, he is affected by the emotions exhibited by his grandmother and his mother. In childlike honesty, he helps everyone deal with their feelings openly as they learn a lesson of love.

Point of Interest Not Mentioned in the Story

- Many of Eve Bunting's books reflect the social concerns of our time. Because of advances in medicine and science, people on the average are living longer. Many families are forced to put their loved ones in nursing homes, for they don't have adequate medical knowledge to care for them. Sometimes this causes emotional stress on an entire family. Eve Bunting tries to enlighten the reader as she shares the experiences of this family.

Memorable Story Quote

"I look up at the balloon and I wonder why the word on it ever embarrassed me. It's the best word there is."

Activities for *Sunshine Home*

ACTIVITY 1: Bouquet Book Report

ACTIVITY 2: Visit a Local Nursing Home

ACTIVITY 3: Cheerful Greeting Cards

ACTIVITY 4: Writing Extension—"Honesty Is the Best Policy"

ACTIVITY 5: Mood Words

ACTIVITY 6: Balloon Messages

ACTIVITY 1
Bouquet Book Report

Sunshine Home is a touching story about a boy who visits his grandmother in a nursing home for the first time. He brings her a bouquet of sweet peas he picked and a balloon his father bought. Invite students to retell the story by making a bouquet of either sweet peas, balloons, or both.

Supplies

- sweet-pea pattern, page 198
- balloon pattern, page 198
- glue
- scissors
- construction paper, 12" x 18" (30 cm x 45 cm)
- ribbon (optional)
- pencils

The Writing Process

Brainstorm with students answers to these questions.

- *Who* was in the story?
- *Where* did the story take place?
- *Why* was there a story at all?
- *What* was the main problem? (for example, the family's struggle to deal with Gram in a nursing home) *How* was it resolved?

With the class, list on the chalkboard the sequence of story events. Keep the list simple, and to the point. Whenever possible, use students' own thoughts and ideas. Below are suggested events in order.

1. Timmie and his parents prepare to visit his grandmother in Sunshine Home. Timmie picks a bouquet of sweet peas.

2. Timmie's dad buys a balloon for him to carry. It says "Love." Timmie is embarrassed.

3. At the home, Timmie notices his mother talking to Gram in an unusually cheery voice.

4. Timmie gives Gram the gifts, and she introduces him to her friends.

5. Timmie and his parents tell Gram goodbye.

6. As soon as they leave, Timmie's mother bursts into tears.

7. Timmie rushes back in to leave his school picture with Gram and finds her crying, too.

8. Timmie wonders why they pretended to be happy.

9. Timmie runs outside to get his parents to come back and discuss their true feelings with Gram.

10. Timmie learns that *love* is the best word there is.

Distribute to each student ten copies of the sweet pea or balloon pattern. Ask students to write or illustrate each story event on one sweet pea or balloon, numbering them in order. Have students cut them out.

Assembling the Bouquet

1. Give each student a sheet of 12" x 18" (30 cm x 45 cm) construction paper. Tell them to glue down their sweet peas or balloons in story order toward the top of the paper.

2. With a marker or crayon, have students draw in the stems of the sweet peas or strings of the balloons to make a bouquet. You might let students glue on ribbon to "tie" the bouquet together.

3. Have students title their bouquets of flowers or balloons *"Sunshine Home* by Eve Bunting."

Sweet-Pea and Balloon Patterns

ACTIVITY 2
Visit a Local Nursing Home

When Timmie and his family visit the nursing home, all of Gram's friends gather around. It is obvious that they are glad to have visitors. This would be the perfect opportunity to visit a nursing home.

Procedure

1. Contact a local nursing home and ask when an appropriate time for a visit might be. You might describe the book you are reading, explaining your interest to visit. Make arrangements with your school for the field trip, too.

2. Send a letter home with information regarding the field trip. (See letter below.)

3. Before the field trip, prepare something that children can share with the nursing-home residents. A song is a great idea. It doesn't cost anything, each resident can have one, and it is sure to bring a smile. Practice singing a favorite class song.

4. Also discuss correct behavior. Make sure children understand that they need to act with respect and politeness. Also, if any of your students have visited a nursing home, like Timmie did, invite them to tell their classmates about it.

5. After the field trip, talk with students about the experience. How did it feel to make the nursing-home residents happy?

Extra! You might have students send a large group card or banner to the home, thanking them for allowing your class to visit.

Dear Family,

We have been reading books by writer Eve Bunting during our author studies. Many times her books address current social issues. In her book *Sunshine Home*, she tells a heartwarming story about a young boy who visits his grandmother in a nursing home for the first time. As a culminating activity, we would like to visit a nursing home, too. We are planning to go to _____ on _____. We feel this will be a good opportunity for students to bring cheer to the residents. We need your permission for your child to go. Thank you for your encouragement.

Yours truly,

P.S. If you might want to be a chaperon for our trip, please write your phone number so we can contact you.

ACTIVITY 3

Cheerful Greeting Cards

It is very important for children to be thoughtful of senior adults. *In Sunshine Home*, Timmie brings his Gram cheer in the forms of a bouquet of sweet peas and a balloon. Encourage students to make greeting cards for residents of a nursing home or for an older person at home.

Supplies

• construction paper
• colored paper or fabric scraps
• crayons or markers

Procedure

1. Discuss with students how the gifts Timmie took to his grandmother made her happy.

2. Invite students to create cheerful greeting cards for residents of a nursing home or for an older family member. Brainstorm appropriate messages, such as "Thinking of you" or "Wishing you a happy day."

3. Give each student several sheets of plain or colored paper. Show them several ways to fold the paper to represent a card. Provide colored paper or fabric scraps for extra decoration.

4. Have students write and decorate their cards, making sure they include their names and the school's name.

5. Encourage students to present their cards to older family members or send the cards to the nursing home you visited, checking with the administration for a list of names. Make sure no one gets left out!

ACTIVITY 4

Writing Extension—"Honesty Is the Best Policy"

In *Sunshine Home*, Timmie's mother and grandmother are not very honest about their feelings, pretending to be happy while they are really sad. Timmie helps them show their true feelings. Encourage students to think about a time when they did not allow their true feelings to show and to write what happened.

The Writing Process

1. Reread page 25 of *Sunshine Home*. Talk with students about how Timmie helped his mother and grandmother understand what they were really feeling. Explain that although there are times when you should consider other people's feelings before you speak or act, usually telling the truth is the best policy. Why was it better in this story?

2. Invite students to write about a time when they discovered that telling the truth was the best choice. Guide their writing with the following prompts.

- *What* was the situation?
- *What* was the conflict or problem?
- *Who* was involved?
- *How* did telling the truth help the situation?
- *What* was the end result?

3. Have students conclude by writing why telling the truth in this situation worked best. Be aware that this may be a sensitive topic for some students. Keep each essay between you and the student who wrote it.

ACTIVITY 5

Mood Words

The mood of *Sunshine Home* changes as the feelings of the characters are revealed. Challenge students to examine how Eve Bunting uses powerful language to involve her readers in these mood changes.

Procedure

1. Explain to students that the mood of a story is the feeling the book evokes, often guided by the emotions of the characters. Point out how Eve Bunting reveals the mood through descriptive language.

2. Reread *Sunshine Home* with your students. Have them discover and list words that help describe the mood. Make a class hanger chart (Appendix, page 261) with the heading "Mood Words." Some words or phrases to be included are listed below.

3. Encourage students to list these words or phrases in their Writing Journals to refer to when writing on their own.

embarrassing	burst into tears	terrified
peppy	chipper	sparkly
scared	choking up	
cheery	bright	

ACTIVITY 6

Balloon Messages

The balloon that Timmie took his grandmother relayed a powerful message. Simple words or phrases can make important statements. Have students display a message of their own on a balloon.

Extra! A balloon bouquet to your principal or other people in school might be fun.

Supplies

- balloon pattern, page 202
  - pencils
    - real balloons (optional)
      - permanent markers (optional)
        - ribbon (optional)

Procedure

1. Discuss with students that the message on Timmie's balloon was an important part of the story.

2. If students could send a message printed on a balloon, what would they write? Who would they give it to? Pass out the balloon pattern on page 202 for students to write their messages. Display the balloons around the room or give them to the person for whom the message is intended.

3. If materials allow, give each student a real balloon. Help them blow them up, then write their messages with permanent marker.

4. Attach curly ribbons and deliver.

ACTIVITY 6

Balloon Pattern

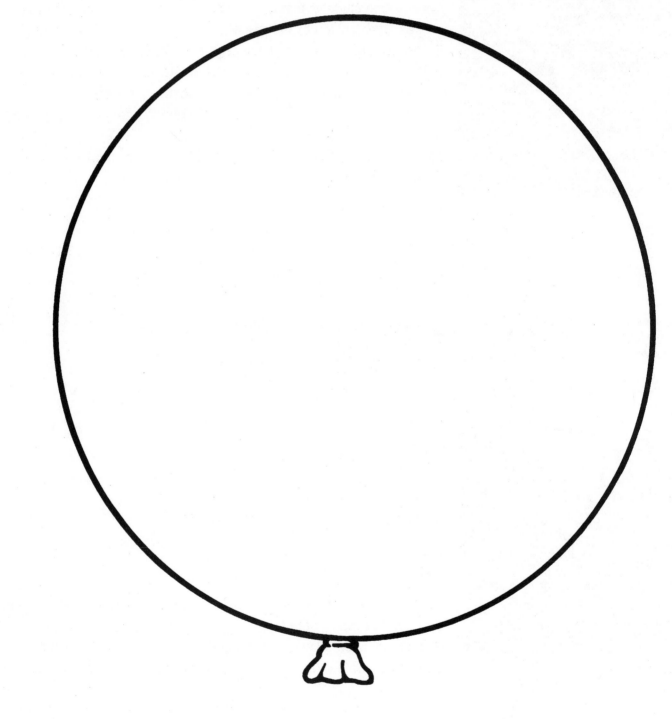

Patricia McKissack

Patricia McKissack is an inspiring author whose stories come from her heart and her rich cultural heritage. Patricia, often along with her husband Fredrick, writes moving and sometimes whimsical stories that reflect the past. In an effort to share her African American heritage with young readers, Patricia McKissack is a passionate storyteller whose books not only entertain but also inform.

Interesting Facts About the Author

Birth: Patricia McKissack was born on August 9, 1944, in Nashville, Tennessee.

Family: Patricia was born to Robert and Erma Carwell. In 1964 she married Fredrick McKissack, a neighbor she'd known most of her life. They have three sons—Fredrick Lemuel and twins Robert and John. Patricia and Fredrick currently reside in Missouri.

Education: Patricia graduated from Tennessee State University with a Bachelor of Arts degree in 1964. In 1975 she received her Master's from Webster University.

Beginnings as an author:

As an eighth-grade English teacher in Kirkwood, Missouri, Patricia wanted to teach a unit on African American writer Paul Lawrence Dunbar. Searching for a biography about him proved fruitless. So, Patricia decided to write a biography about him for her class. Many more biographies followed, along with other types of literature. Her biography of Paul Lawrence Dunbar was published in 1984. She and her husband have coauthored numerous selections as well.

Other Interests: Patricia enjoys gardening.

Common Threads to Look for Throughout Her Books

- Patricia often writes with her husband, Fredrick.

- Many of Patricia McKissack's books focus on the culture and heritage of African American history.

- Patricia and her husband realize that the challenge of achieving racial equality that she and other African Americans of her generation faced in the 1960s is difficult for children today to understand. She and her husband strive to enlighten children about the past through their books. As Fredrick explains, "The reason that we write for children is to tell them about these things and to get them to internalize the information, to feel just a little of the hurt, the tremendous amount of hurt and sadness that racism and discrimination cause—for all people, regardless of race."

Books by Patricia McKissack

- *Who Is Who?*
- *Paul Lawrence Dunbar: A Poet to Remember*
- *The Apache*
- *The Aztec*
- *The Inca*
- *The Maya*
- *Flossie and the Fox*
- *Our Martin Luther King Book*
- *Who Is Coming?*
- *Nettie Jo's Friends*
- *Mirandy and Brother Wind*
- *Monkey-Monkey's Trick*
- *Jesse Jackson: A Biography*
- *A Million Fish—More or Less*
- *The Dark-Thirty: Southern Tales of the Supernatural*

Books by Patricia & Fredrick McKissack

- *Sojourner Truth: Ain't I a Woman?*
- *Martin Luther King, Jr.: A Man to Remember*
- *Mary McLeod Bethune: A Great American Educator*
- *Booker T. Washington: Leader and Educator*
- *Carter G. Woodson: The Father of Black History*
- *Frederick Douglass: Leader Against Slavery*
- *George Washington Carver: The Peanut Scientist*
- *Jesse Owens: Olympic Star*
- *Langston Hughes: Great American Poet*
- *Louis Armstrong: Jazz Musician*
- *Paul Robeson: A Voice to Remember*
- *Ralph J. Bunche: Peacemaker*
- *Marian Anderson: A Great Singer*
- *Rebels Against Slavery: American Slave Revolts*

Nettie Jo's Friends

Nettie Jo is a flower girl at cousin Willadeen's wedding, and she desperately wants to take her doll, Annie Mae. However, her doll needs a new dress, and Nettie Jo's mother does not have time to make one. Nettie Jo decides to make the dress herself. In searching for a needle, Nettie Jo helps three animals, who, in the end, help her out.

Point of Interest Not Mentioned in the Story

- Patricia McKissack has a magical way of using personification—attributing human characteristics to animals. Introduce or reinforce this writing technique as you read the story.

Memorable Story Quote

"'*Thank you* for helping me hear better,' said Miz Rabbit.

'*Thank you* for helping me see clearer,' said Fox.

'*Thank you* for helping me roar louder,' said Panther.

'Might you be needing this?'"

Activities for *Nettie Jo's Friends*

ACTIVITY 1: Paper-Doll Book Report

ACTIVITY 2: Show and Tell of Friendship Toys

ACTIVITY 3: Friendship Chain

ACTIVITY 4: Friendship Interview

ACTIVITY 5: The Food Chain

ACTIVITY 1
Paper-Doll Book Report

The events in *Nettie Jo's Friends* are delightful. The relationship between Nettie Jo and the animals will captivate your students. Invite them to retell the story events on paper dolls.

Supplies

- paper-doll pattern, page 207
- tape or glue
- manila paper, 12" x 18" (30 cm x 45 cm)
- scissors
- markers or crayons
- pencils

Extra! These paper-doll chains make a great border for a Patricia McKissack bulletin board. Display other projects on the bulletin board during your author study.

Assembling the Paper Dolls

1. To avoid frustration, the teacher *must* model each step as students complete the paper-doll chain.

2. Give each student a piece of manila paper. Have them cut the paper in half lengthwise. Show them how to tape the ends together to form one long 36" (90 cm) strip.

3. Measure a 5-inch section, then accordion-fold the strip six times, making seven equal sections.

4. Reproduce a paper-doll pattern for each student. Have students trace the pattern on the top folded section. The hands and feet *must* touch the edges of the paper. Demonstrate how to *carefully* cut out the paper dolls so they form one long chain.

The Writing Process

Brainstorm with students answers to these questions.

- *Who* was in the story?
- *Where* did the story take place?
- *Why* was there a story at all?
- *What* were the main problems? (for example, Nettie Jo's need to find a sewing needle) *How* were they resolved?

With the class, list on the chalkboard the sequence of story events. Keep the list short, simple, and to the point. Whenever possible, use students' own words. Below are suggested events in story order.

1. Nettie Jo wants to take her doll, Annie Mae, to her cousin's wedding, but the doll needs a new dress.

2. Nettie Jo sets off into the woods to search for a needle. She finds many things, which she puts in her burlap sack.

3. Nettie runs into Miz Rabbit, who cannot hear. Nettie Jo ties Miz Rabbit's ears above her head. Miz Rabbit hears Fox and runs.

4. Nettie Jo continues putting things in her bag, but still no needle. She runs into Fox, who cannot help her. He can't see because of the sun's glare. Nettie Jo gives him a hat.

5. Nettie Jo asks Panther to help her, but Panther has lost his voice. Nettie Jo gives him a horn. Panther runs off to chase Fox.

6. Nettie Jo goes home, discouraged. Miz Rabbit, Fox, and Panther come to thank her for her help.

7. Nettie Jo sees something shining on the ground. Her animal friends have left her a sewing needle!

Direct students to write or draw one story event on each paper doll.

ACTIVITY 1
Paper-Doll Pattern

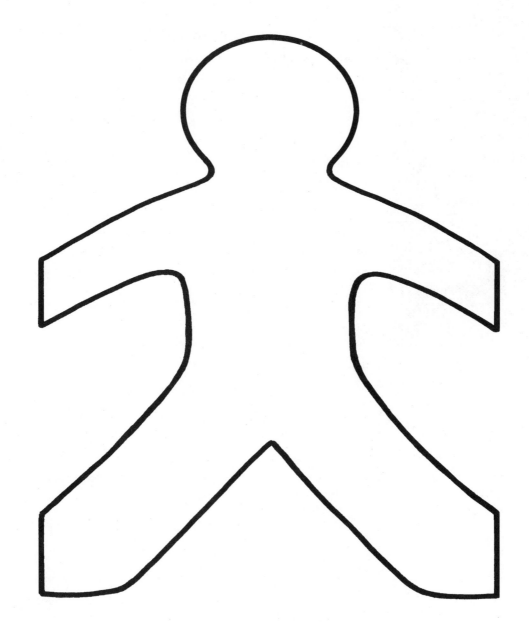

ACTIVITY 2
Show and Tell of Friendship Toys

Nettie Jo was very fond of her doll, Annie Mae, and she went to great lengths to make sure the doll was included in the wedding. Most children have or have had special toys that they were attached to. Invite students to share their special toys during this friendship show-and-tell.

Procedure

1. Discuss with students how Nettie Jo felt about Annie Mae. Ask them to tell about stuffed animals or other toys that they are fond of.

2. Choose a day for show and tell and encourage students to bring in the stuffed animals or toys. You might send home the parent letter at the bottom of this page to alert families of the activity. If children feel embarrassed or awkward about sharing their own favorite toys, suggest that they bring in a cherished toy from a sibling or perhaps even a parent.

3. In class, invite students to share the history of their special "friends."

4. Culminate by passing out writing paper and encouraging students to write about and illustrate their special toys.

Dear Family,

We have been studying children's author Patricia McKissack. Her book *Nettie Jo's Friends* is about a little girl and her special doll, Annie Mae. Many children have special toys or stuffed animals that they treasure as friends.

On _____ , we will have a Show and Tell of Friendship Toys. At this time I would like for children to bring in a favorite "friend" to share with the class. Please help your child choose and remember to bring in the special friend.

Thank you for your help!

Sincerely,

ACTIVITY 3

Friendship Chain

Nettie Jo did many kind deeds for the animals she met in the woods. Which kind deeds have children done for friends? Which kind deeds has someone done for them? Encourage students to write about them.

Supplies

- same-size strips of construction paper
- pencils
- tape

Procedure

1. Brainstorm with students the kind things they do for their friends and the kind things their friends do for them. You might share some kind things that friends do for you to get children started.

2. Give each student a small strip of colored construction paper, the perfect size for making paper chains. Tell each student to write a kind friendship deed on the strip.

3. Have one student share what he or she has written as he or she makes the strip into a circle, taping the ends together. One by one, encourage students to share their kind friendship deeds as they add their construction-paper circle to the chain.

4. Display the chain in your classroom. Encourage students to add to the chain when someone does something nice for them. Watch your friendship chain grow!

ACTIVITY 4

Friendship Interview

Friendships are something that everyone treasures, even adults. Children may not realize that adults have friends, too. Encourage students to interview adults about their friendships.

Procedure

1. Discuss with students the importance of friendships. Conclude that adults too have friendships that are just as important to them as children's friendships are.

2. Invite students to interview an adult, such as a parent, neighbor, or an older family member, about friendship. Suggest that students tape-record their interviews. Allow students to use the interview sheet on page 210 as a guide.

3. Give students several days to conduct their interviews. Set a date and encourage students to share their interviews with the class.

ACTIVITY 4

Friendship Interview

Interviewer _____ **Person Being Interviewed** _____

1. Who is your special friend? _____

2. How long have you known him or her? _____

3. Where and how did you meet her or him? _____

_____

_____

4. What is special about your friend? _____

_____

_____

_____

5. What do you like to do with your friend? _____

_____

_____

6. Tell me about a memorable time you had with your friend. _____

_____

_____

ACTIVITY 5

The Food Chain

In *Nettie Jo's Friends* the animals seemed to be chasing each other. The fox was chasing the rabbit, and the panther was chasing the fox, a pattern similar to the food chain. Introduce students to nature's food chain of animals and plants.

Supplies

- paper plates
- string
- tape
- crayons or markers

Procedure

1. Write the term *food chain* on the chalkboard and challenge children to tell you what it means. Confirm that the food chain is the pattern that animals follow for feeding.

2. Write some examples on the chalkboard. You might start your food chain with the sun. Below is one example.

- The sun is food for what? (plants)
- Plants are food for which animals? (rabbits)
- Rabbits are food for which animals? (foxes)
- Foxes might be food for which animals? (panthers)

3. Point out that different habitats have food chains with different animals. Assign a habitat to groups of four to investigate. For example

• The ocean (plankton; small fish, like herrings; bigger fish, like tunas; large fish, like sharks)

- The African savanna (sun, plants, antelopes, lions)
- The pond (plants, insects, fish, herons)
- The coral reef (plankton, fish, crabs, octopuses)
- The desert (insects, spiders, lizards, snakes)

4. Of course, these are just examples. Encourage students to explore other habitats to learn more. Accept all reasonable answers.

5. Pass out four paper plates to each group, along with string and tape. Tell each group member to choose an animal to draw on the plate, then to attach the plates with string.

6. When ready, encourage groups to share their paper-plate food chains with the class. Display the food chains in your science center.

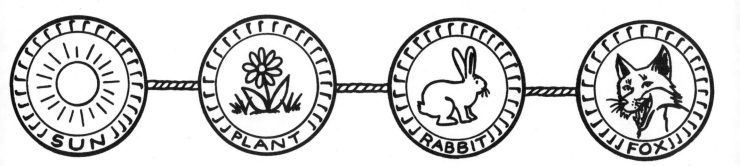

A Million Fish—More or Less

Patricia McKissack uses exaggeration in A Million Fish—More or Less. After listening to Papa-Daddy and elder Abbajon swap exaggerated tales, young Hugh Thomas conjures up a tall tale of his own. Your students will enjoy this story as they learn to recognize exaggeration in literature.

Points of Interest Not Mentioned in the Story

- Patricia McKissack enjoyed listening to tales told by her own grandfather. Suggest to students that she might have learned how to exaggerate when telling a story from him.

- Dena Schutzer's vivid illustrations bring life to the story. Her childlike paintings are ones your students can easily relate to.

Memorable Story Quote

"'Tell us, now, was it *really* a million?' A smile broke across Hugh Thomas's face, and he winked his eye. 'More or less,' he answered. . . .'"

Activities for *A Million Fish—More or Less*

ACTIVITY 1: A Fishy Story Book Report

ACTIVITY 2: Tall Tales—More or Less

ACTIVITY 3: How Much Is a Million?

ACTIVITY 4: Writing Extension—A Million Fish

ACTIVITY 1
A Fishy Story Book Report

This is the fish story of all fish stories as Patricia McKissack takes exaggeration to the limit! Encourage students to retell the story events with this fishy project.

Supplies

- fish pattern, page 214
- long dowel rods or sticks collected from outside
- string
- pencils

Alternate! Instead of using sticks, children can use string only, attaching all the dangling fish to one long length.

The Writing Process

Brainstorm with students answers to these questions.

- *Who* was in the story?
- *Where* did the story take place?
- *Why* was there a story at all?
- *What* was the main goal? (for example, Hugh Thomas's desire to swap good swamp tales with the best of them)
- *How* was it achieved?

With the class, list on the chalkboard the sequence of story events. Keep the list short, simple, and to the point. Whenever possible, use students' own thoughts and ideas. Below are suggested story events in order.

1. As Hugh Thomas fished, he listened to Papa-Daddy and Elder Abbajon tell about the strange events on bayou Clapateaux.

2. They told of a wild turkey weighing 500 pounds, a lantern that had been left by the Spanish conquistadors in 1542, and a giant cottonmouth snake that chased them into a pool of quicksand.

3. Hugh challenged their stories. But Papa-Daddy and Elder Abbajon said they really happened . . . more or less.

4. After hearing these exaggerated tales, Hugh fished alone. The three fish he caught turned into a million in his mind. Along with other exciting events.

5. Atoo, grand-père of all the alligators, appeared and threatened Hugh. Hugh threw half his catch back.

6. Hugh next encountered Mosley, the raccoon, who also wanted some fish. He challenged Hugh to a jump-rope contest. Two bears turned the rope, which was a 24-foot snake. Hugh won, but the raccoon and his friends took half the fish.

7. Hugh was then attacked by a flock of crows. They took some fish.

8. The neighbor's cat tricked Hugh out of all but three fish.

9. Hugh met up with Papa-Daddy and Elder Abbajon. They praised him for catching the three fish.

10. Hugh tells them he caught a million fish. After being questioned, Hugh says he really did catch a million fish . . . more or less.

Give each student ten copies of the fish pattern. Tell the students to cut out the fish, then number them from one to ten.

ACTIVITY 1

Assembling the Fishing Pole

1. Provide students with long dowel rods or have them bring in medium-sized sticks from their yards or found around the school grounds. Stress to children that the sticks are not toys. Students should not poke or tap their classmates with them.

2. Give each student a long length of string and instruct him or her to cut it into pieces of varying lengths.

3. Tell students to tape the strings to the mouths of the fish cutouts.

4. Direct them to tie the other end of the strings to the end of their sticks, which now have become fishing poles.

5. Display the fishing poles around the room.

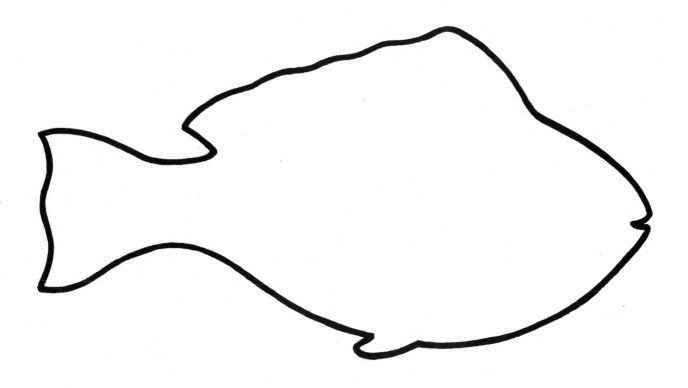

ACTIVITY 2

Tall Tales—More or Less

Papa-Daddy and Elder Abbajon swapped bayou tales while "rowing out of the gauzy river fog." Hugh Thomas listened to the tales grow as each man outdid the other. Challenge students to participate in one-upmanship as they write a group tall tale.

Procedure

1. Discuss with students the exaggeration in *A Million Fish—More or Less*. Explain that many tall tales are made up of exaggerated characters and events, like Paul Bunyan. The story of Johnny Appleseed, who actually was a real person, has been exaggerated over time, describing how Johnny planted all the apple trees from the East Coast to the Ohio Valley.

2. Divide the class into small groups. Write the following story starter on the chalkboard for groups to copy.

> It was a steamy August afternoon. A boy was riding his bike down a dusty road when he heard a loud noise. He stopped and turned around to see what it was. There, just three feet away, stood _____ .

3. Challenge the first student in each group to finish the sentence, then to add a few more sentences to the story. Set a time limit of, say, three minutes for each writer.

4. Call time. Have the first student pass his or her papers to the next group member to continue the story. Repeat until all group members have had a chance to write.

5. Provide time for students to write an ending for their stories. Then invite groups to read their tall tales to the class. You might bind the stories into a class tall-tale book.

Extra! You can also conduct this activity as an oral project. To write a class tall tale, go around the room as children dictate sentences to you.

ACTIVITY 3

How Much Is a Million?

Hugh claims to have caught one million fish. Do students think this is possible? Invite them to find out just how much a million is.

Supplies

- fish pattern
- scissors
- box or fish tank

Procedure

1. Invite a child to come to the board to write the number 1,000,000.

2. Challenge children to tell you what the rest of the zeros stand for, for example, one zero = ten, two zeroes = hundred, three zeroes = thousand.

3. Ask children if they think a million is a lot. Let them have fun finding out.

4. Give children the fish pattern. Tell them that if each child cuts out four fish, they will have a hundred fish (for a class of 25). Have children do so, placing all the fish in an empty box or fish tank.

5. How many fish would they each need to cut out in order to have a thousand fish? (40) How much fuller would their fish tank or box be? (Mark a spot ten times higher.)

6. Keep going until children realize just how much a million is!

Extra! A great tie-in is *How Much Is a Million?* by David M. Schwartz, illustrated by Steven Kellogg (Lothrop, Lee & Shepard, 1985). As the author and illustrator come up with combinations for a million, children realize just how much a million is.

ACTIVITY 4

Writing Extension— A Million Fish

What would Hugh—or anyone for that matter—really do if he caught a million fish? Invite children to write about it in a short story.

The Writing Process

Talk with children about Hugh and his imaginary one million fish. Now suggest that Hugh really did catch this many fish. What would he do with them? What would the students do with them? Pass out writing paper for children to write short stories describing what they would do with a million fish. Guide their writing with such questions as these.

- Where would you put all your fish?
- Would you give your fish to a friend? to whom?
- Would you donate your fish? to whom?
- Would you keep some as pets? how many? Where would you keep them?

Mirandy and Brother Wind

Mirandy and Brother Wind is a light-hearted fantasy of a young girl who tries to catch the wind for a dance partner in her first cakewalk. Patricia McKissack captures the reader as she personifies the wind.

Points of Interest Not Mentioned in the Story

- The cakewalk is an African American dance introduced by the slaves. Couples would dance in a square or circle around judges who would critique them on moves, appearance, and grace. A winning couple was chosen and given an elaborately decorated cake. (See the Author's Note in *Mirandy and Brother Wind* for more information.)

- Patricia McKissack feels it is important to bring the past to life for young readers. She was inspired to write this story by a picture taken of her grandparents at a cakewalk in 1906.

- The illustrations for *Mirandy and Brother Wind* are by Jerry Pinkney. He is one of the authors featured in this book of author studies (see page 91).

Memorable Story Quote

"*Swish! Swish!* . . . Brother Wind was back. He come high steppin' through Ridgetop, dressed in his finest and trailing that long silvery wind cape behind him. *Swoosh! Swoosh! Swoosh!*"

Activities for *Mirandy and Brother Wind*

ACTIVITY 1: Windsock Book Report

ACTIVITY 2: Writing Extension 1—Personification

ACTIVITY 3: Wind Science

ACTIVITY 4: Dancing Jubilee

ACTIVITY 5: Writing Extension 2—How to Catch the Wind

ACTIVITY 6: Adjectives

ACTIVITY 7: Story Snapshots

ACTIVITY 1
Windsock Book Report

The story line in *Mirandy and Brother Wind* will introduce your students to the cakewalk. The personification of the wind adds a delightful tone. Let students make windsocks to retell the events of the story.

Supplies

- windsock pattern, page 219
- string
- butcher-paper strips in various colors
- glue
- stapler

The Writing Process

Brainstorm with students answers to these questions.

- *Who* was in the story?
- *Where* did the story take place?
- *Why* was there a story at all?
- *What* was the main goal? (for example, Mirandy's desire to dance with the wind)
- *How* was it achieved?

With the class, list on the chalkboard the sequence of story events. Keep the list short, simple, and to the point. Whenever possible, use students' own thoughts and ideas. Below are suggested story events in order.

1. It was springtime, and Brother Wind was blowing. Mirandy was going to her first cakewalk, and she wanted to dance with the wind.

2. Mirandy asked her neighbors how to catch the wind.

3. Mirandy told Ezel that she was going to dance with the wind. Ezel said he was going to ask Orlinda.

4. Mirandy tried to catch Brother Wind with pepper and a blanket.

5. Mirandy went to a "conjur woman" to get a potion to catch the wind. She gave Mirandy a scarf to wear at the cakewalk.

6. Mirandy caught the wind in a bottle of cider, but the wind escaped. She caught it again in the barn.

7. The cakewalk began. Mirandy danced with Ezel after Orlinda made fun of him.

8. Ezel and Mirandy won the cakewalk, and Grandmama said, "Them chullin' is dancing with the wind!"

Give each student eight 1" x 18" (2.5 cm x 45 cm) strips of butcher paper. Have them number the strips one to eight. Guide them to write one story event on each strip.

Assembling the Windsock

1. Give each student a windsock pattern to color. Demonstrate how to glue the butcher-paper strips in story order, from left to right, to the bottom of the windsock.

2. Then show students how to close the windsock by taping the edges together.

3. Ask students to attach string, then hang from the ceiling.

ACTIVITY 1

Windsock Pattern

ACTIVITY 2

Writing Extension 1— Personification

In *Mirandy and Brother Wind*, Patricia McKissack makes nature come to life as she personifies the wind. The carefree relationship between Mirandy and the wind offers a great opportunity for you to introduce or reinforce personification.

The Writing Process

1. Discuss personification with students. Make sure they understand that personification means bringing human qualities to nonhumans, for example, the wind in this book.

2. Challenge students to think of other stories they know that have personification. For example, *The Three Bears, The Wind and the Sun, The Wizard of Oz, Beauty and the Beast*.

3. Instruct them to choose a form of nature to personify, such as the sun, the moon, fog, a tree, plants, the rain, snowflakes.

4. Have students first draw a pictures of the "humanized" nature forms. Then encourage them to write short paragraphs about their pictures.

5. After volunteers share their stories, collect children's work and bind it into a class book to place in your reading center.

ACTIVITY 3

Wind Science

Wind is an important aspect of this story. But how does wind form? Invite students to watch this experiment to find out.

Supplies

- hot plate
  - crepe-paper streamer

Procedure

1. Review with children the important role the wind plays in this story. Why would Mirandy want to dance with the wind? Why might she imagine that it is a living thing? Invite children to share their ideas about the wind.

2. Then ask children if they know why the winds blow. Inform children that wind is moving air. We normally don't think of air as taking up space or moving around, but it does.

3. But how does air move? Share with children that air differs in temperature. Hot air expands and rises, and cooler air moves into replace it. Air moving around in this way creates wind.

4. You can show students air in motion, even though they can't see it. Turn on a hot plate. *Keep children at a safe distance!*

5. Hold a crepe-paper streamer above the plate. Be careful that the streamer does not touch the plate!

6. As the hot air from the warming plate rises, children should begin to see the streamer gently twist from the moving air. *Caution children not to try this experiment at home!*

ACTIVITY 4

Dancing Jubilee

In *Mirandy and Brother Wind*, Mirandy and Ezel danced with grace and style, winning the cakewalk. Invite your students to hold their own dance recital.

Supplies

- music that children select
- playing device

Procedure

1. Recall with students that in the story the cakewalk was a dance contest. Invite students to come up with their own dances for a class dance recital.

2. Divide the class into groups. Tell the groups to work together to choose music or a particular song that they would like to dance to.

3. Inform children that their dances need not be fancy but should reflect the tone of the music. For students who may not feel comfortable dancing, suggest that they come up with hand motions for their song or that they play supporting roles as the other members dance. To further inspire children, suggest that they are creating this dance routine for a music video.

4. Set aside time for the groups to rehearse. Then invite them to share their dances with the class.

Extra! Videotape children's dance routines to create your own class music videos!

Extra! To stay true to the story, you might judge each group's dances, awarding special prizes to all groups, such Most Creative, Most Appropriate to the Song, Most Hand-Claps, and so on.

ACTIVITY 5

Writing Extension 2— How to Catch the Wind

Because Mirandy was so determined to catch Brother Wind, she consulted friends and tried a variety of approaches. Speculate with children how they would catch the wind.

The Writing Process

1. Reflect with students the different ways Mirandy tried to catch the wind. How would your students do this?

2. Invite students to write about one of their wind-catching ideas. Pass out writing paper and prompt children's writing with such guiding questions as these.

- *Why* would you want to catch the wind?
- *How* would you do it?
- *What* would you do with the wind once you caught it?

3. When students are satisfied with their writing, encourage them to add illustrations, too.

4. Invite students to share their stories with the class. You might post the stories on a bulletin board titled "Our Class and Brother Wind."

ACTIVITY 6

Adjectives

Patricia McKissack is a master at using words that paint pictures in her readers' minds. Challenge your students to notice the adjectives she uses and how they enrich her work.

Procedure

1. Review with students that adjectives are describing words. Explain that adjectives not only help writers describe things, but they also help bring a writer's work to life.
2. With the class, reread *Mirandy and Brother Wind*. Ask students to listen for the adjectives, perhaps raising their hands as they hear them.
3. List the adjectives on a coat-hanger chart. (See list below.) Encourage students to copy the list of adjectives into their Writing Journals to use in future writings.

long, silvery wind cape
cool cabin window
morning pink
clumsy boy

good-natured smile
family cow
whitewashed cottage
colorful scarves

birthday nickels
prettiest girl
see-through scarves
big willow tree

snowball tree
flickering candlelight
big triple-decker cakes

ACTIVITY 7

Story Snapshots

The cakewalk was a special event for Mirandy and her neighbors. Suggest that someone had a camera at the cakewalk. Encourage students to put together a snapshot album of the event.

Supplies

- index cards
- black construction paper
- scissors
- glue
- manila paper
- hole punch
- yarn
- pencils and crayons or markers

Procedure

1. Flip through the book with the class to point out the scenes of the cakewalk. Ask students to imagine that one of the guests had a camera. What snapshots might he or she have taken?
2. Invite students to draw snapshots of the cakewalk on index cards.
3. Instruct them to mount the cards on black construction paper, trimming the edges to create a slight border.
4. Help children arrange and glue their snapshots onto sheets of manila paper.
5. Invite volunteers to create a photo-album cover.
6. Punch two holes on the left side of each page and the cover and bind together with yarn.
7. Display the Mirandy photo album in your school library to entice other students to read the book.

Flossie and the Fox

Flossie and the Fox is the charming story of a little girl who cleverly outsmarts a fox on her way to run an errand. Again, Patricia McKissack uses humor and rich language to hook the reader, making readers laugh and want to read on.

Point of Interest Not Mentioned in the Story

- This book is dedicated to Patricia's grandfather, who was a great storyteller and probably a great inspiration to her. Many of Patricia's stories come from the tales her grandfather told her as a child.

Memorable Story Quote

"'Top of the morning to you, Little Missy,' the critter replied, 'and what is your name?'"

Activities for *Flossie and the Fox*

ACTIVITY 1: Egg-Basket Book Report

ACTIVITY 2: Cornhusk Dolls

ACTIVITY 3: Grandparent Names

ACTIVITY 4: The Dog Family

ACTIVITY 5: Puppet Play

ACTIVITY 6: Fox Fables

ACTIVITY 7: Animal Clichés

ACTIVITY 1
Egg-Basket Book Report

In *Flossie and the Fox*, Flossie is taking a basket of eggs to Miz Viola when she is stopped by a cunning fox. Flossie proves that she is actually more clever than he. Invite students to retell the story with this basket of eggs.

Supplies

- egg patterns, page 225
- basket pattern, page 226
- scissors
- glue
- pencils
- crayons or markers

The Writing Process

Brainstorm with students answers to these questions.

- *Who* was in the story?
- *Where* did the story take place?
- *Why* was there a story at all?
- *What* was the main problem? (for example, Flossie being stopped on the way to deliver eggs)
- *How* was it resolved?

With the class, list on the chalkboard the sequence of story events. Keep the list short, simple, and to the point. Whenever possible, use students' own thoughts and ideas. Below are suggested events in order.

1. Big Mama asked Flossie to take eggs to Miz Viola.

2. Flossie took the shorter way through the woods.

3. Flossie treated the fox respectfully, but told him she did not believe he was a fox.

4. The fox tried to prove he was. He showed her his thick fur. Flossie said he was probably a rabbit.

5. He showed her his long pointed nose. Flossie said he was probably a rat.

6. He asked a cat to tell Flossie he was a fox because of his sharp claws and yellow eyes. Flossie said he was probably a cat.

7. He showed her his bushy tail. Flossie said he was probably a squirrel.

8. Then the fox said he could run fast.

9. Flossie said she didn't care. But Mr. McCutchin's dogs were running toward him.

10. The fox shouted, "I am a fox!" Flossie said, "I know."

Pass out the egg patterns. Instruct students to number the eggs from one to ten and to write each story event in the proper egg. Tell students to cut the eggs out.

Then pass out the basket pattern. Invite students to color the baskets and cut them out. Instruct them to glue their eggs "inside" the baskets in story order. Display the egg-basket book reports on a bulletin board.

ACTIVITY 1

Egg Patterns

Egg-Basket Pattern

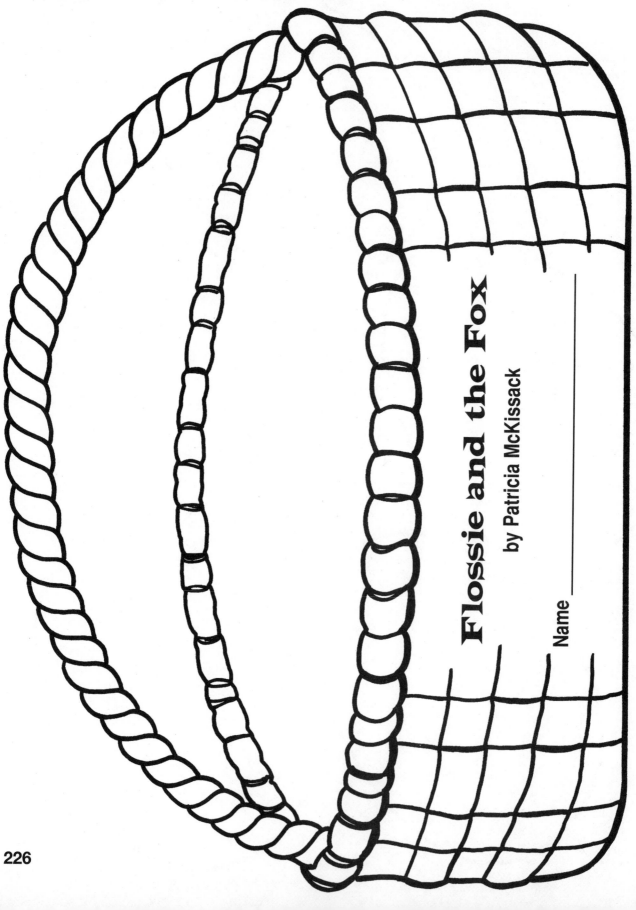

Flossie and the Fox

by Patricia McKissack

Name _____

ACTIVITY 2

Cornhusk Dolls

At the beginning of this story, Flossie tucks a straw doll in a hollow log before rushing to see Big Mama. Invite students to make their own cornhusk dolls.

Supplies

- package of dried cornhusks
- 1" (2.5 cm) plastic-foam balls
- string
- pipe cleaners (optional)
- fabric scraps
- yarn
- fine-tipped markers

Procedure

1. Ahead of time, soak the cornhusks overnight to make them pliable.

2. In class, give each student a plastic-foam ball and two cornhusks. Demonstrate how to cover the ball first with one cornhusk, then the other. Help them tie a string around the base of the ball to form a neck and then secure the cornhusks.

3. Provide children with a third piece of cornhusk, torn lengthwise. Show them how to tightly roll the husk, forming a straight long piece. This will be the arms. Rolling the cornhusk around a pipe cleaner enables you to bend arms into interesting positions.

4. Help students insert the arms directly under the neck string. Using additional string, assist children in securing the arms. The arms can now be bent into position.

5. Sit children around a table of fabric scraps and yarn. Tell them to use permanent markers to draw faces on their dolls and the fabric and yarn scraps to create clothing and hair.

Extra! This makes a great autumn project or gift at holiday time!

ACTIVITY 3

Grandparent Names

In *Flossie and the Fox*, Flossie calls her grandmother Big Mama. In *Mirandy and Brother Wind*, Mirandy calls her grandmother Grandmama. Grandparents are special people, usually with special names. Invite students to share the names they call their grandparents.

Procedure

1. Point out to students the different names Mirandy and Flossie call their grandparents. What do students call their grandparents? Invite them to share the names.

2. Provide students with writing paper. Encourage them to write the name they call their grandparents, telling something special about them, and how the name evolved (if they know).

3. Encourage students to add to the page by drawing pictures of their grandparents. Let children take the pages home to share with families.

ACTIVITY 4

The Dog Family

Students might not realize it, but the fox is actually part of the same animal family as that of one of their beloved pets—the dog. Encourage students to investigate the dog family and the other animals that belong to it.

Supplies

- posterboard
- markers or crayons
- children's nonfiction nature books and encyclopedias

Procedure

1. Turn to the pictures of the fox in the book. Ask students to look carefully at its features. Does the fox look like an animal they are familiar with?

2. Confirm for students that the fox is part of the dog family. Have students notice similarities, such as overall body structure.

3. Divide the class into groups and challenge them to find other animals of the dog family, for example, red fox (from the story), arctic fox, fennec fox, coyote, gray wolf, dingo, dhole, maned wolf. You might assign these so that no two get duplicated. There is also the raccoon dog, the crab-eating fox, the bush dog, and the hunting dog. Many of these dogs are quite rare. Assign such dogs to more advanced students.

4. Tell students to gather information from nonfiction nature books and encyclopedias. A trip to the school library might be in order.

5. Then encourage groups to arrange their information on posters. Suggest that they draw the animal at the top, then list all the interesting things they learned.

6. Set aside time for groups to share their posters with the class.

ACTIVITY 5

Puppet Play

The dialogue between Flossie and the fox is perfect for puppet plays. Invite students in groups to put on puppet plays of this story.

Supplies

- fox pattern, page 229
- drawing paper
- craft sticks
- tape
- markers or crayons

Procedure

1. Divide the class into groups to put on puppet plays. Besides Flossie and the fox, other puppets could include Big Mama and the orange tabby.

2. Pass out the fox pattern for students to color, cut out, and tape to a craft stick.

3. On drawing paper, encourage them to create Flossie and the other characters, cutting them out and attaching craft sticks.

4. Then let students rehearse their puppet plays. Suggest that one group member be the narrator, reading the story as the puppeteers act it out.

5. Drape a table with a blanket to serve as the puppet stage. Then invite groups to share their puppet reenactments.

Fox Pattern

ACTIVITY 6

Fox Fables

Outwitting a seemingly clever fox is a common story line for many animal fables. Invite students to read some to the class.

Stories children might find in the Aesop's fables include these.

- *The Fox and the Grapes*
- *The Fox and the Goat*
- *The Fox and the Woodcutter*
- *The Fox and the Stork*
- *The Fox and the Crow*

Procedure

1. Start by talking about the fox character in this story. What is so remarkable about him? Lead students to understand that the fox is considered a clever animal. In this story a girl uses her own cleverness to outsmart the fox.

2. Inform students that many tales have been told about the wily fox. Working in pairs or groups, invite students to find such a tale. A great place to start is with a collection of Aesop's fables. Another popular children's book is *Chanticleer and the Fox* by Barbara Cooney (Thomas Y. Crowell, 1958), which also won the Caldecott Medal. This story has been adapted from the *Canterbury Tales*.

3. Encourage students to come up with creative ways to retell their fox fables. For example, they can read the story, act it out, tape-record a radio show with sound effects, create a "slide show" to be narrated, or perhaps even use the fox pattern to put on a puppet show.

4. Give groups plenty of time to prepare their fox-fable presentations. When ready, invite the groups to share their stories.

ACTIVITY 7

Animal Clichés

"Sly as a fox"; "Clever as a fox"—these clichés have been around for a long time. Which other animal clichés can students think of? Brainstorm with students such animal clichés for students to add to their Writing Journals.

Procedure

1. Share the above clichés with the class. Do they think the clichés are true? What have they learned about the fox from the story?

2. Brainstorm with students other animal clichés. There are many. For example, big as a whale, quiet as a mouse, proud as a rooster, busy as a bee, busy as a beaver, smart as an owl, hungry as a bear, strong as an ox, and so on. List children's ideas on a coat-hanger chart.

3. Instruct children to write the title "Animal Clichés" in their Writing Journals, then to list the clichés. Suggest that they refer to the list when looking for an appropriate animal simile with which to compare something.

Bill Martin, Jr.

Young readers find Bill Martin, Jr.'s books entertaining. Full of repetition, rhyme, and predictability, his books offer success for beginning readers. And because of this repetition and rhythm, the fluency of young readers is enhanced. Some of Martin's stories are simply pattern stories, while others hold deep meaning.

Interesting Facts About the Author

Birth: Bill Martin, Jr., was born on March 20, 1916, in Hiawatha, Kansas. He was the son of William and Iva June (Lilly) Martin.

Education: Bill Martin, Jr., graduated from Kansas State Teachers College (now Emporia State University) with a Bachelor of Science degree. In 1957 he graduated from Northwestern University with a Master of Arts. He continued there to receive his Ph.D. in 1961.

Early life: As a young boy in Kansas, Martin lacked essential reading skills. He made it through school with the help of several special teachers, gaining much of his knowledge by oral instruction. One of his favorite teachers read to the class twice daily. In high school he found his niche in drama, for it centered around spoken rather than written language.

Martin didn't read a book from cover to cover until he was in college. Through the instruction of a college professor, his reading and writing abilities improved.

Beginnings as an author: After college, Martin taught journalism, English, and drama. He then served in World War II in the U.S. Air Force, where he became a newspaper editor. It was during this time that he wrote his first children's book. At first the book was a slow seller. It wasn't until First Lady Eleanor Roosevelt mentioned the book on the radio that it became a success, selling more than half a million copies.

Career: From 1955 to 1961, Martin was an elementary school principal in Winnetka, Illinois. Starting in 1960 he worked as an editor for a publishing company, creating materials for elementary classrooms. His technique of treating language as "chunks of meanings" has become very popular with teachers. Since 1967, Bill Martin, Jr., has been a freelance writer and editor. He travels extensively, encouraging teachers to continue their enthusiasm for educating children.

Common Threads to Look For Throughout His Books

- Many of Bill Martin, Jr.'s books, including three of the four in this study, were coauthored by John Archambault and illustrated by Ted Rand.

- Martin wants children to enjoy language. He encourages them to read in groups of words to better gather meaning. In an effort to enhance the meaning and flow of written language, the lines of text in his books break where he feels they naturally should.

Other Interests: Martin enjoys storytelling and folk singing.

Award Highlights

- *The Ghost-Eye Tree* was selected as a Children's Choice Book by the International Reading Association (1986) and the Children's Book Council (1987).

- *Barn Dance!* was selected as a Children's Choice Book by the International Reading Association (1986) and the Children's Book Council (1987). It was also a Reading Rainbow book.

- *Knots on a Counting Rope* was also featured on *Reading Rainbow*. It was chosen as a Notable Children's Trade Book in Social Studies by the Children's Book Council and the National Council on Social Studies, 1987.

Books by Bill Martin, Jr.

- *Brown Bear, Brown Bear, What Do You See?*
- *Polar Bear, Polar Bear, What Do You Hear?*
- *The Eagle Has Landed*
- *A Ghost Story*
- *The Happy Hippopotami*
- *Monday, Monday, I Like Monday*
- *Old Mother Middle Muddle*

- *Listen to the Rain*
- *Up and Down on the Merry-Go-Round*
- *The Magic Pumpkin*
- *Chicka Chicka Boom Boom*

Books written by Bill Martin, Jr., and John Archambault

- *The Ghost-Eye Tree*
- *Barn Dance!*
- *Knots on a Counting Rope*
- *White Dynamite and Curly Kidd*
- *Here Are My Hands*

Books written by Bill Martin, Jr., and his brother Bernard Martin

- *The Little Squeegy Bug*
- *Chicken Chuck*
- *Rosy Nose*
- *Smoky Poky*
- *Bunny's Easter Gift*
- *Hook and Ladder No. 3*
- *Lightning, a Cowboy's Colt*
- *Silver Stallion*
- *The Brave Little Indian*

Bill Martin, Jr. has written books too numerous to mention. The above list is just a sampling. Consult your library for a more extensive list.

The Ghost-Eye Tree

In The Ghost-Eye Tree *a mother in need of milk sends her young daughter and son on a nighttime journey. The only problem is the big oak tree they must pass. It is known to have a huge ghost eye! The events that follow are both exciting and humorous. Your students will enjoy this adventure story.*

Points of Interest Not Mentioned in the Story

• The relationship between brother and sister is very common and probably recognizable to your students. One minute they are at each other, and the next they are clinging together. Even though Ellie picks on her brother about his hat, she is the one who finds it when it is lost.

• Your students might not be familiar with the idea of a milkman. Explain that many years ago, milk was not purchased in stores, but delivered to your home. If you needed milk at night, you had to visit the milkman, just as Ellie and her brother did in *The Ghost-Eye Tree*.

Memorable Story Quote:

"Oooo . . .

"The halfway tree . . .

"the Ghost-Eye tree . . .

"shook its arms . . .

"and reached . . .

"for ME!"

Activities for *The Ghost-Eye Tree*

ACTIVITY 1: Hat Book Report

ACTIVITY 2: Favorite Clothes Day

ACTIVITY 3: Ghost-Eye Tree Art Project

ACTIVITY 4: Children's Play

ACTIVITY 5: Our Ghost-Eye Tree

ACTIVITY 6: Writing Extension—Scary Time

ACTIVITY 7: Their Bark Is Worse Than Their Bite

ACTIVITY 1
Hat Book Report

The Ghost-Eye Tree is a fun story about a brother and sister who venture out on a dark, scary night. The boy's hat plays an interesting part. Your students will enjoy retelling this story with this hat book report.

Supplies

- hat cover pattern, page 235
- stapler
- hat writing paper, page 236
- scissors

Assembling the Book

1. Reproduce and pass out the hat cover page to students. Tell them to write in their names. Allow them to color and decorate the hat covers to individualize them, then cut them out.
2. Reproduce nine hat writing pages for each student to cut out.
3. Tell students to stack the pages together and staple them across the top to make the hat book.

The Writing Process

Brainstorm with students answers to these questions.
- *Who* was in the story?
- *Where* did the story take place?
- *Why* was there a story at all?
- *What* were the main problems?
  (for example, needing to pass the Ghost-Eye tree)
- *How* were they resolved?

With the class, list on the chalkboard the sequence of story events. Keep the list short, simple, and to the point. Whenever possible, use students' own words. Below are suggested events in story order.
1. One dark night, Mama asked my sister and me to get a bucket of milk.
2. I put on my hat. My sister made fun of it.
3. We had to pass the Ghost-Eye tree. I was scared.
4. We passed the tree and nothing happened. I looked mighty tough in my hat.
5. We made it to the milkman's just fine. He commented on my hat. Now we had to pass the Ghost-Eye tree again.
6. I thought I heard something! My sister insisted it was nothing, but the Ghost-Eye tree looked at me!
7. We ran all the way home.
8. I lost my hat! Ellie went back alone to get it.
9. Since that scary night, I try not to be around when Mama needs milk.

Tell students to write one story event on each page of their hat books. Encourage students to describe the events in their own words. Invite students to share their books with a partner, in small groups, with the whole class, or with another class.

ACTIVITY 1

Hat Cover Pattern

The Ghost-Eye Tree

by Bill Martin, Jr., and John Archambault

Name _____

Hat Writing Page

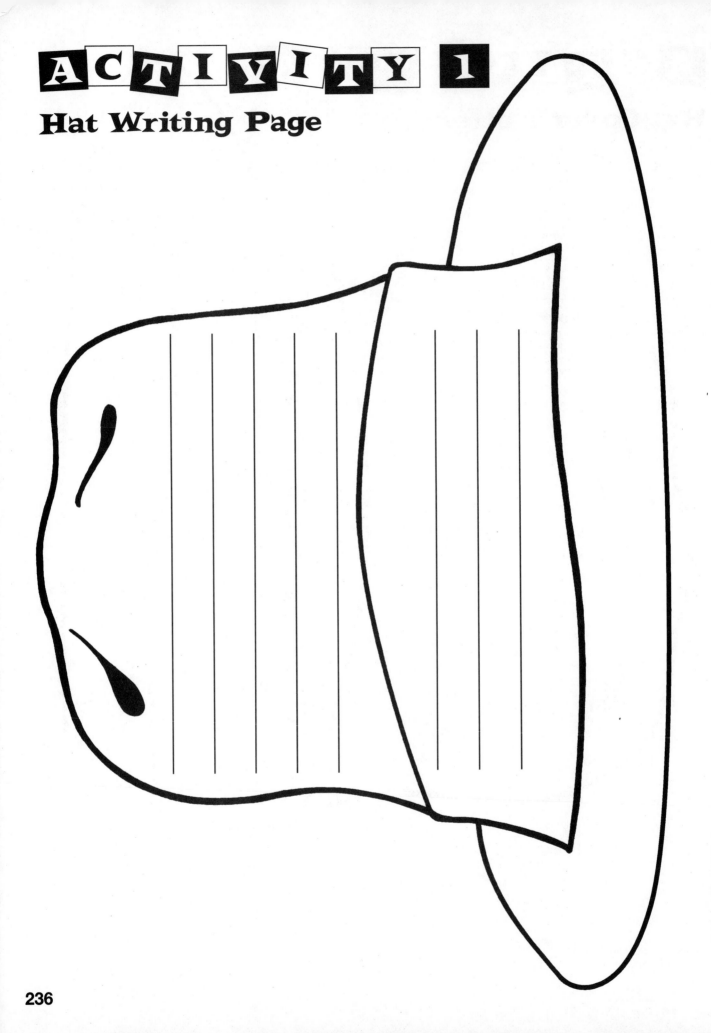

ACTIVITY 2

Favorite Clothes Day

The brother in *The Ghost-Eye Tree* had a special passion for his hat. Most children have articles of clothing that they are particularly fond of. Invite students to share special clothing items with their classmates.

Procedure

1. Recall with students how the brother in the story felt about his hat. Encourage students to share favorite clothing items they have. For example, they might have a favorite shirt they bought as a souvenir during a family vacation, a lucky pair of socks, or perhaps a hat like the one in the story.

2. Inform students that you have planned a special day for them to bring in their favorite articles of clothing. Tell students the date and perhaps send a letter home, alerting family members of the activity.

3. On your special clothing day, encourage students to talk about the background of the clothes, where they got them, and why they are special.

4. Culminate by letting students write about their clothing items, drawing pictures of them too, perhaps using the lined hat pattern page.

5. Display children's work on a bulletin board. Choose a favorite hat-related story quote to accompany the display.

ACTIVITY 3

Ghost-Eye Tree Art Project

The focus of this book is a large, mysterious oak tree the children must pass on their way to the milkman's. Let students make their own Ghost-Eye trees.

Supplies

- blue construction paper, 9" x 12" (22.5 x 30 cm)
- black construction paper, 9" x 12" (22.5 x 30 cm)
- yellow construction paper, 3" x 3" (7.5 cm)
- purple crayon
- white chalk
- glue

Procedure

1. Invite students to make a reproduction of the Ghost-Eye tree from the story. Provide each student with the above materials.

2. Have students look at pictures of the tree in the book. Encourage them to take special notice of its shape. How could they achieve this look? (continued)

3. Guide students to *tear* the black paper vertically into the shape of the tree. (Tearing the paper instead of using scissors creates an authentic effect.) Have them glue the tree to the blue paper vertically.

4. Then guide students to *tear* the yellow square of paper into the shape of the moon for the ghost eye, gluing the moon to the appropriate place near the tree. Suggest that students might have it peeking from behind the tree.

5. Show students how to use the purple crayon and white chalk to add depth and dimension to their pictures.

6. Invite students to choose a few favorite lines from the story that signify the tree and to write them in white chalk on their pictures.

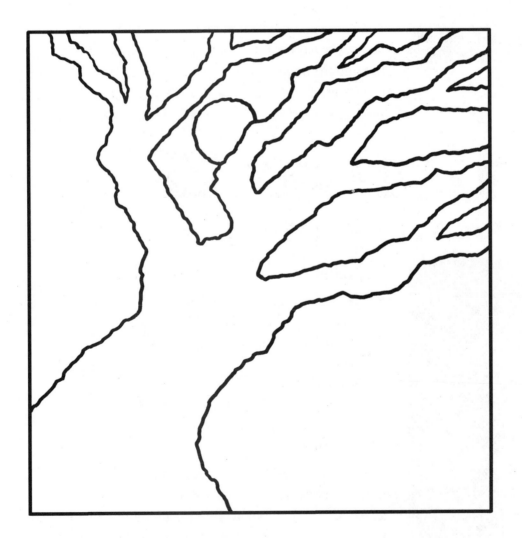

ACTIVITY 4
Children's Play

The rhyme and repetition in this story make it fun for students to chant and act out. Let students act out the story or participate in choral reading.

Extra! Read the story several times so that students can play different roles. Or assign pages to groups of students to present a choral reading of the story.

Supplies

- bucket
- hat

Procedure

1. Choose a person to be the narrator. (The teacher may need to take this role.)

2. Choose students to be the mother, the sisters, the brother, and the milkman. Remaining students will be the tree.

3. Clear a large area in your classroom. In a strategic place, let the "tree" students join together to form the tree. Some may need to stand on chairs or tables. Others may stand, and others may kneel. Their raised arms will be the branches. Let them practice swaying back and forth as if the wind is blowing, whispering "Oooooo" for sound effects. Make sure children are acting safely.

4. Instruct the narrator to read the text while the characters act out their parts.

ACTIVITY 5
Our Ghost-Eye Tree

Your students probably find the events in this story thrilling. Invite them to share their favorite parts.

Supplies

- brown butcher paper for the tree
- tape or glue
- yellow construction paper, 9" x 12" (22.5 x 30 cm)
- pencils

Procedure

1. Ahead of time or with volunteers' help, make the trunk and branches of a wall-sized tree out of brown butcher paper. Tape it to a wall in your classroom.

2. Give each student a sheet of yellow construction paper and have him or her tear it into the shape of a ghost eye. Encourage each student to make the eye as large as possible.

3. Now invite students to write about or illustrate their favorite parts from *The Ghost-Eye Tree*, using one side of their ghost eyes only.

4. When complete, let students tape or glue the eyes to the tree. Label the tree with the book title and author.

Extra! *Sky Tree* by Thomas Locker, *Rosie and Michael* by Judith Viorst, and *Cherries and Cherry Pits* by Vera B. Williams also require class trees. You might save this tree to use again for these activities.

ACTIVITY 6

Writing Extension— Scary Time

The brother and sister in the story were afraid to walk by the Ghost-Eye tree. What things have your students been afraid of? Encourage them to write about or retell a scary moment or object.

The Writing Process

1. Review with students how the brother and sister were frightened of the tree at night. Which items have students found frightening in the past? Or have they ever experienced a scary moment that was like something out of a real-life ghost story? Let students freely tell their stories in class.

2. Then pass out writing paper and encourage students to write about and draw a time when they were afraid. Prompt their writing with the following guiding questions.

- Where were you when you were afraid?
- Who were you with?
- What made you afraid?
- What did you do?

3. Invite volunteers to share their stories with the class.

ACTIVITY 7

Their Bark Is Worse Than Their Bite

Although the brother and sister in the story were afraid of the tree, trees are really not scary objects. In fact, it's quite the contrary! Trees are wonderful plants that are necessary for life on Earth. Invite students to get closer to trees by making bark rubbings.

Supplies

- drawing paper
- crayons
- trees

Procedure

1. Recall with students that the Ghost-Eye tree was a central figure in this story. Inform children that trees are central figures in real-life on earth, too.

2. Tell children that they are going to have a chance to get closer to trees by making bark rubbings. Provide students with drawing paper and dark-colored crayons.

3. Take the class outside to a tree-rich area. Working in pairs, have children help each other place the paper on the tree, then rub a crayon over the paper.

4. Back in class, invite children to compare the patterns of their bark rubbings. How many different patterns do they see?

5. Culminate by asking children what purpose they think bark serves. Explain that bark protects the tree. It keeps the wood inside safe, allowing the nutrients that travel inside the tree trunk to get to the branches, leaves, and roots safely.

Barn Dance!

In Barn Dance! a young boy lies awake in his bed and hears noises coming from the barn. He jumps from his window and races to the barn to investigate. And what a sight he sees! All the animals and the scarecrow have gathered for a night of dancing! As the scarecrow plays the fiddle, the boy and the animals dance the night away.

Points of Interest Not Mentioned in the Story

- Unlike most of the books featured in this collection of author studies, *Barn Dance!* is pure fantasy. The scarecrow and animals take on human characteristics as they talk and dance.

- Square-dancing is enjoyed by many people throughout the country. This would be a great time to invite your physical education teacher to integrate square-dancing into the curriculum.

Memorable Story Quote

". . . when the night owl said,

'Come a little closer . . .

Come a little closer . . .

Listen to the night.

There's magic in the air . . .'"

Activities for *Barn Dance!*

ACTIVITY 1: Barn Book Report

ACTIVITY 2: Barn Diorama

ACTIVITY 3: Choral Reading

ACTIVITY 4: Writing Extension 1—Magic of the Night

ACTIVITY 5: Painting Watercolor Scarecrows

ACTIVITY 6: Writing Extension 2—Personification Comics

ACTIVITY 7: Animals of the Night

ACTIVITY 1
Barn Book Report

Barn Dance! is a frivolous story about a young boy and his night in the barn dancing with the animals. Your students will enjoy retelling the events of this fantastical night.

Supplies

• barn cover pattern, page 243
• stapler
• scissors
• barn writing page, page 244
• markers or crayons

Assembling the Book

1. Reproduce and pass out the barn cover pattern to students. Invite them to write their names on the line, color the pattern in, and cut it out.
2. Then give each student nine barn writing pages. Show students how to stack the pages together, placing the cover on top.
3. Help them staple their books down the left wall of the barn.

The Writing Process

Brainstorm with students answers to these questions.
- *Who* was in the story?
- *Where* did the story take place?
- *Why* was there a story at all?
- *What* was the main problem? (for example, the sounds coming from the barn and the boy's desire to discover what they were)
- *How* was it resolved?

With the class, list on the chalkboard the sequence of story events. Keep the list short, simple, and to the point. Whenever possible, use students' own thoughts and ideas. Below are suggested story events in order.
1. A full moon is out. The boy hears the owl say, "Come a little closer . . . there's magic in the air."
2. The boy follows the sound of a violin to the barn.
3. The scarecrow was playing a fiddle and welcoming the animals into the barn. The boy sneaked in.
4. The crow called to begin the dance, and everyone grabbed a partner.
5. The boy danced until he had a hole in his sock.
6. The pigs whirled until they were dizzy and fell.
7. The owl began to hoot "Mornin's comin' closer."
8. The boy ran from the barn, slipped past the dog, and tiptoed through the kitchen and up to his room.
9. He flopped in his bed, thinking about the barn dance.

Instruct students to write one story event on each page of their books. Challenge them to use their own words to explain what happened. Have students take their barn book reports home to share with families.

Barn Cover Pattern

Barn Dance

by Bill Martin, Jr., and John Archambault

Name _____

ACTIVITY 1

Barn Writing Pages

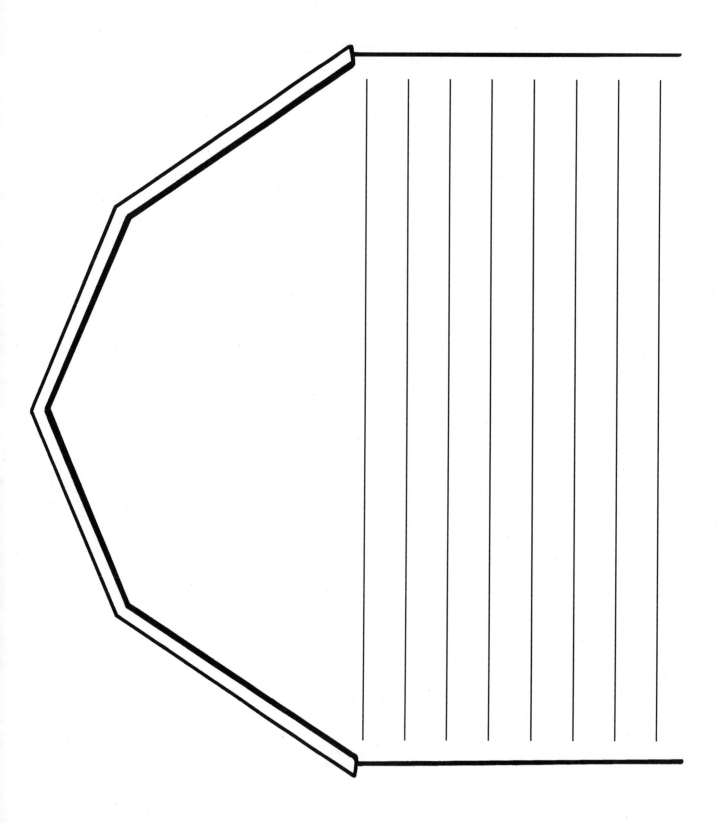

ACTIVITY 2

Barn Diorama

The images of the animals dancing after everyone has gone to sleep are ones that students might want to remember. Invite them to turn shoeboxes into the barn to create *Barn Dance!* dioramas.

Supplies

- shoeboxes
  - barn patterns
    - construction paper
      - scissors
        - glue or tape
          - crayons or markers
            - craft sticks
              - other art scraps

Procedure

1. Flip through the book with the class and talk about the fun scenes of the animals dancing in the barn.

2. Invite students to create dioramas to remember the barn dance. Ahead of time, ask children to bring in shoeboxes from home. Have some on hand for children who forget.

3. Sit children around art tables and encourage them to create the barn scene inside their shoeboxes. Suggest that they make animal cutouts from construction paper to stand in the shoebox. They could also line the back of the shoebox with craft sticks to represent the barn walls. Challenge students to use other art scraps as well to bring the barn dance to life. You might obtain some square-dance music from the school music teacher to set the mood for your art activity.

4. To finish off their dioramas, pass out the barn cover pattern from page 243, three for each student. Have students color them, cut them out, and glue them to the sides of the shoeboxes.

ACTIVITY 3

Choral Reading

The text in *Barn Dance!* is fun to read. The rhyme and foot-stomping rhythm make it perfect for choral reading. Invite students to read along with you.

Procedure

1. Talk to students about the rhythm in this book and the language the author uses to create it.

2. Seat children around you where they can easily see and read the text.

3. Have them read the book along with you while they clap or tap their feet, getting into the rhythm and festive mood of the story.

Extra! Check with your school music teacher for appropriate music to play in the background.

ACTIVITY 4

Writing Extension 1— Magic of the Night

The boy in this story hears noises outside his window that pique his curiosity. Many children's imaginations run wild when they hear things in the night or other noises they can't explain. Invite students to write about and illustrate such noises.

The Writing Process

1. Reflect with students how the boy's imagination ran wild when he heard noises in the night. Elicit from students noises one might hear, for example, owls, insects, trains, rain, wind, cars, fans, people talking, footsteps. Let students share any noises they might have heard at night. What did they imagine these noises to be?

2. Provide students with writing paper. Encourage them to write about and illustrate noises they have heard at night and the incredible images their imaginations conjured up.

3. After students share their stories, collect all the papers into a class book. Title it "The Magic of the Night." Place the book in your class reading center.

ACTIVITY 5

Painting Watercolor Scarecrows

Ted Rand's spirited watercolor illustrations add life to this already fun-filled book. The scarecrow is a lively character. Allow students to create their own scarecrows in watercolors.

Supplies

- watercolors, preferably a set for each student or for pairs of students
  - manila or other art paper
    - paintbrushes
      - cups of water

Procedure

1. Flip through the book to view the illustrations with children. Ask them to pay special attention to the scarecrow. Explain that these pictures were painted with watercolors. Help children notice how the colors fade in and out, changing shades.

2. Invite students to create their own watercolor scarecrows. Give each child a sheet of paper, a set of watercolors, a paint brush, and a cup of water. Allow plenty of time for students to work and plenty of paper for do-overs. You might suggest that students sketch their scarecrows in pencil first, then cover over the pencil with paint.

3. Set the paintings aside to dry. Then mount them on posterboard and display them. Be sure students sign their work.

ACTIVITY 6

Writing Extension 2— Personification Comics

In *Barn Dance!* the animals have human characteristics as they dance in the barn at night. This is a great time to teach personification. Challenge students to try this fun literary device.

Extra! Let students draw additional personified objects and animals to create complete comic strips.

The Writing Process

1. Write the word *personification* on the chalkboard and draw from students what it means. Lead students to understand that personification is when a nonhuman takes on human characteristics, such as the animals dancing in *Barn Dance!* (You might underline the root word, *person*.) Brainstorm with students other books in this author study in which animals or objects have been personified, such as *Nettie Jo's Friends* and *Mirandy and Brother Wind* by Patricia McKissack. Talk about how personification is a fun literary device.

2. Challenge students to try it. Pass out manila paper and have students draw pictures of animals or objects that have been personified.

3. Then ask them to draw a speech balloon above the character and to write a sentence for their animals or objects to say.

4. Let students share their drawings and sentences with the class.

ACTIVITY 7

Animals of the Night

The animals caught dancing in *Barn Dance!* are animals that usually sleep at night. But many animals actually prefer to sleep during the day. Encourage students to investigate these nocturnal animals.

Supplies

- children's nonfiction nature books
  - encyclopedias
    - drawing paper
      - markers, crayons, pencils

Procedure

1. Ask children if they think all animals are awake during the day and sleep at night. Explain that, no, many animals are nocturnal.

2. Elicit from students animals they think are nocturnal, for example, owls, bats, raccoons, skunks, moths, fireflies, mosquitoes, frogs, some mice, crickets. List their ideas on the chalkboard. Make sure they consider insects, too.

3. Invite students to choose an animal and investigate why it is nocturnal. You might share that many animals find it is safer to look for food at night, when predators—including people—are asleep.

4. Have students draw pictures of their animals, then write what they learn beneath it. Combine students pages' into a class book of nocturnal animals.

Knots on a Counting Rope

Knots on a Counting Rope *is the touching story of a blind Native American boy and his aging grandfather. Over and over again the boy asks to hear the stories of his own life, beginning at his birth. Each time his grandfather tells the stories, he ties a knot on a rope. He assures the boy that when the rope is full of knots, he will know these stories by heart. This book depicts the passing of traditional oral stories that link generations.*

Points of Interest Not Mentioned in the Story

- The story never overtly states that the young boy is blind. Help students discover this on their own.

- In this story the counting rope symbolizes the passage of time.

Memorable Story Quote

"Boy-Strength-of-Blue-Horses,

"you have raced darkness and won!

"You now can see with your heart,

" . . . Your courage lights the way."

Activities for *Knots on a Counting Rope*

ACTIVITY 1: Counting Rope Book Report

ACTIVITY 2: Counting Ropes of Our Own

ACTIVITY 3: Similes

ACTIVITY 4: Writing Extension 1—Describing Colors

ACTIVITY 5: Writing Extension 2—Autobiographies

ACTIVITY 6: Adjectives

ACTIVITY 1
Counting Rope Book Report

Knots on a Counting Rope is a tale of family relationships and traditions. The events in the young Native American boy's life, retold by his grandfather, are a statement of courage. Encourage students to retell these events on their own counting ropes.

Supplies

- knot title page, page 250
- knot writing paper, page 251
- scissors
- glue
- pencils
- strips of brown butcher paper, 2 in. x 4 yd (5 cm x 4 m)

The Writing Process

Brainstorm with students answers to these questions.
- *Who* was in the story?
- *Where* did the story take place?
- *Why* was there a story at all?
- *What* was the main goal?
  (for example, the young boy's desire to know the stories of his life)
- *How* was it achieved?

With the class, list on the chalkboard the sequence of story events. Keep the list short, simple, and to the point. Whenever possible, use students' own thoughts and ideas. Below are suggested story events in order.

1. Tell me again of my birth, Grandfather.

2. You were born, sick and frail, on a stormy night.

3. In the morning, blue horses came from the mountains and gave you strength to live. You were named Boy-Strength-of-Blue-Horses.

4. You will always be surrounded by dark mountains, but there are many ways to see. You can touch and feel and hear.

5. Tell me about my horse, Grandfather.

6. You named your newborn horse Rainbow because of the sign in the sky. You have trained her well.

7. Tell me about the race, Grandfather.

8. You rode bareback like the wind to finish the race.

9. Now that I have told you the story again, I will tie another knot. My love will always surround you with the strength of blue horses.

Give each student nine knot writing pages. Have them write about or draw one story event on each knot, numbering the events, too.

Assembling the Counting Rope

1. Give each student a strip of brown butcher paper to represent the counting rope, as well as the knot title page. Tell students to glue the knot title page to the top of the rope.

2. Then instruct students to glue the events in order down the rope.

3. Display the counting ropes in your school hallway or library for others to learn about the story.

ACTIVITY 1

Knot Title Page

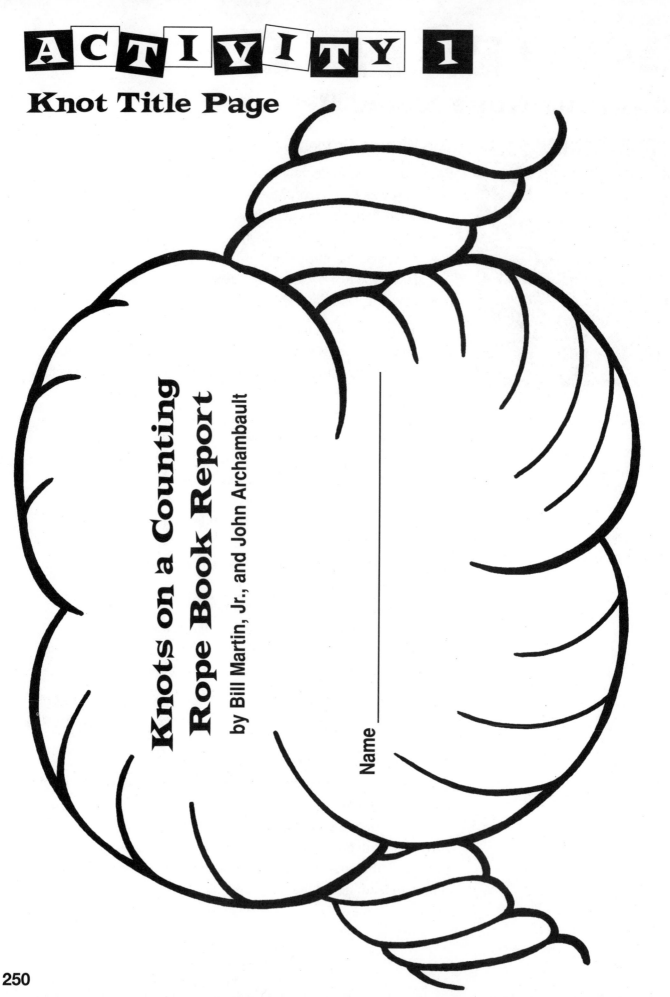

Knots on a Counting
Rope Book Report

by Bill Martin, Jr., and John Archambault

Name _____

ACTIVITY 1

Knot Writing Page

ACTIVITY 2

Counting Ropes of Our Own

Most children have probably heard special stories about their births and early childhoods. Encourage students to make their own personal counting ropes as they ask their parents or other family members to tell them stories about their early lives.

Supplies

- Events of My Life, page 253
- twine

Procedure

1. Discuss with students how important the counting rope was to the young boy and his grandfather. Talk about how the rope symbolized the passing of time and helped the boy learn about his past. Ask students to share stories they have been told about their own childhoods by parents, grandparents, or other family members.

2. Invite students to create their own counting ropes by learning some stories about their pasts. Give each student a yard of twine and the Events of My Life page, along with the letter below.

3. Instruct students to take the pages and twine home and to ask their parents or other family members to share four events about the children's lives, starting with their births. Instruct students to tie a knot in the rope each time they hear a new story and write or have parents write about the events on the activity pages.

4. In class, students sit in a circle to share their stories, using their counting ropes to symbolize each one.

Dear Family,

We have been studying children's author Bill Martin, Jr. His book *Knots on a Counting Rope* is about a grandfather who tells his grandson stories about the boy's life, beginning at birth. For each telling, the grandfather ties a knot on a counting rope. The grandfather assures the boy that when the rope is full of knots, the boy will know the stories by heart.

In keeping with this theme, I am sending a small counting rope home with your child. Please share with your child at least four stories about his or her life, beginning at birth. Each time you tell a different story, help your child tie a knot in the rope and assist, if necessary, in writing down the stories.

Please have your child bring the counting rope and the event page to school on _____ . Stories will be shared with the class on that date.

Thank you for your cooperation!

Sincerely,

ACTIVITY 2

Events of My Life

Name _____

Event 1

_____

_____

_____

_____

Event 2

_____

_____

_____

_____

Event 3

_____

_____

_____

_____

Event 4

_____

_____

_____

_____

ACTIVITY 3

Similes

Bill Martin, Jr., uses similes throughout this book. Challenge students to discover these similes to incorporate in their own writings.

Procedure

1. Make a coat-hanger chart (Appendix, page 261) for your classroom and title it "Similes." (You may have already made a simile chart for a previous activity. If so, add to it.)

2. Challenge students to tell you what a simile is. Confirm that a simile is a figure of speech comparing two things by using the words *like* or *as*. For example, *the bed was as hard as nails.*

3. Reread *Knots on a Counting Rope* with the class and have students listen for the similes, perhaps raising their hands as they hear them. For example, "No, but you rode like the wind."

4. Encourage students to write their similes in their Writing Journals.

ACTIVITY 4

Writing Extension 1— Describing Colors

The grandfather in this story helped his grandson to "see" color in special ways. Challenge students to look at color in different ways, too.

Supplies

- What Is _____ ?, page 255
  - assorted colors of construction paper
    - glue
      - pencils

The Writing Process

1. Review with students how the boy's grandfather helped him "see" colors. Read with them the passage from the book that describes blue. You might write the passage on the chalkboard for students to use as a model.

2. Give each student a What Is _____? page. Have them choose a color and fill in the blanks, following the model from the book.

3. After students share their color descriptions, mount them on colored construction paper. Display the color descriptions around the room.

Name _____

What Is _____?

_____? . . . _____?

_____ is _____ . . .

the _____ . . .

the _____ . . .

the _____ . . .

O, I see it!

_____! _____!

_____ is _____!

I feel it . . .

in my heart!

ACTIVITY 5

Writing Extension 2— **Autobiographies**

Once the boy's counting rope is complete, he will know all about his life. Perhaps he might like to tell his life story in an autobiography. Introduce students to this writing genre by encouraging them to write autobiographies.

The Writing Process

1. Talk with the class about all the things the boy now knows about his past. Suggest that one day he might want to tell others about his life. One way to do so would be to write an autobiography. You might dissect the word to show children what it means. (*Auto* means "self," and *biography* is the written story of someone's life.)

2. Invite children to write their own autobiographies. If your students completed the Events of My Life activity sheet, encourage them to use those stories. Have students describe their lives up until this current day.

3. Let students take their papers home to share with families.

Alternate! If you feel this activity invades children's privacy, ask children to write autobiographies for the boy in the story. Remind them that the boy's life should be told from his point of view. Suggest that students include how the boy feels about his blindness as well as his grandfather and his horse, Rainbow.

ACTIVITY 6

Adjectives

The adjectives in *Knots on a Counting Rope* provide the reader with vivid pictures of the characters and story setting. Challenge students to recognize the adjectives and to add them to their Writing Journals.

Procedure

1. Explore adjectives with the class. Emphasize how adjectives bring life to literature. Reread *Knots on a Counting Rope,* and have students listen for all the interesting adjectives.

2. List the adjectives on a chart as you read them. (See the list below.)

3. Encourage students to record the adjectives in their Writing Journals. Suggest that they refer to their lists when looking for appropriate adjectives to use in their own writings.

strange night

wild storm

wounded wind

dark mountains

dark curtain

hot sweat

heart-pounding afraid

wet foal

great, blue horses

long nights

cold rain

dusty sweat

Brown Bear, Brown Bear, What Do You See?

Brown Bear, Brown Bear, What Do You See? is a predictable children's book written to enhance reading success and fluency. It is used by many preschool teachers to encourage reading. The book is very easy for young children to memorize and "read" along with. Since Brown Bear, Brown Bear, What Do You See? is below the reading level for most of the students targeted in this author studies book, we are using it as a writing focus. The activity will encourage students to write predictable books for children.

Points of Interest Not Mentioned in the Story

- Even though this book was written for very young children, the author was 51 years old when it was published.

- The illustrations are by well-known author and illustrator Eric Carle.

- A modified sequel to *Brown Bear, Brown Bear, What Do You See?* was written in 1991. It is *Polar Bear, Polar Bear, What Do You Hear?*

Memorable Story Quote

The activity for this book involves having the students write a children's book using *Brown Bear, Brown Bear, What Do You See?* as a pattern. The memory quote will come from the student's own books.

ACTIVITY
Writing Children's Books

Brown Bear, Brown Bear, What Do You See? is a children's book with an easy pattern. Invite students to write, edit, and "publish" their own children's books using such a pattern. Please note that because of the writing, editing, illustrating, and publishing process, this project might require an entire week.

Procedure

1. Read with students *Brown Bear, Brown Bear, What Do You See?* Discuss the repetition and pattern of the text.

2. Also read *Polar Bear, Polar Bear, What Do You Hear?* Discuss how the pattern is the same, although the subject and action are different.

3. Encourage students to write, edit, illustrate, and "publish" a simple children's book using this pattern. Have them start by choosing a theme, for example, sports, a sports figure, a cartoon or book character, friends, nature, toys, and so on.

4. Then have students write rough drafts of their books. Help them edit, perhaps asking classmates for editing help.

5. Once students are satisfied with their stories, allow them to type their books on a computer in book form. Remind them that only two sentences should appear on each page. The type should be large.

6. Instruct students to illustrate their stories with big, colorful drawings.

7. Ask students to make front and back covers for their books out of construction paper.

8. Bind each book with ring binders. (These can be purchased at an office-supply store.)

9. Have students share their books with the class. Arrange for them to read their books to students in lower grades.

Extra! If resources allow, laminate the pages of each book, including the front and back covers. Help students cut out the pages, then bind them together.

Appendix

Authors' Addresses

Patricia Polacco
c/o Agent: Edythea Selman
14 Washington Pl.
New York, New York 10003

Robert Munsch
c/o Annick Press
15 Patricia Ave.
Willowdale, Ontario
Canada MEM1H9

Judith Viorst
3432 Ashley Terrace N.W.
Washington, D.C. 20008

or c/o Agent: Carolyn A. Larson
Lescher & Lescher
67 Irving Place
New York, New York 10003

Brian and Andrea Pinkney
315 St. John's Place
Brooklyn, New York 11231

Jerry and Gloria Pinkney
41 Furnace Dock Road
Croton-on-Hudson, New York 10520

Patricia McKissack
All-Writing Services
P.O. Box 967
Chesterfield, Missouri 63006-0075

Thomas Locker
Attn: Author Mail
Dial Books for Young Readers
375 Hudson Street
New York, New York 10014

Eve Bunting
1512 Rose Villa
Pasadena, California   91106

Vera B. Williams
c/o Greenwillow Books
William Morrow & Co.
1350 Ave. of the Americas
New York, New York 10019

Bill Martin, Jr.
c/o Henry Holt & Co.
115 West 18th Street
New York, New York 10011

Coat-Hanger Chart

Supplies

- coat hanger
- butcher paper
- tape
- scissors

Directions

1. Cut a rectangle of butcher paper 18" x 48" (45 cm x 120 cm).

2. Center over the top of the hanger. Fold the top corners over to the back of the hanger and tape in place.

3. Hang your coat-hanger chart on a hook. Use it to list words and student ideas for many of the activities in this book.

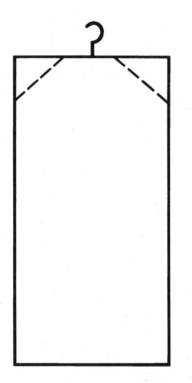

Venn Diagram

Name _____

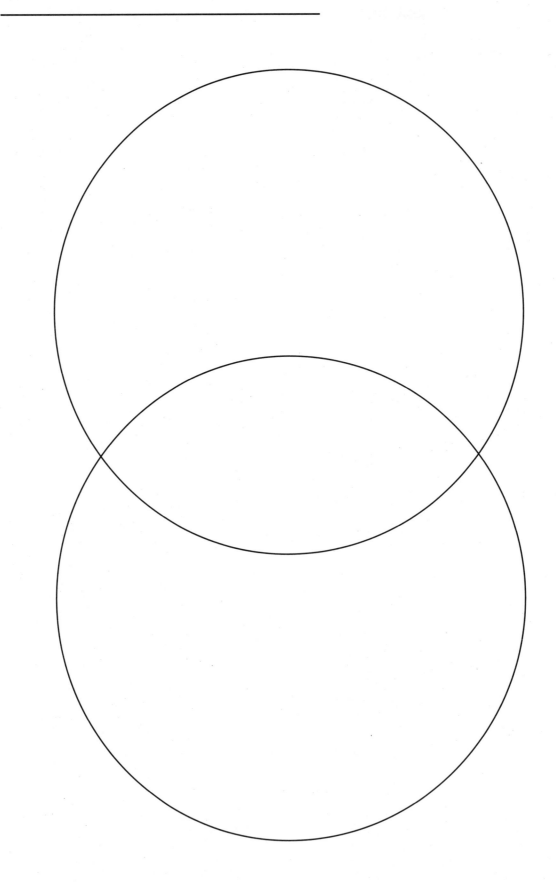

Time Line

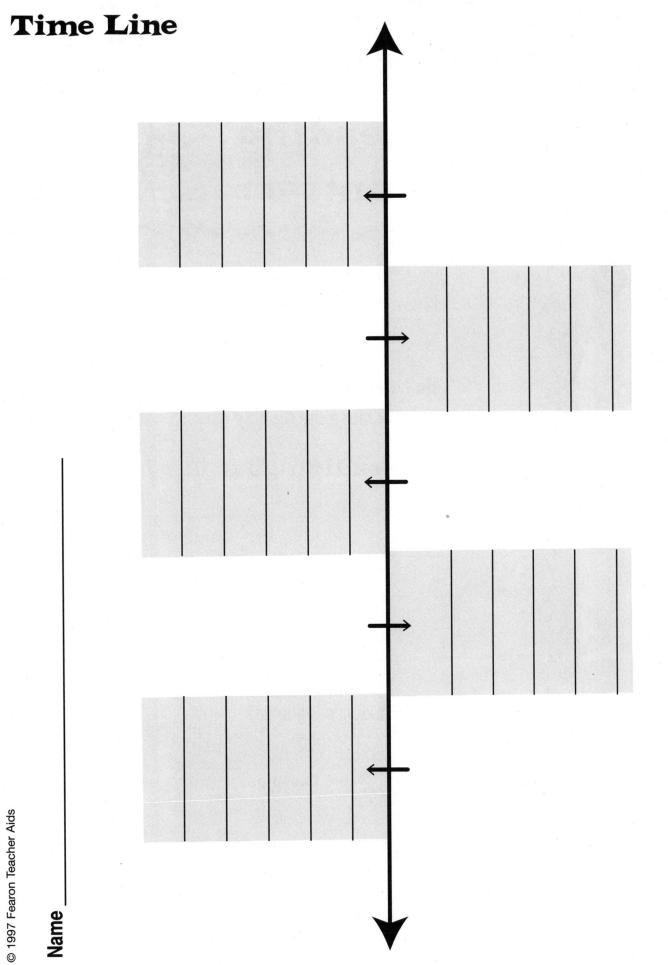

Name _____

Reading Contract

I, _____,

Name

do hereby promise to try my
best to achieve my reading goal.

My reading goal is

_____

_____

_____

_____

_____

Student's Signature

_____

Teacher's Signature

_____

Date

Congratulations!

This certificate, presented by _____
Name of School

is awarded to _____
Student's Name

for achieving a reading goal of _____

We are very proud of you!

_____
Teacher's Signature

_____
Date

Reading Award

Student's Name

**is a
star reader!**

Award

Student's Name

has done an award-winning job!

Title _____

Illustrator _____

Author _____

Summary _____

_____

_____

_____

Comments and opinions _____

_____

_____

Here is a picture about my book.

Name

_____

Date

_____

268

Biographical Information

Researcher (student) _____   Date _____

Name of Author

_____

Date and Place of Birth

_____

Early Life

_____

_____

_____

Teenage Years

_____

_____

_____

Young Adult Life

_____

_____

_____

Adult Life

_____

_____

_____

Postcard Outline

Peacock Pattern

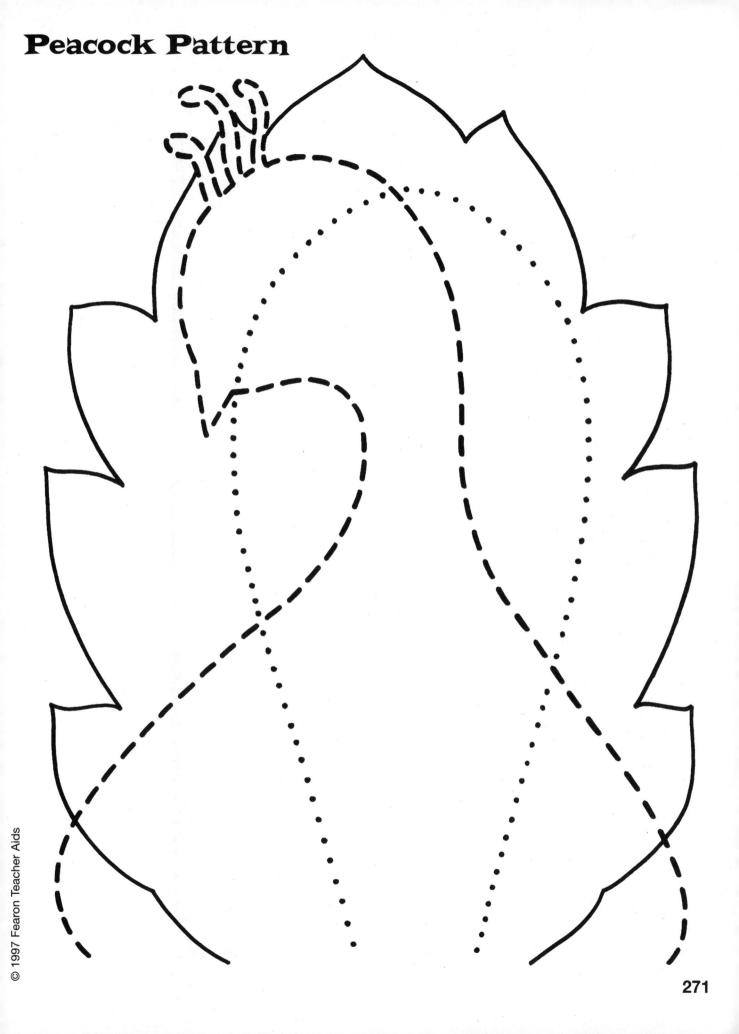

Resources

Kid Pix Around the World: A Multicultural Computer Activity Book
by Barbara J. Chan (Addison Wesley, 1993).

Meet the Author series (Richard C. Owen Publishers, 1994).

Something About the Author. Kevin S. Hile, ed. (Gale Research, 1996).

The Family Treasury of Jewish Holidays by Malka Drucker (Little, Brown, 1994).

"True Pictures" by Gabrielle Lyon. *Teaching Tolerance*. Fall 1996.